# THE PILGRIM FATHERS

AÑO·DOÑ·1651
ÆTIS·SVÆ·57

EDWARD WINSLOW
FROM AN AUTHENTIC PAINTING

# THE
# PILGRIM FATHERS

## THEIR CHURCH AND COLONY

BY

WINNIFRED COCKSHOTT

ST HILDA'S HALL, OXFORD

WITH TWELVE ILLUSTRATIONS

AND A MAP

NEW YORK: G. P. PUTNAM'S SONS
LONDON: METHUEN & CO.
1909

*First Published in 1909*

# PREFACE

TO write on the history of the Pilgrim Fathers, a subject to which many scholars have devoted their lives, and about which a novice can hardly hope to discover any new fact, perhaps needs some apology. But some have written only for the learned, others to defend a creed, or to illustrate the growth of American colonization; it is many years since a popular book was published on the subject as a whole, and possibly the name of the Pilgrim Fathers is better known than their history.

Wherever it was possible I have tried to consult original sources of information, and to verify even the best accepted facts and opinions. In the case of the Dutch Archives this has not been possible, and I am deeply indebted to " The Pilgrims in England and at Leyden," by the late Dr H. M. Dexter and his son, on which I have relied entirely for extracts from the Amsterdam and Leyden records. Professor Osgood's " American Colonies in the Seventeenth Century " also gave me many valuable clues to the labyrinth of the Records of New Plymouth.

The question of Dutch influence on Separatism in England and on the Pilgrims in particular, seems to me both interesting and important, linking as it does the great Republic of the seventeenth century with that of to-day. For this reason I have given rather an unusual amount of attention to the life of the Pilgrims in Holland, but am aware that the subject still needs fuller and more adequate treatment than mine.

v

Dates have been given in New Style, except that for convenience of verification I have given my references to the English State Papers and the Plymouth Records as they are given in the Calendar of State Papers, and in the 1855 edition of the Records respectively.

Much of the actual writing has been done out of reach of a good library, and this must be my apology for any imperfect references.

I should like to thank Miss Burrows, St Hilda's Hall, and Mr. E. Armstrong, M.A., Queen's College, very gratefully for their advice and suggestions on many technical points.

WINNIFRED COCKSHOTT

OXFORD, 1908

# CONTENTS

## PART I—THE PILGRIM CHURCH

### CHAPTER I

Introduction—Separatism explained by the character of the English Reformation. Importance of foreign influences. Reformation under Henry VIII., Edward VI., and Mary. Position of Elizabeth—Effect of her settlement was to check Calvinism. The Puritans—Their aim to make the Reformation intellectually complete. Vestiarian Controversy—Disciplinarian Controversy. Treatment of Puritans by Elizabeth. The Separatists—Their aim to make the Reformation a practical reality. James I.—His Settlement. Value of the work of the Separatists, temporary and permanent.

### CHAPTER II

Separatism a demand for practical religion—Stages in the development of Separatism. Earliest churches—Robert Browne—His life and teaching. Henry Barrow—His views compared with Browne's—His life and literary work—His execution.

### CHAPTER III

The church of the Pilgrim Fathers at Scrooby. Character of the district—The Great North Road—The Manor. Leaders of the movement — Brewster — Life at Cambridge — With Davison — As Postmaster at Scrooby. Clifton—Bernard—John Robinson—The Scrooby congregation—William Bradford.

### CHAPTER IV

Persecution of the Scrooby church—Holland the obvious refuge—Difficulties of the journey—Religious freedom of Amsterdam—Prosperity of Holland. Life of the Pilgrims in Amsterdam transitory and unsettled—Decision to remove to Leyden.

# CONTENTS

# PART II—PLYMOUTH COLONY

## CHAPTER X

## CHAPTER XI

## CHAPTER XII

## CHAPTER XIII

# LIST OF ILLUSTRATIONS

xi

# CHIEF AUTHORITIES

BRADFORD. History of the Plimoth Plantation. (Facsimile MS.) London and Boston, 1896.

„ Letter Book. (Mass. Hist. Soc.) Boston, 1863.

WINSLOW. Hypocrisie Unmasked. London, 1646.

MOURT'S RELATION. (Edited by Dexter.) Boston, 1865.

WORKS OF JOHN ROBINSON. (Edited by Ashton.) London, 1851.

STATE PAPERS. Domestic, Elizabeth and James I. ; Colonial, Seventeenth century.

PLYMOUTH RECORDS. (Edited by N. B. Shurtleff.) Boston, 1855-57.

DEXTER. Congregationalism. New York, 1880.

„ Pilgrims in England and at Leyden. London, 1904.

A. YOUNG. Chronicles of the Pilgrim Fathers. Boston, 1841.

ARBER. Story of the Pilgrim Fathers. London and Boston, and N. Y., 1897.

OSGOOD. American Colonies in the Seventeenth Century. London and N. Y., 1904.

The following have also been consulted :—

ZURICH LETTERS. (Parker Soc. Pub.) Cambridge, 1842 and 1845.

ORIGINAL LETTERS. (Parker Soc. Pub.) Cambridge, 1846-47.

BACON. Pacification and Edification of the Church of England.

GARDINER. History of England, 1603-1642. London, 1883.

ROBERT BROWNE. True and Short Declaration. (Reprinted in *Congregationalist*, 1882.)

„ „ New Year's Guift. (Reprinted, London, 1904.)

„ „ Treatise of Reformation, etc. (Reprinted, London, 1903.)

„ „ Retractation. (Reprinted, London, 1907.)

„ „ Book which Sheweth, etc. Middelburgh, 1582.

CHAMPLIN BURRAGE. True Story of Robert Browne. London, 1906.

HENRY BARROW. Four principall and waighty causes of Separation. (Reprinted, London, 1906.)

„ „ Brief Discovery, etc.

„ „ Brief Description, etc.

„ „ Plain Refutation, etc. N. p., 1606.

„ „ Conferences. N. p., Dort? 1590.

xiii

HENRY BARROW.  Examinations in Harleian Miscellany and Egerton Papers.

LELAND.  Itinerary.  Oxford, 1712.

MULLINGER.  History of the University of Cambridge.  Cambridge, 1884.

JOYCE.  History of the Post Office.  London, 1893.

COTTON MATHER.  Magnalia Christi Americana.  1702.

HUNTER.  Founders of New Plymouth.  (Mass. Hist. Soc.)  Boston, 1852.

FROUDE.  History of England in the Seventeenth Century.  London, 1872.

WADDINGTON.  Congregational History.  London, 1874.

RELATION OF A VOYAGE TO HOLLAND.  Harleian Miscellany, vol. ii.

ROGERS.  Holland.  London, 1891.

MOTLEY.  United Netherlands.  London, 1868.

GUICCIARDINI.  Low Countries.  London, 1593.

FYNES MORYSON.  Itinerary.  London, 1617.

      „         „      Shakespeare's Europe.  Reprinted 1900.

BAILLIE.  Dissuasive from the errours of the time.  London, 1645.

BARCLAY.  Inner life of the religious societies of the Commonwealth. London, 1877.

CLYFTON.  Advertisement.  N. p., 1612.

LAWNE.  Prophane schism of the Brownists.  London, 1612.

      „      Brownism turned inside outward.  London, 1613.

G. JOHNSON.  Discourse of some troubles, etc.  Amsterdam, 1603.

F. JOHNSON.  A Christian Plea.  N. p., 1617.

DEXTER.  True Story of John Smyth.  Boston, 1881.

DELICES DE LEIDE.  1712.

HARRISON.  Elizabethan England.  (Ed. Furnivall.)  1886.

HALL.  Society in the Elizabethan Age.

AIKIN.  Court of James I.

NICHOLS.  Progresses of Elizabeth and James.

BRYCE.  American Commonwealth.  London and N.Y., 1899.

CARLETON LETTERS.  London, 1775.

WORKS OF CAPTAIN JOHN SMITH.  (Ed. Arber, English Scholars' Library.)

PALFREY.  History of New England.  London, 1859-61.

GORGES.  Briefe Relation.  London, 1622.

A. YOUNG.  Chronicles of Massachusetts.  Boston, 1846.

WINTHROP.  Early History of Massachusetts.

MORTON.  New English Canaan.  Amsterdam, 1637.

R. WILLIAMS.  Key to the Languages of America.  London, 1643.

      „      Reply to Mr Cotton's Letter.  London, 1644.

R. WILLIAMS.   Bloudy Tenent, etc.   N. p., 1644.
   ,,          Letters. (Mass. Hist. Soc.)   Boston, 1863.
NEW ENGLAND'S FIRST FRUITS.   London, 1643.
WONDER-WORKING PROVIDENCE.   London, 1654.
INCREASE MATHER.   Relation of trouble with the Indians.
PRINCE'S MASON.   (Mass. Hist. Soc.)   Boston, 1869.
HARLEIAN MSS., 360, 6849, 7041, 7042.
LANSDOWNE MSS., 33.
ADDITIONAL MSS., 29,546, 25,460, 28,571, 6394.

(The additional authorities are given roughly in the order in which they are used in the chapters. Authorities which have been very casually consulted are mentioned only in the footnotes.)

"Out of small beginnings great things have been produced, and as one small candle may light a thousand, so the light here kindled hath shone to many."—BRADFORD.

# A HISTORY OF
# THE PILGRIM FATHERS

## PART I.—THE PILGRIM CHURCH

### CHAPTER I

#### THE ROAD TO SEPARATISM

THE history of an enterprise so weighted with consequences as that of the Pilgrim Fathers can hardly find an impartial reader. The results have been too vast, have touched men too vitally, not less in social life than in religion and politics, and as the results are judged, so the story is read.

The obvious thing which they did, that which they accomplished during their own lives, was to found the first successful colony in New England, and to establish the credit of Congregationalism. From these two things, and the way in which they did them, have sprung institutions, methods of government, social customs, and habits of thought, which have gone far to influence the present life, not only of New England, but of the United States, and which England has not hesitated to imitate and adapt.

In establishing democratic government in Church and State, the Pilgrims bequeathed to America some of the institutions which have done most to make her great, and to those who look at this side of their work, every stage in their history seems one more step on towards freedom and light. But they bequeathed also a conscience, and others, remembering the gloomy and restricted atmosphere, the false standard of life that resulted from it, feel that it was not a temple of liberty, but rather a prison house that these men set themselves to build.  And so, fairly or unfairly, almost everyone is biassed in one direction or another.

Shorn of its great results, the story of the Pilgrim Fathers is not always an exciting one.  If we look to the hundred years which include all their history and that of the colony of Plymouth as a separate State, it will be found to concern itself with small and trivial events, with some very great men, but with many others who seem ordinary, rather narrow-minded, and decidedly uncultured. There was nothing famous about most of them, except their consciences, but these consciences have coloured the lives of a people and its literature.

They were not immediately influential, though they did exercise a quiet influence over thought, even before they reached America.  But their movement sprang up in a remote part of England, its members had been of little importance previously, and when they left the country not a trace of their community remained.  Even in America, where they had greater scope and freedom, they were still so few and so weak that it was long before the influence of their colony, or of their religious principles began to spread and to react upon their native land. And they were quickly overshadowed by colonies, more wealthy and powerful.  When they had barely passed into a third generation, before the last of the *Mayflower* passengers was dead, the Pilgrim colony at Plymouth was united to Massachusetts, and its separate influence, its individual policy were at an end.

But no piece of history can be isolated; the Pilgrims had a great past as well as a great future, and in its relation to the seventeenth century, to the history of the Reformation in England and abroad, their story finds an interest only added to, and not created by its great results.

The seventeenth century came upon Europe like a gust of wind, sweeping away the dead leaves of the past and leaving the trees bare for the springtime of modern life. The Separatist movement, to which the Pilgrims belonged, was part of a general revolt against uniformity; men were growing more and more conscious of their importance as individuals, and asserted their individuality by questioning everything, not only in religion, but in art, politics, science and philosophy. They would have no more of the submission and uniformity of thought which had been the ideals of the Middle Ages. And each of those impulses towards expansion which were hall-marks of the seventeenth century, the instinct for liberty, civil and religious, for freedom of speech and of the press, for colonization, and at the same time for an intense national unity, had its share in the course which the Pilgrims took. Later in their history, Calvinism acted as a reactionary check, its discipline carried them back very nearly to the ideals of the Middle Ages, and the more firmly its domination was established in New England, the more these impulses towards individual liberty were obscured.

Beyond what it owed to the spirit of the age, there was much in the movement that was essentially English. The Pilgrims were true types of their nation; Henry VIII. was not more ruggedly independent of the Pope than they were of the Church; Raleigh and Drake did not face the perils of strange lands and seas with greater courage than they. "May not and ought not," writes their historian Bradford, when arrived at Cape Cod he views their perils past and to come, "may not and ought not the children of these fathers rightly say, our fathers were English men, which came ouer this great ocean, and were ready to perish in this wildernes?"[1] So far as England was concerned, the rise of the Pilgrim Fathers was the coming of the little cloud no bigger than a man's hand, a first breath from

[1] Bradford MS., p. 47.

the tempest that was soon to shake and test the foundations of every institution in the land.

To English people there must be a special interest in the typical character of their enterprise, illustrating as it does the national mind and character of that day, and further in seeing the working out of that mind and character under different conditions, and under religious and political institutions which England has considered and rejected. In this way their story, instead of being a kind of excrescence on English history, becomes an essential feature.

But there was a great deal in their work that was certainly not English. When they reached America, their institutions and modes of thought were such as they could never have learnt in England at that date; and anyone noticing the districts from which the Separatists came, the people who influenced them, and the way in which they spent the years before they reached America, must conclude that they owed an enormous debt to the Dutch. It was this mixture of influence that made the Pilgrims so different from the later New England settlers, for Holland, highly civilized, trained to liberty, and amazingly tolerant, had great lessons to teach, and the Pilgrims, more than any others, had opportunities to learn them.

Of the many aspects which their work has for us now, the Pilgrims themselves saw only its religious one. If any scrap of illusion remains that they established, or ever claimed to establish, religious freedom, it must be banished for ever; such an aim would have been as sinful in their eyes as in the eyes of the greatest Catholic or Anglican bigots of the day. All they claimed was liberty to worship after their own fashion, not because such liberty is due to every man's conscience, but because their fashion was the right one; and though they were more broad minded and kindly than many, toleration in any modern sense was as far from their minds as from the minds of their persecutors. And yet their Separatism, and the Reformation Church from which they separated, each marked a stage towards toleration, because by them diversity of religious belief forced its way into recognition. The Reformation had taught that a creed need not be universal throughout Christendom; Separatism taught that it need not even be national, and this was a fair way towards realising the rights of an individual conscience.

But the Separatists admitted no such rights, and only advanced another claimant to the position of the true Church. There is no need here to question the justice of that claim, for even those who cannot admit it can value the central feature of their work, the connection they insisted upon between religious profession and moral life.

The state of England under the Reformation shows clearly enough why it was necessary so to insist, and explains both the uprising and the growth of the Separatist Churches.

One gets a little tired of hearing that the Reformation in England was mainly a political one, and that it was imposed upon the people from above, but these facts really do account for a great deal. The Reformation for a long time was not a reality in England ; for many generations after it became nominally a Protestant country, its people had little sympathy with, or even knowledge of, true Protestant principles; and as the country was so backward, the most complete work of Reformation was in every case done by those who had come under foreign influences. "All these people," said Barrow, writing of the English National Church in 1590, "with all their manners, were in one day with the blast of Queen Elizabeth's trumpet, of ignorant papists and gross idolaters, made faithful Christians and true professors." [1] There had, however, been more preparation for Protestantism than Barrow's condemnation implies. The pendulum of reform had swung backwards and forwards, touching Calvinism on

[1] Brief Discovery, p. 19.

the one side and Roman Catholicism on the other, since the days when Henry VIII., fuming at restraint, asserted the national independence in matters ecclesiastical as well as civil. Some of his subjects, urged by the spirit of independent inquiry and criticism which filled the air, seized the opportunity of a breach with Rome, to demand the reform of many abuses, and the insertion in the Church service of some doctrinal changes savouring of foreign Protestantism. But only a very small part of the nation wished for any changes; Henry himself, like Elizabeth after him, desired above all things national independence and national unity. He was unwilling to permit the introduction of new doctrines which by creating disputes would war against this unity, and so long as he lived he did his utmost to stem the current of independent thought and opinion. It flowed with all the greater force after his death. Edward VI. himself was a strong Protestant, and he was largely under the influence of Cranmer and Somerset who were Calvinists in doctrine, if not in matters of Church government. The first Prayer Book of Edward VI. was composed with the aid of many leading reformers; it was based upon the old Latin services, aiming however at greater simplicity and a more congregational character, and it took the Scriptures and the example of the Primitive Church as its test. The Prayer Book of 1552 went still further towards Protestantism, and widened the breach between the old and new religion by attempting to deny the Real Presence.

But this was going too far for the majority of Englishmen. In spite of so much Protestant legislation the people were still Romanist at heart; many of the parishes were sadly neglected, the people were often unable to read, and so new influences could have little effect. Hooper writes to Bullinger in 1549, "a great portion of the kingdom so adheres to the Popish faction as altogether to set at nought God and the lawful authority of the magistrates; so that I am greatly afraid of a rebellion and civil discord. . . . The state of our country is indeed most deplorable." Men looked askance at the changes of doctrine, at the wholesale destruction of images and decorations in the churches which they loved, and the tremendous enthusiasm on Mary's accession voiced the dislike to these innovations, the disgust at Edward's ministers, and their self-seeking policy, and the jealousy of foreign reformers who had had so large a share in the new Establishment.

Mary's reign however was one long horror. Hundreds were slain directly or indirectly on the plea of religion, hundreds fled to the Continent, and her death was a relief alike from persecution, alliance with Spain, and Papal subjection. The new religion was a more living thing after Mary had trampled on it, than it had ever been under the fostering care of the previous government.

And then came "the blast of Queen Elizabeth's trumpet," and men waited eagerly to hear the orders which should follow it. The English Reformation had felt its first impetus from abroad in Calvinism, an influence which had touched those in high places rather than the mass of the people, and which Elizabeth at once set herself to check. Obviously her position was a very difficult one. On the one hand she had the large body who still remained Catholic, on the other the crowds of exiles hastening back from the Continent, and the many who had been in seclusion in England during Mary's reign, and who now came to the fore, all hoping for Protestantism. Even the Protestants were not united, save in their antagonism to Rome, for the English exiles at Frankfort had split into two schools of thought in 1554, and though most of them disliked ceremonial, there was every shade of opinion about its real importance.

Elizabeth's own views were very clear. She wanted to return to the position taken up by Henry VIII., of national independence and national unity ; but unlike Henry VIII. and Edward VI., she did not wish the Church to be a department of the State, but to have its own sphere of jurisdiction, subject to her as national sovereign, but otherwise independent. To preserve the national unity, she at first announced that one form of service was to be used in all churches, and that all must go to church, but that opinion should be practically free. By this means she hoped to avoid persecuting those who still clung to the old religion, and to wait until the old generation should die out and the newly established Church should prove its claims to the allegiance of a younger race. She wished to adopt the Prayer Book of 1549 as the standard for the English church service, but there was a difficulty about this. Most of the divines who were not Romanists, had lived abroad and were by now very nearly Calvinists, and even the Prayer Book of 1552 seemed to them very backward in reform. So Elizabeth's Prayer Book was a compromise based mainly on that of 1552, but slightly exalting ceremonial. The Forty-two Articles which had been drawn up in 1553 by Cranmer and various foreign reformers, were reduced to thirty-nine, but no important change was made in them.

Elizabeth's next difficulty was to find Bishops to carry out her policy. In Matthew Parker, who became Archbishop of Canterbury, she had just the moderate man she wanted, but the other possible candidates were much more Calvinistic than she liked, and only the necessity of filling the sees vacated by the Marian Bishops made her appoint such men as Grindal, Cox, and Jewel. They on their side were hardly more willing to accept appointments, feeling that they were thereby pledged to a policy they neither understood nor approved. Many were the groans they uttered to their friends in Zurich, and greatly they longed for the old peace of their life there, with its congenial companionship, and freedom from responsibility. "Oh Zurich! Zurich!" writes Jewel to Peter Martyr, "how much oftener do I now think of thee than ever I thought of England when I was at Zurich . . . we are yet strangers

in our own country."[1]  Some of them felt this so strongly
that they declared that even a dog from Zurich would be
a welcome sight.  But they waived their scruples, and did
violence to their inclinations, rather than desert the cause
of English Protestantism, and Elizabeth knew very well
that the form of Reformation which they would have preferred would speedily have driven many of her subjects
back into the arms of the Pope.

Thus compromises were made on both sides ; both in
the liturgy and the hierarchy, Elizabeth found herself urged
to a further point of reform than she really liked, and she
determined to go no farther.  The Act of Uniformity, and
laws against recusants were strictly enforced, and in 1566
Elizabeth, scandalised by the irregularities of service which
she had noticed during her royal progresses, permitted
Parker to issue a book of Advertisements, enforcing a
minimum of ceremonial observance, and forbidding
unlicensed preaching.

By her settlement Elizabeth had checked the influence
of foreign Protestantism, but she had chained her officers
to a policy which they could only support half-heartedly.
It seemed to many people too, that she had lessened the
reality of the Reformation in England.  Protestantism
implied the shifting of responsibility from the Church and
its officers to every human being, and now they thought
that the great promise of Protestantism, the personal
relation between God and the individual, was being
obscured once more by a machinery of offices and
observances.

It now became a direct question with everyone whether
he could or could not conform to the Church of England
thus established.  Up to this time, the Reformation had
been helped on by a number of people with very different
views, all eager to help in the work, and all under the
impression that their individual consciences, their individual interpretations of the Scriptures, were to count

[1] Zurich letters, I. p. 23.

But the Puritans soon found that they had more to fight about than ceremonies and vestments. It was of no use to make the Reformation intellectually complete for the few, when the many knew practically nothing about it at all. They saw that Protestantism had little real hold on the country and that the Romanist Church, invigorated by the reforms of the Council of Trent, and the zeal of the Jesuits, was making brave attempts to include England in the Counter Reformation. In 1568 was founded the Jesuit College at Douay, mainly for the education of English Catholics, who were taught and kept entirely free of charge, if they would promise to return to England as Roman Catholic missionaries.

They saw, too, that the people of England were terribly neglected and ignorant, and that little good teaching could be obtained for them. The many religious changes of the last few reigns, had caused a dearth of suitable candidates for Holy Orders; Jewel writes in 1559, "In the meantime there is a dismal solitude in our universities. The young men are flying about in all directions, rather than come to an agreement in matters of religion." [1] Laymen and foreigners were often given charge of parishes and there is frequent testimony of the bad character of many beneficed clergy, and of the dire ignorance of all who lived under non-resident and non-preaching ministers. [2]

Undoubtedly the position of the Bishops was difficult. They themselves were in many cases anxious for reform, but they were hampered by the Queen's Romanist tendencies, and they had to maintain the Established Church with a very insufficient supply of clergymen. The Church of England was indeed at this time a mere skeleton of rules and regulations, the dry bones waiting to be clothed with living flesh and blood. All the zeal and fervour of Protestantism was to be fouud in the ranks of the Puritans, and the best hope of the Church was to open her arms a little wider and embrace them all.

[1] Zurich letters, I. p. 40.　　　[2] S. P. Dom. 1565? vol. xii. 108.

A magnificent opportunity soon offered itself. There arose in Northampton about 1571, under the auspices of the parish clergyman and the Mayor of the town, a religious association, whose object, together with some inquisitorial investigation of people's manners and morals, was the holding of meetings called Prophesyings, for the discussion of theological subjects and the training of un-practised speakers. These Prophesyings spread rapidly from town to town, and Archbishop Grindal, seeing their value, and unwilling that it should be lessened by any abuses, drew up rules for their regulation. They were to be definitely under the direction of the Bishops, who could exercise a veto on the speakers, and no attack on the institutions of the Church was to be tolerated. No fewer than ten of the Bishops approved and encouraged these meetings, but Elizabeth, fearful of the free discussion they permitted, and dreading the introduction of new and heretical opinions, put an abrupt end to them in 1577. The Bishops were commanded to suppress all Prophesyings, and Grindal, who ventured to show the Queen the dangers of such a proceeding, was disgraced for the rest of his life.

Bacon, when urging the resumption of the Prophesyings in the early years of James I., admitted certain objections to them. It was possible, by so inveighing against a dumb ministry, to withdraw reverence from the liturgy, making it seem of no account ; it was possible, too, that men were so anxious for a preaching ministry, that they were not critical enough about the quality of the preaching. "For God forbid," writes Bacon, "that every man that can take unto himself boldness to speak an hour together in a church, upon a text, should be admitted for a preacher, though he mean never so well." [1] But he contended that "the silencing of ministers by this occasion is, in this scarcity of good preachers, a punishment that lighteth upon the people as well as upon the party." [2]

[1] Pacification and Edification of the Church of England.
*Ibid.*

Certainly the value of the Prophesyings greatly outweighed their drawbacks, and with their suppression, all hope of including the main body of the Puritans within the Church was at an end.   They had ceased to hope for any active measures of reform from the Bishops, and in their despair, they began an attack on the whole system of Episcopal government.   Many of them, influenced by the friendships they had made abroad, and seeing in Calvinism a logical system which would be the best weapon against Rome, had undoubtedly preferred the Presbyterian form of government from the first, and looked upon Elizabeth's first Bishops as deserters and renegades.   But there is no evidence that they tried to impose it until they had lost all patience with their lukewarm, half-hearted efforts, and all faith in the reformation power of a Church so governed.

They now commenced what is known as the Disciplinarian Controversy, in which they frankly tried to discredit the hierarchy, to prove it unauthorised by Scripture, and to discover a form directly ordained by the Word of God.

Naturally they turned to Calvinism.   Calvin in his " Institutes " had drawn up a model of church government, often known as the " Holy Discipline," and this was now urged in opposition to Episcopacy.   He had asserted that a separate ministry was an ordinance of God, and that only ministers duly called and ordained might preach and administer sacraments ; that a legitimate ministry was one in which suitable persons were appointed with the consent of the people, guided by other pastors, who finally ordained the elected one by the laying on of hands.

From such passages as 1 Timothy v. 17, Romans xii. 6-8, and 1 Corinthians xii. 28, he deduced five orders, three of which were extraordinary and had lapsed.   The remaining two, pastors and teachers, were for all time. With them was to be joined a senate of governors, or elders, for the government of the church, whose special business was discipline. They were to be the representatives of the congregation, who must not rule as a body for fear of confusion; but as the power of excommunication really rested with the whole church, this must not be used by the elders without the people's consent. The position of the elders was, indeed, a fruitful source of discord.

There were also to be minor officials, such as deacons and widows, who looked after the sick and poor; and the churches collectively were to be controlled by a Presbytery, classis, Synod, General Assembly, and Moderator.

In 1572, the first English Presbytery was established at Wandsworth in Surrey, and classes were gradually introduced in different parts of the country. The claims of Presbyterianism were upheld in the "Admonition to Parliament," which opened the Disciplinarian Controversy. The Admonition demanded a Church rightly reformed, shown by pure preaching, sincere sacraments, and a faithful discipline, the three marks which Calvin had said denoted a Church of the living God. It further demanded the restoration to the Church of its ancient officers, and the abolition of Popish abuses remaining to the Prayer Book, and it stated the objections to vestments and other matters.

The authors of this Admonition were imprisoned, and their appeal denounced in a reply by Whitgift, but it was quickly followed up, and in the years that followed, Cartwright, Travers and Udall published able expositions of the Holy Discipline, pleading always that the Scriptures were a sufficient model of Church government, and a perfect rule of all actions. Many counter attacks were made by the Church, most of them abusive, some few courteous.

Here, again, was an almost hopeless controversy; different minds read the Scriptures differently, and since each side claimed that their polity was based on divine authority, and since there was in reality a good deal of human institution in both, it was impossible to come to any satisfactory conclusion. Hooker, the ablest defendant of the Church of England, happily took a different line. He maintained that though the Scriptures were supreme as to doctrine, they were not intended as a rule of discipline or government, that the practice of the Apostles need not be an invariable law to the Church in all ages. In fact he maintained that the Church was a society, capable of making laws for her wellbeing in accordance with the general commands of the Scriptures, and of appointing ceremonies and establishing order within its limits, and that all born and baptised into the Church must obey.

Nothing could have been more displeasing to Elizabeth than the Presbyterian form which nonconformity threatened to take, for its claims touched the power of the State, both with regard to the use of ceremonies and the interference of the civil power in discipline. Cartwright held that the ministry should dictate both as to doctrines and ceremonies, and Calvin expected the State to support the Church in discipline, since both were presumably working together to carry out the will of God. But this position would have been difficult, even with a State Church, and where the Church which claimed to be thus supported was *not* the State Church, but only a small body of men whom the State did not wish to recognise, it became impossible.

Certainly Elizabeth had no idea of tolerating principles so limiting and disintegrating to her jurisdiction; and the attacks on nonconformists were not by any means confined to literature. In the time of her struggle with Roman Catholic powers, the Queen had been less severe with the Puritans than the Papists, amongst whom her chief danger lay. But after the death of Mary Queen of Scots, and still more after the defeat of the Armada, she felt herself independent of the Puritans, her natural dislike to them revived, and after the death of Grindal she employed Whitgift, as Archbishop of Canterbury, to stamp out nonconformity in the kingdom. She charged him "to restore the discipline of the Church, and the

uniformity established by law, which by the connivance
of some prelates, the obstinacy of the Puritans, and the
power of some noblemen, is run out of square." [1]

By the Court of High Commission, scarcely less
arbitrary than the Spanish Inquisition, and by the oath
" ex officio," through which men sworn to speak the truth
could be made to accuse themselves and their friends,
Elizabeth finally gave the lie to her original promise that
thought and opinion should be free.  The second generation of her Bishops too was more convinced of the
infallibility of the English Church, and less sympathetic
towards scruples than their predecessors had been, and
Whitgift found enough of them to carry out his work.

In 1593 even the House of Commons, which formerly
had inclined to some licence with regard to uniformity of
church government, came over to the Queen's point of
view, influenced perhaps by the violent attacks on the
Church in the Mar-prelate libels.  It was enacted that
any recusant, or any who should deny the Queen to have
any authority whatever in ecclesiastical causes, or who
should frequent conventicles, should be imprisoned, and
if obstinate should be banished from the realm within
three months, and lose his goods and lands.  Any who
should not submit and leave the realm within the three
months, or should return without licence, was guilty of
felony, punishable by death without benefit of the clergy.

This was the extremest point of persecution, and meanwhile a new party had arisen.

For a long time, although there had been great discontent with the conduct of the Church, and consequently
with its polity, there had been practically no Separatism.
The Puritans remained within the Church, so far as they
were permitted to do so ; some of them conformed, some
of them did not, but all hoped to urge on a reformation
within the Establishment.  How they expected the Bishops
to abolish themselves in favour of elders ; how they

[1] See Strype's " Life of Whitgift," p. 114 et seq.

2

expected the State to minimise its control over the Church
to the necessary extent, it is hard to imagine, but so it was.

But Puritanism was not enough for all.  All claims to
establish a true Church, so far, had been based upon proof
of continuity from the Primitive Church, which was extremely hard to establish without the help of the hierarchy.
Then every scheme had included within the Church all
who had been baptised, without respect to character, and
finally every scheme hitherto proposed was made practically useless by its dependence on the civil power for
initiative and support.

It was those who saw the hopelessness of the efforts of
Cartwright and his fellows, and who felt that they could
wait no longer for something to be done to remedy neglect
and immorality, who split off into the various sects known
as the Separatists.

The subtle developments of foreign Protestantism were
touching England once more, and this time its influence
worked upon the common people, and in a way which
appealed to them.  Those who listened were not, as the
disciples of Calvinism had been, men in high places ; they
were unhampered by ambition, and looked at the problem
of reform with different eyes.  They would not shrink
from drastic remedies, for they knew that the Church of
England was doing very little for them, and they were
not chiefly interested in the theory of a Church, but in its
work.  They wanted something direct and immediate,
which should help them and their neighbours, and they
cared nothing at all for a scheme which might be complete
and ideal at headquarters, but which never reached them.

The objections of the Separatists to the Church of
England went far deeper than mere dislike to ceremonies
and prelatical power ; they aimed at a visible Church of
saints upon earth, and in their eyes the purity and reality
of a Church was lost if it included, even nominally, within
its ranks, the infidel and the evil doer ; if it were to be
hampered in its choice of ministers and its duty of

discipline by any power outside the congregation; and if it were to depend for maintenance on anything but the willing gifts of the devout. As to the Puritans who refused subscription to rites and ceremonies, and bemoaned abuses in the Church, the Separatists thought they were merely straining at a gnat and swallowing a camel, since they waited for the arm of the State to effect a reformation, and were willing to have the whole land, good and bad, once more included in the Church, making it as impure as ever. The Separatists demanded a spiritual and not a political reformation, and would have no man in the Church who had not experienced such a regeneration.

The Act of 1593 helped to draw the line between them and the Puritans; many of the Separatists fled to Holland, the rest fixed their hopes on the next sovereign.

But James I. soon showed that there would be few reforms to meet the wishes of the nonconformists. As he had been trained by Scotch Presbyterians, and had pleaded for Cartwright and Udall, their hopes ran high, and he was met on his way from Scotland by a Puritan deputation bearing the Millenary Petition. Its demands were far more moderate than those of earlier documents, such as the "Admonition to Parliament," and although not sufficiently representative of public feeling to be granted as they stood, many of them merited serious consideration. James at first seemed inclined to give them this consideration, in spite of the opposition of Universities and Bishops; but at the Hampton Court Conference, which he called to consider the Petition, he took fright, thinking no doubt that the doctrine of independence of the civil power would be advanced, and showed an attitude towards the reformers which was not only hostile but most insulting.

The Separatists in exile had also presented a document, stating their differences with the Church of England, and praying for lenity; and so many petitions on religious matters came to the King from all parts of the country, that he became seriously annoyed, and issued a Proclamation bidding his subjects repose themselves, and leave such things to his conscience.

The lack of results from the Conference, the new Prayer Book with its royal Proclamation against innovations, the conservative acts of Convocation, crushed all hopes. A code of Church canons was set forth, to which all were bound to conform within four months, or "dispose of themselves and their families some other waies." [1]

So there was as little hope for the Separatists in England as there had been in the days of Elizabeth. James had less excuse for his persecution than she had had. Her Church policy seems harsh and cruel from a modern standpoint; but weakness leads men to persecution, and indeed the nation was in such peril in her early days that, if the scruples of a comparatively small number were leading to disunion, they might well seem blameworthy, even to a far-seeing statesman. A much-quoted passage from the State papers illustrates the condition of England. "The Queen poor; the realm exhausted; the nobility poor and decayed; good captains and soldiers wanting; the people out of order; justice not executed; all things dear; excesses in meat, diet, and apparel; division among ourselves; war with France; the French king bestriding the realm, having one foot in Calais and the other in Scotland; steadfast enemies, but no steadfast friends." [2]

Protestantism abroad had seemed synonymous with disloyalty; the Queen had for examples of religious disunion France, divided by the civil wars of the Huguenots and the Holy League; and the Netherlands, split up into Protestant Holland and Roman Catholic Flanders, and whilst her danger from France and the Pope was so imminent, she was determined that "division among ourselves" should be as little as possible, and that she would keep England united and strong. To blame Elizabeth

---

[1] Proclamation, July 16th 1604.
[2] S.P. Dom. vol. vii. 73, Dec. 27th 1559.

for coercion in religious matters, is neither here nor there. The Puritans and most of the Separatists were just as much in favour of such coercion as she was herself, they merely objected that she was using pressure in a wrong direction. The future career of the Puritans, both in England and Massachusetts, showed plainly enough that it was not religious liberty that they claimed, but Puritan domination.

Again, it must be remembered that the Church of England was a very new organization, which had hardly had time to settle itself on any firm basis. It was essentially a compromise, made up of some Romanist ceremonial, a little reformed doctrine, and a great deal of royal supremacy. Time alone could adjust the balance between these elements, and until they were thoroughly welded together, and until the principles of the Established Church should be better known to the nation at large, Elizabeth was probably wise in allowing as few innovations and as little legislation concerning it as possible. Great changes bring to the fore extreme and dangerous men; there was a tendency to " that negative and contradictory humour of thinking they are then rightest when they are unlikest the Papacy; then nearest to God when farthest from Rome ; " [1] and but for Elizabeth's resolute support of the Church as established at the commencement of her reign, it might have been committed to doctrines and measures which would have imperilled its future usefulness. One may pity the harshness and blindness of her efforts to obtain conformity, and regret that she was not more urgent in the reform of real abuses ; in the matter of the Prophesyings she undoubtedly made a serious mistake, but it is difficult to criticise her general policy in the face of results, for when James came to the throne England was in a vastly different position, both at home and abroad, and the Church had attained that strength which should have resulted in toleration. Now was the time for those domestic reforms which had been pushed into the back-

[1] Sandys.

ground during more pressing dangers; now was the time
to do something to allay the religious discontent which
was growing beyond bounds, and to make some sadly
needed improvements in the educational and religious
condition of the country.

The need for change had been felt before Elizabeth's
death, and at his accession, Bacon appealed to James I. on
behalf of the Church.  He protested against the idea that
innovation in Church matters was bad policy, since there
is a tendency to corruption there as well as in the State;
laws must be made to stem it, and no time is so good for
correcting abuses as the beginning of a new reign.  And
he pleaded eloquently that all reformation need not be
after the same pattern, and that some licence should be
permitted with regard to rites and ceremonies.  "For
howsoever politic considerations and reasons of state may
require uniformity, yet Christian and divine grounds look
chiefly upon unity."[1]   Many of the abuses he condemned
were those which the Puritans petitioned against, many
of his suggested remedies would have met with their
approval; he wanted to include within the Church, if
possible, all who would fight for Protestantism, being
"partly persuaded that the Papists themselves should not
need so much the severity of penal laws if the sword of
the Spirit were better edged, by strengthening the
authority, and suppressing the abuses in the Church."[2]

James did not ignore Bacon's advice, he even took some
steps towards investigating matters for himself.  But the
demands of the Puritans seemed to him a direct attack
on his own power, his self love and vanity were wounded
and he missed his opportunity.  As he gradually grew to
identify his own royal prerogative with the power of the
Bishops, the great Puritan struggle became inevitable, and
all chance of pacification was at an end.

Like Elizabeth, James aimed at maintaining the in-

---

[1] Pacification and Edification of the Church of England.
[2] Ibid.

tegrity of the Church of England, and in a very narrow sense he succeeded, though at enormous cost. It was perhaps too much to expect that he would see with the eyes of Bacon, but his policy would seem a worthier one had it included even some slight measure of licence to nonconformity which would have diminished the number of those who filled the English prisons, and fled from persecution over seas, and still more had it included a real zeal for reform which would have gained for the Established Church a degree of respect even from those who disapproved of its constitution and government.

After centuries have passed, it is possible through all the mistakes and failings of the Church and the Separatists, to see a beautiful ideal on either side.

Nothing could be more noble, more divine, than the conception of a Church which had room even for the weakest and the most frail, which would hold out a hand to any who turned to her for help, though they should fall again and again. And this was the principle of the National Church. But the Church was temporarily living far below her ideal. The general standard of conduct was so low that Church membership has come to mean little or nothing. Too many worldly considerations had entered into the Reformation settlement, too much time was spent in elaborating the widespread and complicated machinery, which promised to be permanent, but which worked so slowly that generations lived and died without feeling its touch.

The Separatists, on the other hand, had great immediate advantages. Their task as they saw it was so simple ; they had to think of no extensive scheme, but only to work among the two or three gathered around them, directly, and with no hampering machinery. They too had their great ideal ; their Church was to be a Church of saints upon earth, which should be a light and example to those without; but it was an ideal which, in human hands, led to a narrow and judging spirit.

Their strength lay in the practical work which they did, and in the protest which their Church embodied. They taught that to be a member of a Church should mean something in a man's life, that it was a privilege which he must earn, and which should not come as a matter of course.

For a time they were left to uphold the ideal of a spiritual life, and no one can fail to appreciate the greatness of their work. But when the Church of England became a living thing, and her spiritual life grew with her, the value of their protest necessarily grew less. Others were working for the same ends, though their methods might be different; the peculiar task of the Separatist Churches was accomplished, and they fell into rank amongst the honourable Churches of Christendom.

# CHAPTER II

## THE EARLIEST SEPARATIST CHURCHES

THE whole meaning of Separatism in its early days was a demand for practical religion, for some relation between the spiritual profession of a Church, and the lives of its members. Many people within the Anglican Church had looked around for this, and failed to find it; had been convinced that such a state of things was wrong, and had suggested this system or that as a remedy. They hoped, as the Church of England still hopes, to make the lives of the people correspond with their profession as Church members, but the Separatists had no faith in such a scheme. There were apparently so few who wished to live spiritual lives, the Church gave so little opportunity for disciplining themselves and others, and the good were apt to be contaminated and overpowered by the bad.

Their plan was different. They thought they would begin at the other end and form the nucleus of a Church out of the spiritual few, and so work from this centre that the whole visible Church should be spiritual, and should live out its profession as an example to all.

This was to found a Church on an entirely new basis, independent of any historic continuity, or any authorization from civil powers; and the scheme involved entire freedom from outside control, that it might regulate its own discipline, and keep itself pure and free from contamination.

It was an assertion of the idea that to belong to this Church or that was not an end in itself, but a help towards right living in this world, and salvation in the next. During their early life in England, the Separatist Churches were very much alike, they were so to speak *merely* Separatist, the further principles of their polity not having been yet worked out. Next came for most of them a period of exile abroad, during which they became differentiated, their new ideas crystallising into one shape or another, largely according to the personality of their leaders. Finally, the Churches returned to England or America, as more or less complete and distinct sects.

Governor Bradford says [1] that the first Separatist church in England was that in which John Rough, minister, and Cuthbert Symson, deacon, were burned alive by Bonner ; but this church under Mary was rather an attempt to continue the national Protestantism of Edward VI. than an assertion of congregational rights.

Later, under Elizabeth, an independent church was formed within the walls of Bridewell prison. About one hundred people had met together in Plumbers' Hall in June 1567, to celebrate a wedding, and to hold a religious service after their own fashion. This was strictly illegal ; they were surprised by the sheriff and his officers, and a number of them arrested. Once in Bridewell, instead of realising the enormity of their act, they put a seal upon it by uniting into a separate church, with Mr Fitz as their pastor and Rowland as their deacon. Both these men, and it is to be feared many others, died in prison, but the church thus founded lived on.

But, although there are traces of various Separatist communities in the early days of Elizabeth, they had not as yet formulated their claims to be considered true Churches. They separated because they disliked the national assemblies too much to remain in them, and they ran the risk of being considered outcasts. Then they searched the Scriptures for support, and as the result of

[1] Dialogue in Young's "Chronicles."

that appeal the principles of Congregationalism, the claims of its adherents to be not only truly a Church, but *the* true Church of apostolic times, were first enunciated.

It was the independent mind of Robert Browne which first dared a theoretical justification of Separatism, at a time when the idea of one Church for all Christendom had only just been abandoned, and when the idea of several Churches within one nation seemed impossible; and from him its recorded history may be said to date.

There are many varying estimates of Browne's character and aims, and indeed he must have been perplexing, even to his contemporaries full of apparent contradiction, of mingled greatness and weakness. To many historians he was never more than a restless, revolutionary democrat, "Trouble-church Browne," always warring against the established order, always resisting authority, no matter whose it might be, and yet unwilling to pay the penalty of his own defiance. Later writers, studying those of his works which were then known, saw him to have been very earnest and eager for truth, impulsive and ill balanced perhaps, visionary and impractical through his too high ideal of human nature, but one who had a higher and clearer perception of Christ's rule on earth, than any other of his day. They felt it impossible to accept the earlier condemnations of Browne, however much known facts seemed to justify them, and seized upon the plea of insanity to account for inconsistency and weakness. But gradually new facts have come to light, and old ones have been discredited; above all some of Browne's hitherto lost writings have been found, and he stands now before us as a man who mistook his own strength and the strength of his convictions, but not as a cowardly traitor to his cause, nor yet as a man whose acts were invalidated by long insanity. It is said that he was a musician, "a singular good lutenist," and he had a musician's sensitive, highly-strung nature. To those who will look beyond the surface weaknesses of his life, his story must have a deep and melancholy interest, with its contrasts between an energetic mind and a delicate body, between the obloquy which fell upon him personally, and the gradual strengthening of the cause which he had done so much to promote.

Browne's position refutes a common idea about the Separatists, that they were all of low birth, having nothing to lose by dissent. He was a native of Tolethorpe in Rutland, and belonged to a family of wealth and influence. His ancestors were merchants of the Staple in 1376, and from that time onward they come into prominence again and again. Lord Burghley was his kinsman, and interested himself considerably in his career, saving him many times from the heavy hand of the law, though, as was to be expected from a privy-councillor, he probably sided with the ecclesiastical authorities in attempting to force conformity upon him. Robert Browne was born probably about 1550 : he was "brought vp in schooles and in the Uniuersitie of Cambridge,"[1] where he took his degree in 1572. At this time there were many men in Cambridge who preached extreme Puritan doctrines ; in 1570 Cartwright was forced to resign the Lady Margaret Professorship on account of the nature of his teaching, which undoubtedly persuaded others to a Separatism which he was not willing to adopt himself. The danger of the Cambridge Puritanism was beginning to be realised ; that the future ministers of the Established Church should be thus impregnated with feelings of disloyalty and doubt towards its institutions was perilous. Almost all the great Separatist leaders in after years were Cambridge men ; the pupils went further than their teachers, and frightened those teachers in many cases back to orthodoxy.

Even in these early days, Browne's views were suffi-

[1] True and Short Declaration.

ciently advanced to get him into trouble, and in 1575
he seems to have begun to "teach schollers," probably
feeling that he was too unorthodox to take orders.   For
about three years he taught thus, whether in London or
in the country is uncertain,[1] but his teaching, according to
his own account, was of rather a revolutionary nature, for
the condition of the National Church was already preying
upon his mind, and he did not scruple to criticise it.

The plague broke out in 1578, and Browne was
summoned home, but after a few months he went to
Cambridge, to the house of Mr Richard Greenham of
Dry Drayton, who encouraged him to preach publicly.
With regard to the authority of the Bishops, Browne
seems to have started where many Puritans ended, for
he very early decided that they had no right to grant
licences to preach.   He hesitated to accept a parish in
Cambridge, because this would involve ordination or
licence by a Bishop, and when his brother bought for
him the Bishop's seals which were to establish him there,
Robert burnt one and lost the other.   He preached in
this parish until January 1580, but never took charge
of it, in spite of the requests of his congregation; he
objected to their grounds of church government, and
sent back the money they would have given him.   In
January 1580 he fell ill, and during his sickness was
forbidden to preach any longer.

From this time he began gradually to formulate the
system on which all future Congregational churches were
based.   He decided that ordination was an abominable
institution, and that the "kingdom of God Was not to
be begun by whole parishes, but rather of the worthiest,
Were they neuer so fewe."[2]   This was the very corner-
stone of the future system.

Having evolved his theory, Browne lost no time in
putting it into practice.   He had heard much of some

---

[1] See Baillie's "Dissuasive."
[2] True and Short Declaration.

reformers in Norfolk, and there, together with Robert
Harrison, a Cambridge friend who became Master of
the Hospital in Norwich, he formed a church of the
"very forwarde." At this time he was living with
Harrison, and probably began teaching again. He
convinced Harrison, who was at first inclined to
conformity, that faith was wrought by the preaching
of those sent by the Lord, and by them only; he
expounded to his hearers the necessity of separation
from the ungodly; and he abused in no measured terms
the set and stinted services of the English Church.
"Their stinted service is a popish beadrovv full of vaine
repeticions, as if seauen paternosters did please the Lord
better then syx: and as if the chattering of a pie or a
parate vvere much more the better, because it is much
more thē enough. Their tossing to and fro of psalmes
and sentēces is like tenisse plaie, vvhereto God is called
a Iudg vvho can do best and be most gallant in his
vvorshipp: as bie organs, solfaing, pricksong chaūting,
bussing and mumling verie roundlie, on diuers handes.
Thus thei haue a shevve of religion, but in deed thei
turne it to gaming, and plaie mockholidaie vvith the
vvorship of God. For the minister and people are
bridled like horses, and euerying appointed vnto them
like puppies," etc.[1]

By teaching and preaching, he gathered around him
a company who liked his views, and feeling the need of
some closer organisation, on an appointed day they met,
and covenanted together with the Lord, to cleave together and to separate from the wicked. They chose
their teachers, and agreed as to the manner of their
services, they arranged for the maintenance of mutual
discipline, and the redress of abuses, and agreed to
further the kingdom of God in themselves, their households and friends, and "whosoeuer vvas worthie."

Browne's new polity was first advocated on account

[1] True and Short Declaration.

of its possibilities of reform, not yet on the plea that it was more scriptural. He himself says that he gave up the parish system "with manie teares," feeling that "no man can serue twoe contrarie maisters."[1]

He had much in common with the Puritans; like them he was shocked at the worldliness of those who entered into communion with the devout; like them he thought that the Bishops who tolerated such a state of things were no true ministers of God. Like them too, he held that it was the duty of a Christian to seek the utmost purity of belief and life, but in the means he took to realise this ideal, he became a Separatist. For whereas at the meeting of the Presbytery in Wandsworth, it had been timidly asked whether the ministers might proceed to the work of Church reformation, without the help or leave of the magistrate, and the question had been answered in a decided negative, Browne had not a doubt that it was their right and duty so to do.

What his views were at this time may be gathered from the works published a year or two later in Holland. "A True and Short Declaration" gives his autobiography up to 1583; and his early views on Church polity, on the need for separation, and on the relation of the Church to the civil power are expounded both in this and in the three treatises in which he defended his position in 1582. He taught that a true Church need not try to prove continuity, for any assembly of believers, who have separated from the irreligious, and whose members unite in a public covenant with God and each other, becomes by that act a perfect Church. He taught that the need for purity of life was so urgent, and the necessity of separation from corrupt Churches so great, that there was no obligation to wait for the authority of the civil power, which had given no hope of reform. Of the Magistrates he wrote, "yet haue they no ecclesiasticall authoritie at all, but onelie as anie other Christians, if

[1] True and Short Declaration.

so they be Christians."[1]  The Lord's Supper was to
be the seal of the Church, to be received only by the
worthy separated from those "unmeete to receaue."
Thus Browne threw to the winds the conservative
scruples of the Presbyterians and Puritans, creating a
Church on an entirely independent basis.

With regard to church government he followed the
Scriptures in choosing a pastor, teacher, elders, deacons,
and widows, but the one Head of the Church was Christ,
who should manifest His supremacy and exercise His
power through every member of the congregation.[2]
Hence the charge of democracy.

All were to have a share in the mutual discipline, and
the church was to be associated with other true churches
in a bond of mutual friendliness and help.  But it would
not look to the secular power, nor to any ecclesiastical
power outside the congregation, either for the calling of
ministers or for the exercise of discipline, and thus it
was a truly Congregational church, distinct from both
Episcopalianism and Presbyterianism.

Naturally these principles, when put into practice in
the Norfolk Church, brought Browne into collision with
the ecclesiastical authorities.  Moreover, he did not con-
fine his ministrations to Norwich, but seems to have
travelled about Norfolk, rousing the people with "corrupt
and contentious doctrine."  Bury St Edmunds in particular
felt his influence; twice Bishop Freak of Norwich complained of him to Lord Burghley,[3] and twice he was
imprisoned in London.

Alarmed at the first imprisonment, Browne's followers
thought of fleeing into Scotland, but Browne, writing from
prison, dissuaded them, thinking it cowardly, and unwise
too, since Scotland was too conformable to England.
Then they suggested Jersey or Guernsey, and this Browne

---

[1] Reformation without Tarying, etc., p. 4.
[2] Book which Sheweth, Def. 48.
[3] Lansdowne MSS., xxxiii. 13020.

liked better, though he thought there was no need for such haste to leave England.

But the church was too often without its leader, and in 1582, after Browne's second imprisonment, it migrated to Middelburg for greater safety.

There were an enormous number of Dutch people in Norwich, and perhaps some in Browne's own congregation. On November 21st 1583, the Mayor and Aldermen of Norwich sent to the Council a certificate of the strangers in their city, to the number of 4679, being Dutch refugees and others.[1] They had been invited by the English to try and revive the decaying worsted manufactures, and to remedy the consequent poverty of the town, and they had a flourishing church of their own there. They may have influenced Browne's opinions. It is noticeable that, unlike most writers of his time, he shows no aversion to the Anabaptists, who on account of their early excesses in Germany and Holland, were looked upon with quite unmerited horror. Many of his opinions, indeed, were singularly like theirs; in doctrine he was orthodox, but the idea of a church composed of believers only, into which none but believers should be baptised, was one of their principal tenets  Southwark too, where Baillie avows that Browne taught, after leaving Cambridge, had a large Dutch population; a long list of the names of Lowcountrymen living there being published in 1586.[2]

It may have been that these affinities led to his choice of a retreat, but more likely it was the memory of Cartwright that suggested it, for Cartwright had worked in the Channel Islands, and now had a church in Middelburg which they may have joined for a short time on their arrival. A few of the congregation stayed in Norwich. George Johnson, in 1603, speaks of the church there, with Hunt as its Pastor, as elder sister of the Amsterdam church.

---

[1] S.P. Dom. vol. clxiii., Nov. 21, 1583, no. 69.
[2] *Ibid.* vol. cxc., Dec. 1586, no. 86.

Browne's church had but a short and inglorious life in Middelburg, the history of which he tells himself in the "True and Short Declaration."[1]

If it joined Cartwright at all, it was not for long. it soon began to hold separate meetings in Browne's' "chamber." The obligation on church members to criticize and discipline each other could not fail to be abused amongst ordinary human beings, and quarrels and recriminations finally broke up the church. Browne laid down his pastorship three several times, and each time was induced to take it up again; finally in despair he left his company to Harrison, and returned with a few followers to Scotland. But during the stay in Holland his most important literary work was done; there he wrote the "Treatise on 23rd Matthew," the "Book which Sheweth," and the "Treatise of Reformation," as well as the "True and Short Declaration." The first three treatises, and two from the pen of Harrison, published soon after they reached Holland, led to a special proclamation from the Queen against "schismatical books and Libels," and Elias Thacker and John Copping were hanged at Bury St Edmunds for distributing and defending them.

After his return, Browne wandered about Scotland and England, possibly went "beyond sea" once more, but little is known of him until in 1585, wearied with his outlawry, his theories pruned by sharp experience, he made some form of subscription to the Archbishop of Canterbury, and became nominally conformable. It is probable that his subscription was so worded as to make considerable reservations possible, but his views seem really to have moderated somewhat. In the few writings known to belong to the later period of his life, although he is vehement as ever about the need for a preaching ministry, and for the true calling of ministers, although he rails as harshly as ever against the mistaking of forms

[1] True and Short Declaration, 21-24.

and ceremonies for realities and truth, he shows more tolerance, and more disposition to respect the law and the magistrates, provided their decrees were not incompatible with conscience.  In other words, he seems to be realising that it would be wiser to follow the law wherever possible, instead of combating it wholesale ; to make the best of existing institutions, instead of overturning all.

His conformity was not indeed very pronounced, and in 1586 he and his wife were cited to appear before the Bishop of Peterborough as recusants.

Soon afterwards, Browne began to teach once more, and became schoolmaster in St Olave's Grammar School, Southwark.   His position was very anomalous ; when accepting the mastership he openly acknowledged certain "distinctions and exceptions" in his promise of conformity; the accusations of his enemy, Bredwell, show how very loose was his adherence to the English Church, yet at the same time he was writing against Barrow and Greenwood, who echoed the extreme Separatism of his earlier years ; defending in some sort the preachers of the Church of England, acknowledging their calling since they could beget faith, and commending their war against abuses. " A letter to Mr Flower,"[1] written for the New Year of 1589, shows the same appreciative attitude towards the Church of England, comparing it favourably with Presbyterianism.  He says that some of his bitterest persecution was as the hands of the Scotch Presbyterians, a testimony very different from that of Penry, who bids his children " Show yourselves helpful and kind unto all strangers and unto the people of Scotland, where I, your mother and a couple of you, lived as strangers, and yet were welcome and found great kindness for the name of our God."

Soon after this, Browne gave up his mastership and sought an office in the Church.  In June 1591 he was instituted to the rectory of Little Casterton, and in

---

[1] Reprinted 1904.  "A New Year's Guift."

September was finally ordained deacon and priest, and became rector of Achurch-cum-Thorpe, which was in the gift of Burghley.

Little is known of his later life, but he was rector there until his death in 1633. Probably he employed curates, and devoted himself chiefly to a little band of unorthodox people within his parish; it is possible that the story of his excommunication and submission, formerly given as the cause of his subscription in 1585, belongs to this period. The story of his death is that as a very old man he struck the constable of the parish, who too roughly demanded the payment of a rate, and for this offence was imprisoned. Too "infirme to goe, too unweldie to ride, and no friend so favorable as to purchase for him a more comly conveyance" he was placed on a feather bed in a cart and carried to Northampton jail, and there he died.[1]

Browne's defection was a sorrow and scandal to all who accepted his views; he earned the fate of most men who adopt a middle course, and was reviled by those on either side. His conformity was too qualified to allay the suspicions of the Church, and to his former followers he appeared "as a coward and one that shrinketh in the wetting."[2] Possibly in his early days he had not worked out his own arguments to their logical conclusion; though he urged separation, possibly like the Puritans he clung in his inmost soul to the roots of the old Church, much as he condemned her outgrowths, and when his own attempts at reform had ended in ignominious failure, he grew to have more respect for her slower and more conservative methods. Browne's calm exposition of his later views makes it impossible to believe that he became permanently insane, but there are some indications, both in his writings and in the traditions which grew up around his name, that his balance may occasionally have been disturbed. A mind capable of ranging so far beyond the

---

[1] Fuller's "Church History," v. 70.
[2] Bredwell, quoted in "True Story of Robert Browne," p. 50.

limitations of his age, must have been without some of
the restraints which hold down ordinary men to safer
planes, and physical suffering and mental excitement
may have unhinged him.   He writes touchingly in 1588,
" For I am poor enough and broken to to much with
former troubles, and therefore had no need of further
affliction " ;[1] few men have suffered more for what they
believed to be the truth, and yet all the honour and glory
of martyrdom was denied him.   But the success of his
work was his true crown, though he might never wear it.
He had set moving forces too powerful for him to arrest,
even had he wished to do so, and soon another man was
found to hasten them on and direct their course.

This was Henry Barrow.   He, like Browne, was a man
of an impetuous and independent mind, but he had had
a legal training, and Browne's writings seem archaic and
mystical beside those of this valuable exponent, so clear
headed and alive to every bearing of an argument.   In
his hands the movement passed, as it must do to be
successful, to a stage where its constructive side was
emphasized more than the other.   Probably on account
of the scandal of Browne's subscription, Barrow, like most
later Separatists, denied all connection with the Brownists,
yet it is difficult to find any essential point in which he
did not agree with them.   He, too, asserted the uncon-
ditional and supreme authority of the Scriptures, interpreted by the help of God's Spirit, he too defined a
church as a faithful people separated from the unbelievers
of the land, gathered by the Word unto Christ, and joined
as members of one body.

The order of church government he declared to have
been immutably ordained in the New Testament ; the
power of ordination was not derived from the Apostles
and Evangelists, but the true Church must call its own ministers and depose them, and must be free from any servile
dependence on the civil power or on ecclesiastical synods.

[1] New Year's Guift, p. 43.

Even its maintenance must have no worldly taint; the ministers must be supported not by tithes, but by the free offerings of their people. The former means of maintenance he thought should be put to civil uses; many of the Separatists suggested education, and this was actually done in Holland.

The difference between the two men was chiefly one of emphasis. In reading Barrow's works immediately after Browne's, one is struck by a difference in the relative stress which they lay upon their points. Both men were impulsive and outspoken to the verge of recklessness, neither of them hesitated to overturn or to destroy, but Barrow was a shade less democratic in his views, a shade more high-church, if such a term can be used. While emphasizing the fact that a minister is still a layman, he gives on the whole more importance to the officers of the church; he admits no equality among church members, though all have a like interest in the Word and the Faith, and all have the right of prophecy; the church is to acknowledge and submit to its leaders. But he was far from adopting the Presbyterian idea of government by elders. "Elders are appointed to see the government and order of Christ observed, not to take yt al into their hands."[1] Discipline was to belong to the whole church, and it appointed and controlled its officers; "every stone hath his beauty, his burden, and his order."[2]

He seems also to lay greater stress on the sacraments as a means of grace, and has a strong sense of the indelible character of baptism, even when administered in a false church. He had a horror of the Anabaptists utterly unknown to Browne, and no doubt shrank from any semblance of agreement with them. So, although he holds that baptism in a false church is no baptism, and that without true baptism no people can proceed to the formation of a true church, thus creating a deadlock, he expressly

---

[1] Brief Discovery, p. 223.
[2] A Description out of the Word of God, etc.

forbids that any should be rebaptised, saying that "The errours and faults of Baptism being purged by repentance, it pleases God, in pardoning the faults, to reserve, and not to have repeated, the outward action."[1]

He is no less congregational than Browne with regard to the rights and duties of a church towards its members. He would not however forbid synods, if they did not interfere with the rights of the congregation, and if every member of the church had a right to be heard in them.

He emphasizes the duty of the Prince in forwarding true religion, and rooting out the false, but he, too, says that "The Churche need not staye for the Prince in the reforminge of any abuse, but may reforme it, though the Prince saye noe."[2] There are a few points in which Barrow does not carry our sympathy with him, where he seems unnecessarily fanatical. He considered it wrong for the Church to have any concern with marriages or burials; he carried his objections to popish ornaments so far that he wished to destroy not only them, but the very buildings and churches in which they had been, and in which the old services had been held. He had, too, a violent objection to pulpits, " a prescript place like a Tub,"[3] and complained that the clergyman "in that his privileged Tub," might preach what he liked, and no one might answer him. He further objected to the names of the days of the week, holding that they were heathen, and ought to be abolished.

As the years went on his eccentricities were more pronounced, and he grew more rigid as Browne had grown more flexible. The difference in their circumstances would account for this; Browne's life was spent in battling with strange experiences, in contact with men of all kinds, whilst Barrow's views came to maturity within the narrow walls of a prison. The two men were born probably about the same year, 1550; Barrow came from

[1] Brief Discovery, p. 119.
[2] Examinations in Egerton Papers, p. 170.      [3] Brief Discovery.

Shipdam in Norfolk, and was connected with Lord Bacon, distantly with Burghley, and possibly also with Aylmer, Bishop of London, one of his bitterest enemies. His family seemed to take little part in the tragedy of his life; we hear of no relatives intervening, either to reproach or help him; save for his friendship with Greenwood he stands utterly alone. He took his B.A. at Clare Hall, Cambridge, in 1567-70; later he became a member of Gray's Inn, but was never called to the Bar. He was much about the Court, and both at Court and University he had opportunities to learn a great deal that was profligate and bad. Bacon says, that he "made a leap from a vain and libertine youth to a preciseness in the highest degree, the strangeness of which alteration made him very much spoken of";[1] and Bradford in his "Dialogues" relates the story of his conversation. "Walking one Lord's day, with one of his companions, he heard a preacher very loud as they passed by the church. Upon which Mr Barrowe said unto his consort, 'Let us go in and see what this man saith that is thus earnest.' 'Tush,' saith the other, 'what! shall we go to hear a man talk?' But in he went, and sat down." So touched and stricken was Barrow by what he heard, that "he left the Court and retired himself to a private life, sometime in the country and sometime in the city, giving himself to study and reading of the Scriptures and other good works very diligently; and being missed at Court by his consorts and acquaintances, it was quickly hinted abroad that Barrow was turned Puritan."[2]

How he took the further step and became a Separatist, we do not know, probably through the influence of his friend John Greenwood, who in his turn may have been influenced by Browne both at Cambridge, and later in Norfolk.

He had been deprived of his benefice in Norfolk, and

[1] Observations on a Libel.
[2] Bradford's Dialogue in Young's "Chronicles," p. 434.

had for some time assisted at the meetings of a conventicle in the house of Lord Rich at Rochford.  The Bishop of London put a summary end to these, and Greenwood came to London, where he, as well as Barrow, knew something of the Separatist church at Southwark, which since the days of Mr Fitz had been often scattered, never entirely rooted out.

In the autumn of 1586, whilst reading the Scriptures to a number of people on the Lord's Day in the house of a friend, Greenwood was arrested and imprisoned for holding a private conventicle.  Barrow visited him in the Clink six weeks later, was detained, and in spite of his protests against the illegality of the arrest, was taken to Lambeth to be examined by the Archbishop, and committed to prison in the Gatehouse.  Soon after he was indicted under a recusancy act of 1581 really intended for Papists, and from this time he was probably never again at liberty until his death in 1593.  He was examined five times in the hope of making him retract his opinions about the Church of England, which he delivered with dangerous freedom, but so far from retracting, he undoubtedly prejudiced his cause by his violence and the utter lack of conciliation in his manner.  He refused persistently to swear upon the book, to call the days of the week by their ordinary names, or to admit even the Lord's prayer as anything but a model, and thus irritated not only Whitgift, but Burghley, who called him a " fantastical fellow " and threatened him with " straiter laws " even than those made for the Papists.[1]

These examinations, and the conferences which followed, served little useful purpose at the time, but, recorded as they were by the prisoners themselves, they give us a vivid picture of Barrow which we could ill afford to do without.  On his knees before his interrogators, he is now the astute lawyer, exact in his phrases, anxious to have proofs in writing of all that is said, giving chapter and

[1] Examinations in Harleian Miscellany, vol. iv. p. 354 (mistake for 352).

verse for all his arguments ; now the passionate enthusiast, yearning to make himself heard of all, to give the message which is burning through him, cost what it may.  He is dogmatical, almost a fanatic, through his sense that to him also, in a lesser degree, has been given the spirit of Christ and the Apostles, that through him the written Word may be interpreted.  Again he is a man of very human frailties, filled with anger against the men who seemed to him to defile their office.  Asked if he knew the Bishop of London, he answered " His name is Elmer, my Lord," and regretted that I laid him not open for a wolf, a bloody persecutor, and an aposta." [1]  When asked the same question about the Archbishop of Canterbury, "The Lord gave me the spirit of boldness, so that I said : He is a monster, a miserable compound ; I know not what to call him, he is neither ecclesiastical nor civil, even the second beast that is spoken of in the Revelation."  He was finding his reference when "the beast arose for anger and gnashed his teeth, and said, ' Will ye suffer him, my lord ? " ' and Barrow was plucked up from his knees by the warden's man, and led back to his cell.

He had great provocation ; confined in a close and horrible prison, deprived for the most part of air, exercise, companionship, and the means to make his own defence, it was no wonder that his temper was irritable and uncompromising.  His reply to Burghley's harshness, " O my Lord ; speak more comfortablie, we haue sorrowes ynough "; his unanswered appeal for the " libertie of the aire," arouse our pity.  He had a true humility, in spite of his hot temper ; and when Burghley accused him of taking the Lord's name too often in vain, he was touched to the quick, and prayed earnestly for grace to set a more careful watch before his lips.

Barrow's ceaseless petition for a public conference with some dignitaries of the Church, in which their differences could be fairly argued out, at length met with a response.

[1] Examinations in Harleian Miscellany, vol. iv. p. 353.

In 1590 conferences were arranged between Barrow, Greenwood and other sectaries, and a number of preachers of the Church of England. The conferences were hardly public, being held in the porter's lodge of the prison, and the preachers were seldom even moderately open-minded, but Barrow made the most of his opportunities, for the burning desire to speak his mind, to set out fairly his true, and as he thought, irrefutable position, overcame all prudence.

No result came from the conferences, and Barrow and Greenwood, seeking some other means of utterance, began their literary work.

The amount which they managed to write and to have printed from their prison was marvellous. Barrow has even been credited with the authorship of the Mar-prelate tracts, but their views on some points seem incompatible with his, and they were probably Puritan rather than Separatist. But apart from these, his literary achievements were enormous, considering the difficulties in the way, the dim and noisome prison, the deadening effect of long confinement, the heavy risks which all who helped him must run. The prisoners were permitted visitors at times, and these must have smuggled out their writings sheet by sheet, to be given to their friends Robert Stokes and Robert Bowle, who paid the expenses, carried them over to Dort in Holland to be printed by "one Hanse," brought them back to England in Stoke's "clock bag," and circulated them so far as the Bishops' vigilance would permit.[1] This traffic came to an end in 1591, when Whitgift's agents intercepted 3000 copies of Barrow's last treatises on their way over from Holland, and when Stokes became a member of the Church of England, and would do no more work for the Separatists. Nothing more was published until the next century; and now, the conferences over, his writings forced to remain unprinted and unknown, Barrow had no voice save in the lamentable petitions which set forth the sufferings of himself and his friends.

[1] Egerton Papers, p. 175.

The church at Southwark, persecuted as it was, had been growing, and had had some valuable accessions. Francis Johnson, convinced by one of Barrow's books, joined it in 1591; and a year later Penry, who began life as a Roman Catholic, and was later the Puritan evangelist of Wales, his native country, also became a member. In 1592 Greenwood was released for a time on bail, and the church was fully officered and reorganised; Johnson was made pastor, Greenwood teacher, Daniel Studley and George Kniveton, elders, Christopher Bowman and Nicholas Lee, deacons. But in about three months its chief members were arrested once more; the prisons were full, sickness and death were busy amongst them, and their petitions sound like the last cries of men who feel that their lives, and something more precious than their lives are being crushed out. " We crave for all of us but the liberty either to die openly or to live openly in the land of our nativity. If we deserve death, it beseemeth the Majesty of Justice not to see us closely murdered, yea, starved to death with hunger and cold, and stifled in loathsome dungeons. If we be guiltless, we crave but the benefit of our innocency, viz.: That we may have peace to serve our God and our Prince in the place of the sepulchres of our fathers." [1]

To the Queen, to Burghley, to Parliament, and to the Privy Council, petitions came from the imprisoned Separatists, but they met with little response, and for Barrow and Greenwood the end was soon to come. They were convicted on March 23rd 1593 for publishing and dispersing seditious books, and condemned to death. Barrow was accused of having declared the Queen's Majesty to be unbaptised, the State to be wholly corrupt, and all the people of the land to be infidels, all of which charged he explained and denied. But there was no forgiveness for him; he had been kept in prison six years before committing the offence for which he died, and his enemies

[1] Petition to the Queen.

were not to be baulked now. Execution was deferred twice, it was said at the intervention of Burghley, who complained that their blood should be shed in a land where no Papist was touched for religion by death; and in the interval, Barrow wrote earnestly to "an honourable lady and countess of his kindred," stating his defence. "Your ladyship, then, will do a right Christian and gracious act to inform Her Majesty of our entire faith unto God, unstained loyalty to Her Majesty, innocency and good conscience toward all men; and so to procure our pardon," or, failing this, removal of "our poor worn bodies out of this miserable gaol (the horror whereof is not to be spoken to your Honour) to some more honest and meet place, if she vouchsafe us longer to live."

This last appeal failed, and on April 6th Barrow and Greenwood "were, early in the morning, hanged." [1] It was not long before Penry, convicted most unjustly, shared the same fate for similar offences, and those members of the London church who were happy enough to regain their liberty, acted on his last words of advice, and made their escape to Holland.

Governor Bradford tells some anecdotes which, if true, would show that Elizabeth regretted her severity towards Barrow and Greenwood. She spoke to Dr Reynolds and to the Earl of Cumberland about them, and the end they had made, but got no consolation, for there was nothing but good to be said of them. Finally "the Queen demanded of the Archbishop (Whitgift) 'What he thought of them in his conscience.'

"He answered 'He thought they were the servants of God, but dangerous to the State.'

"'Alas,' said she, 'shall we put the servants of God to death?' And this was the true cause why no more of them were put to death in her days." [2]

---

[1] S.P. Dom. vol. ccxliv. no. 124, 1593.
[2] Dialogue in Young's "Chronicles."

# CHAPTER III

## THE CHURCH AT SCROOBY

ONLY a very few years after the death of Barrow and Greenwood, when the hopes of the Separatists were at their lowest ebb, there arose at Scrooby in Nottinghamshire the famous church of the Pilgrim Fathers.

There was but little religious persecution in the last years of Elizabeth, for Browne had ceased to be a power; Barrow and Greenwood were dead; their church had escaped from imprisonment to Holland, and it seemed as though extreme Nonconformity were stamped out. As events proved, its effective work was just about to begin. Its vitality lay in the fact that it advanced a practical reform scheme, and was not merely based on intellectual differences of opinion; the deficiencies and abuses that had given birth to it still remained, and so another group of serious people, who resented the neglect of the parishes, the tolerance of evil doers, and the vain insistence on ceremonies, began to see "How not only these base and beggarly ceremonies were unlawfull, but also that the lordly and tyranous power of the prelats ought not to be submitted unto." [1]

The next thing for these people to do, now that Browne and Barrow had pointed the way, was to form a church free from these defects; "they shooke off this yoake of antichristian bondage, and as the Lord's free people, joined themselves (by a covenant of the Lord) into a church estate, in the felowship of the Gospell, to walke in all his wayes made known, or to be made known unto

---

[1] Bradford MS., p. 5.

them, (according to their best endeavours) whatsoever it should cost them, the Lord assisting them: And that it cost them something, this ensewing historie will declare."

According to Bradford's nephew, Secretary Morton, a church estate was first entered into in the Scrooby district in 1602, and Bradford says "These people became two distincte bodys or churches, in regard of distance of place, and did congregate severally, for they were of sundry townes and vilages, some in Notinghamshire, some of Lincollinshire, and some of Yorkshire, where they Border nearest togeather."

These two churches were at Gainsborough and Scrooby, and a date given in the margin by Bradford or Morton fixes the division in 1606; but owing to the secrecy which necessarily attended their formation, and some difference in the evidence of historians, it is doubtful whether the two existed side by side in England, or whether the Scrooby Church was only formed after the Gainsborough people had gone to Holland.

The Pilgrim district in England was a sort of triangle,[1] having for its northern point Austerfield in Yorkshire, with Babworth and Worksop at the base; Scrooby itself being in Nottinghamshire, close to the borders of Yorkshire.

To account for such a church in such a district is very difficult. Its members were not, as in the churches of Browne and Barrow, inhabitants of busy mercantile centres, where the nature of their lives, and the constant foreign intercourse, fostered freedom of thought; they were almost all farmers, scattered over a sparsely populated country. The extreme Reformists could hardly have expected so soon to touch the agricultural population, always conservative and slow to move.

All the importance that Scrooby had, it owed to its position on the Great North Road, the main route from London to Scotland and the North. This was the channel along which flowed all the life that the little village ever

[1] Arber's "Pilgrim Fathers," p. 58.

saw; the current which would sweep past leaving the inhabitants high and dry on the bank, or again, would absorb them into its rush, carrying them on to good fortune or ruin.  Crafts bound on every sort of enterprise passed by, and sometimes a melancholy wreck returned.

Never since the time of the Roman occupation had roads been so inadequate and so badly kept as they were under Elizabeth.  Kemp, a morrice dancer, who danced from London to Norwich in 1600, found the way so foul that sometimes he skipped in mud up to the waist; Ogilby writes that the road from London to Berwick, though one of the most frequented in the Kingdom, was none of the best way ; so probably the name of the Great North Road was much more impressive than the reality.  Arber says, that it was " a mere horse track, and not fenced in, so that the traveller needed a guide to prevent his wandering out of the way." [1]  Thoresby writes of it, as a place easy enough to mistake the way in, but such as it was, in those days of slow travelling and scanty news, it was for the country district the one link with the outside world.

The " mene Tounelet of Scroby " as Leland calls it, was famed also for its Great Manor place, " standing withyn a Mote, and longging to th'Archbishop of York." [2]  This Manor, in which the Pilgrim Church congregated for a year or two before migrating to Holland, has now almost entirely disappeared.  In 1535, an inventory was made of the " implements " in the thirty-nine rooms of the Manor House ; in 1538 Leland, in his " Itinerary," described it as built in two courts, partly of timber and partly of brick, with a flight of stone steps ; but though these records, together with the mention in leases of the various buildings which were to be kept in repair by the tenant, seem to show that it was once of considerable size, successive demolitions have now reduced it to a mere farm-house.  A bricked-up archway, a niche in a wall of unusual thickness, some beams in an outbuilding, which

[1] P. 51.          [2] Leland's " Itinerary," i. p. 29.

SCROOBY MANOR AT THE PRESENT DAY

look as though they might have supported the chapel roof, are almost all the traces that remain to suggest the ancient building. Outside, there are indications of the moat, and mounds where the fishponds have been filled up with débris.

To this Manor House the Great North Road had brought both some of its triumphs and some of its failures. It had belonged to the See of York from very early times, and the Archbishop used it as a residence when he visited the southern part of his domain. Many differences were adjusted there at his informal courts in the thirteenth and fourteenth centuries, and in June 1503 Margaret, the daughter of Henry VII., stayed there for a night on her way to Scotland, where she was to marry James IV. Leland writes that after leaving Tuxford she " drew her way right to Sirowsby (a Manayer of the Reverend Father in God my Lord the Archbishop of Yorke) to her Bedd." There must have been great preparations at the Manor House, for the Princess brought with her a great train of noblemen and ladies, both Scotch and English, besides minstrels, officers " ordonned to make space that more plainly the sayde Queene and her companie might bee better sene," retainers, and a large escort of the chief men of the country. All would be entertained at the Manor, for these were hospitable days, and when James I spent a night at Worksop there was such store of provisions that " it was left open for any man that would to come and take." [1]

No triumphant escort followed a generation later, when Wolsey, driven from Court by the anger of the King, took refuge at Scrooby on his way to York. He was there for some weeks in the autumn of 1530, " ministering many deeds of charity. Most commonly every Sunday, if the weather did serve he would travel unto some parish church thereabout, and there would say his divine service ; and either hear or say mass himself, causing some one

[1] Nichols, " Progresses of Elizabeth and James."

of his chaplains to preach unto the people. And that done, he would dine in some honest house of that town ; where should be distributed to the poor, a great alms ; as well of meat and drink, as of money to supply the want of sufficient meat if the number of the poor did so exceed of necessity."[1] Tradition says that he planted a mulberry tree there, which existed until recently.

There must have been something very desirable about this old Manor ; Henry VIII. stayed there in 1541, and three years later bought it from Archbishop Holgate, but it was soon repurchased for the See. In 1582 Elizabeth attempted to have it leased to the Crown for seventy years, at a rental of £40 a year. Archbishop Sandys, almost broken hearted, remonstrated that to separate Scrooby and Southwell (which she also demanded) from the See for such a rent, would be a loss to it of £70,000 at least, and that, far from misliking his denial, she should think him unworthy to live, should he consent to so great an evil. Elizabeth apparently relented, but in 1603 James I. also made an attempt to get possession of the Manor. Nichols relates that during his progress from Scotland to take his place on the English throne, he stayed one night with the Earl of Shrewsbury at Worksop. On his way there, on entering into Nottinghamshire, he was met by the High Sheriff, who " conducted his Majesty on till he came within a mile of Blyth, where his Highness lighted and sat down on a bank side to eat and drink." James was rather pompous, and possibly this style of entertainment was too rustic for his taste, for soon after, he wrote to the Archbishop, Matthew Hutton, saying that he wished for an abode near Sherwood Forest for use during his passages between the two realms, and that he had noticed Scrooby and Southwell as being suitable. James was extremely fond of hunting ; on his way south he had slain two deer in Northumberland, and had been delighted

[1] Cavendish, "Wolsey," p. 260. Ed. 1825.

by an impromptu hunt, with huntsmen " all in green," got up for his amusement by the Earl of Shrewsbury in Worksop Park, and perhaps he hoped to relieve the tedium of some future journeys in the same way. He offered a more adequate return for the houses than Elizabeth had done, but the transfer was not made, and the Manor to this day is owned by the See of York.

Long before the time of James I., the prospective connection of Scrooby Manor with the Pilgrim Church had been established. The Archbishops were there but seldom, and the expense of keeping up the place was great ; so as early as 1558 parts were demolished, and the rest was leased to one James Byrne. He became receiver and bailiff for the Archbishop, and was bound to provide entertainment for him when he came ; and apparently the Manor became at the same time a house of call for travellers along the Great North Road. The next lease was granted to William Marshall, but he did not become bailiff, for in 1575 this office was given to William Brewster, who then came to live in the Manor House. Probably he had come to the neighbourhood some four years before, when his son William, who was to give such lasting renown to the old house, was a child of about five years old. Scrooby Manor had now become a regular post-house on the Great North Road, and in 1588 the elder William was also appointed postmaster under the crown.

There is no doubt that the Scrooby district was a religious one. There had been many monasteries about it, and if the strong Catholic spirit there was likely to oppose the Reformation at first, as indeed it did in the reign of Henry VIII., still a devout people, once they had accepted new principles, would probably be strenuous about them, and not lapse into indifference. But nevertheless the strength of the revival there, and the form that it took, can only be explained by looking to its leaders and their previous history ; it seems as though the force and energy of a few men, working on a neglected population, had carried the whole thing through, for after the departure of the Pilgrims, not a trace remained in the district of the spirit which had enforced them.

There are three men round whom the early fortunes of the Pilgrims seem to centre, Clifton, Brewster, and Robinson ; and of these, so long as they were in England, William Brewster was the leading spirit.  With one exception, he was the man of most learning amongst them ; during his lifetime he read widely, taught clearly, and even knew something of the printing of books, and at his death he left a large and varied library in English and Latin, dealing with theology, politics, philosophy and general literature.  Without any exception at all, he was the man who had most knowledge of the world, of states-men, and statecraft.  We know little of his progress towards Separatism, but we have Bradford's testimony as to the work he did for it.  He seems to have financed the cause, and to him was due no doubt its spread through-out the scattered neighbourhood.

Brewster's education and training fitted him well for the leading position which he took among the Pilgrims. He was born probably about 1566 ; the place of his birth is unknown, but in 1571 his father was assessed for a subsidy in the township of Scrooby.  In 1590 when his father died, the younger William was an only child ; there were other Brewsters living in the neighbourhood, and they may have been connections, but it is likely that the family came from Suffolk.

Although little is known of them, they seem to have been of good position and well off.  In December 1580, William matriculated at Peterhouse, Cambridge, under Dr Perne, whose skill in keeping his position during the many religious changes of the century, had gained him the reputation of being a turncoat.  Martin Mar-prelate taunts him mercilessly, and his sermon before Elizabeth at Cambridge would have infuriated Browne and Barrow.[1]

---

[1] Mullinger, ii. p. 190.

But he was a good man and a scholar, devoted to his college and the University, and brave in their interests. He resisted stoutly the proposed royal nomination of fellows; he worked hard to improve the University Library, and himself left a large and valuable collection of books and manuscripts to enrich it. Probably it was from him that Brewster first gained his love of books.

If Perne were somewhat elastic in his convictions, Brewster must have come in contact with many men at Cambridge who were very much the reverse. Amongst these were John Udall, who died twelve years later in the Marshalsea, imprisoned for his vigorous writings against the Episcopacy; John Greenwood, who died with Barrow at Tyburn; George Johnson, brother of the pastor of the Ancient Church; and William Perkins, afterwards a famous preacher and writer, who is mentioned by both Robinson and Bradford, and many of whose books were in Brewster's library. When to these names are added that of John Penry, the reputed author of the Mar-prelate tracts; possibly those of Browne and his friend Harrison, it is obvious that the atmosphere into which Brewster entered at Cambridge was very largely tinged with advanced ideas on religious subjects, and whatever may have been his sympathies at the time, his serious and thoughtful mind must have been impressed by them. Theology was the chief study of the University at this date; next came logic and rhetoric; the study of Greek and mathematics was on the wane. But, whatever Brewster learned there, he turned it to good account later in Holland, where Bradford tells us that "he fell into a way, by reason he had the Latin tongue, to teach many students who had a desire to learn the English tongue, to teach them English: and by his method they quickly attained it with great facilitie, for he drew rules to learne it by, after the Latine maner, and many gentlemen, both Danes and Germans resorted to him as they had time

from other studies, some of them being great Men's Sons."[1]
Nothing is actually known of Brewster's life at Cambridge,
nor even how long he stayed there.  Bradford says
"some small time," but considering the number of years
often spent there on a university course, "some small
time" might mean as much as two or three years.

After he left, he went into the service of William
Davison, and so entered upon the second important
part of his training.  Davison may have been an occasional guest at the Manor House, on his numerous
political journeys between London and Scotland in
1583-4, and Brewster seems to have been some sort of
personal attendant to him.  There was nothing de-
rogatory in this ; Sir Henry Killigrew, whose nephew
was likewise with Davison, begs him to "use him in all
things as a common servant,"[2] and in another letter,
advises that he should be kept under, and from idleness.
"He was wont," he writes, "to be called up of a morning,
and given to keep his bed over long, which will do him
no good."[3]  Young men in those days, even of high rank,
had a strict apprenticeship to serve.  Whatever was
Brewster's exact capacity, he showed himself worthy of
trust, for we hear that Davison "found him so discreete
and faithfull, as he trusted him above all others that were
aboute him, and only ymployed him in all matters of
greatest trust and secrecie ; he esteemed him rather as
a sonne than a servante ; and, for his wisdom and godliness, (in private) he would conuerse with him, more like
a freind and familier, than a maister."

Henceforth for several years Davison's fortunes were
Brewster's too, and together they shared some exciting
experiences.  In 1584 Davison was sent to the Hague
to conduct an extremely delicate negotiation.  The Low
Countries were in great danger from Philip II., who was

---

[1] Bradford MS., p. 255.

[2] S. P. Dom., Dec. 29th, 1580, vol. xxvii. no. 65.

[3] *Ibid.* Feb. 22nd, 1578, vol. xxv. no. 74.

bent on crushing out Protestantism and liberty, and they had appealed to Elizabeth to help them. She did not want the expense, nor did she approve of any revolt against a sovereign power, but on the other hand, as head of a Protestant nation, she felt some obligation to help the Dutch, and also she herself would be in greater danger from Philip, should they be wholly reduced. So Davison was sent over to see how little help she need give, and whether there was any hope that France would save her the trouble of giving any help at all. Brewster probably went with him, but they came back without making any terms, and not until Antwerp fell did Elizabeth send back her envoy to promise assistance. She then agreed to send over the Earl of Leicester to help govern the country, to provide some forces, and she was to receive the cautionary towns of Flushing, Brill, and Rammekins as a guarantee for payment. The keys of Flushing were given to Davison, and he handed them over to Brewster for safe keeping " who kept them under his pillow, on which he slept, the first night." When Leicester arrived, full of importance, and vain of the power he was to exercise, he made promises beyond the Queen's instructions, so that Davison, returning to report on what had been done, found that he, as well as Leicester, was in great disgrace. This was the first he had heard of Leicester's unauthorised doings, and probably he had left Holland in good spirits at the success of his work, for so pleased were the States-General with his negotiations, that they had presented him with a gold chain, which he committed to Brewster's care, "and commanded him to wear it, when they arrived in England, as they rid through the country till they came to the Court." He was soon reinstated in the Queen's favour, for all spoke strongly of the great service he had done in the Low Countries, and in 1586 he became Secretary of State.

But Queen Elizabeth's most faithful servants had a

very precarious time ; before long Davison was again
employed in a delicate matter, and needless to say he
got into trouble.   It was about Mary Queen of Scots.
She had now been absolutely convicted of conspiracy
against Elizabeth's throne and life, she was closely imprisoned at Chartley Manor, and Parliament was clamour-
ing for her death, that she might no longer be the centre
of foreign conspiracies and Popish plots.   Elizabeth,
under great pressure, finally signed the warrant, after
suggesting to Davison that Mary's warder, Sir Amyas
Paulet, might save her the odium of the execution by a
secret murder, and it fell to Davison's lot to seal the
warrant and have it carried into effect.   Although he,
knowing the Queen's methods, was most careful to do
nothing which she did not expressly order, no sooner
was Mary dead than Elizabeth accused him of violating
her commands, and sent him to the Tower.   There,
apparently Brewster went too, for Bradford says " He
afterwards remained with him till his troubles, that he
was put from his place about the Queen of Scots ; and
some good time after ; doing him many faithful offices
of service in the time of his troubles."

In spite of his manly and honest defence at his trial,
Davison was imprisoned and fined enormously.   He was
still in prison on August 14th, 1588,[1] but a letter from
him to the Queen "from my poor desolate house in
London," December 1590, shows that he was then at
liberty, though ruined by the fine.   Whether Brewster
left him before the end of his imprisonment is uncertain,
but at any rate he was back at Scrooby early in 1589.

He must have carried back with him a knowledge of
men and of affairs which would be invaluable to him in
later life ; indeed his experiences no doubt determined,
to a great extent, the course which the fortunes of the
Pilgrims took.   He had been in Holland, their future
home for many years ; and must have acquired there

---

[1] S. P. Dom., Aug. 14th ? 1588, vol. ccxv. no. 19.

entirely different views from those prevailing in England, both as to church government and the relations of Church and State ; he had encountered both in literature and in real life some of their chiefest enemies and their chiefest friends. Sir Edwin Sandys, who was their friend at court for many years, he may have known previously, as his father held the Manor House from Sir Samuel Sandys, the son of the Archbishop, but he probably had further opportunities of knowing him in London, for George Cranmer, a great friend of his, was in Davison's service at the same time as Brewster.

Davison's personal influence too was an element to be reckoned with in the development of his religious views. Any Puritan tendencies which Brewster had acquired at Cambridge would surely be accentuated under it, for Davison had long been elder of a Puritan Church in Antwerp,[1] where many English people found refuge in Mary's reign. He was a friend of Cartwright too, and apparently helped him with money, when he was forced to resign his position in Cambridge and live abroad.[2] Although he may never himself have inclined to Separatism, he could sympathise with men of the most extreme views ; he even pitied such fanatics as Coppinger and Hackett, and so grateful were they to him, that they declared he ought to be the first magistrate in England.[3] Probably he was by nature extremely tolerant, for even the Papists disliked Elizabeth's treatment of him, and this natural tolerance could only be increased by his intercourse with the broad-minded Netherlanders.

Apart from any definitely religious influence, Brewster could not fail to learn valuable lessons of fidelity and self-sacrifice during his life with Davison. He was always a good friend and a peacemaker, a man whom all loved and interceded for, and no one could less have deserved

[1] Add. MSS. 6394
[2] S.P. Dom., July 22nd 1586, vol. xxix. no. 125.
[3] *Ibid.* July 19th 1591, vol. ccxxxix. no. 93.

his fate. " Put not your trust in princes, nor in any child of man," might well have been the thought which Brewster took back with him to his quiet country home.

Probably he found his father in failing health when he returned. On his death in 1590, the new Master of the Posts, Sir John Stanhope, not knowing the facts of the case, gave the office of Post at Scrooby to a friend of his relative, Samuel Bevercotes, but William Brewster, supported by Davison, made good his claim to it, on the ground that he had practically held the office and done all the work for eighteen months previously.

A rough system of Posts had been established in Henry VIII.'s reign,[1] exclusively for the use of the sovereign, who had previously had to employ special couriers on affairs of state ; but even after the establishment of Posts by Sir Brian Tuke, the first Master, they were often temporary, during a special emergency only. The first regulation of the Posts was issued by Queen Elizabeth ; for the forwarding of Her Majesty's packets from one stage to another, each Post was required to have four good horses always in readiness, three good leather bags lined with baize or cotton, to carry the letters, and three horns, for every man riding in post was accompanied by a guide, who was to blow his horn "so oft as he meeteth company, or passeth through any town, or at the least thrice every mile." Any packets but those of the Queen were to pass as by-letters, and to go as they could ; the Post was not to go on purpose for them, and was strictly forbidden to attend to them, until he had discharged his official duties. Not until the reign of Charles II. was any proper arrangement made for the transmission of private correspondence.

The history of Posts, and the history of travelling, gradually became complicated, for as the horses were not always needed to carry letters, they were used also to pass on travellers from one stage or post to the next.

[1] Joyce, "History of the Post Office."

The roads were so bad, and so heavy for carriages, that it was still usual for all who could to travel on horseback. At first only travellers on the Queen's business could use the horses, but gradually, under one pretext or another, they were used by private persons too, and private persons began to carry letters. James I. issued further regulations forbidding this illicit carrying without a commission, settling the speed, the load, and the rate of payment of all carriers, and insisting that no traveller should take horses save from the authorised Post houses. So that the resources of travelling, as well as the privilege of letter carrying, were entirely in the hands of the sovereign.

The office of a postmaster was a very important and responsible one, for besides having all the government dispatches under his control, he exercised a sort of supervision over all who travelled through the country, and the Posts became a detective network by means of which conspiracies were checked and any undue excitement noted. A postmaster too was often sorter, letter carrier, and everything else, besides having to deliver letters in his own town, but nevertheless the office was very badly paid, and frequently not paid at all. In 1628, "99 poore men" complained that they had received no wages for nearly seven years. Brewster seems to have been luckier than most, and got his money fairly regularly. With the accession of James I., there was of course much more traffic between England and Scotland, and the importance of the Great North Road and the Posts along it increased accordingly. A copy of the accounts of Sir John Stanhope show that Brewster's wages as Post were raised in July 1603 from 20d. a day to 2s. a day, and the last payment made to him was from April 1st 1607 to September 30th 1607.[1] As he would probably hold his office as long as possible, this date helps to determine the date of the migration to Holland.

Of the years that he spent at Scrooby, Bradford writes

[1] Add. MSS. 25460,

that he was "in good esteem amongst his freinds and the gentlemen of those parts, especially the godly, and religious; he did much good in the countrie wher he lived, in promoting and furthering Religion, not only by his practiss and example and provocking and incouraging of others; but by procuring of good preachers to the places theraboute; and drawing on of others to assiste and help forward in shuch a work; he himselfe most comonly deepest in the charge, and sometimes above his abillitie." It is easy to see what a power this well-educated, studious man, with his wide experience of men and things, would be in the country district, and Brewster set about his missionary enterprise zealously. His position as postmaster helped him; he would be kept in touch with new ideas, would meet men of all opinions; he would always hear how things were going, and how much he could venture with safety; and his large house was an excellent place for meetings, or to shelter his preaching guests.

The most active agent for good whom he would find in the neighbourhood was probably Richard Clyfton, rector of Babworth since 1586. He was a Derbyshire man, educated at Cambridge, and during the time that he held the living at Babworth, he was known as a "forward" preacher, in other words a Puritan and reformer. There is a list extant[1] of sixty parishes in the neighbourhood, amongst which were only twelve ministers "sufficient and painful," the rest being either non-resident, negligent, or even scandalous; and Burghley openly accused the Bishop of Lichfield in Council of having made seventy ministers in one day for money, some tailors, some shoemakers, and other craftsmen,[2] so there was probably ample scope for such men as Brewster and Clyfton, who were both of course still members of the Church of England.

[1] Birch Add. MS. 4293, 41. See also S. P. Dom., 1565? vol. xii. 108.
[2] S. P. Dom., Feb. 27, 1585, vol. clxxvi. no. 68.

In 1601 Richard Bernard became Vicar of Worksop, seven miles from Babworth, and although he was later one of the bitterest enemies of the Separatists, in these early days he greatly sympathised with some of their views, and no doubt his preaching helped to spread them. He was a harsh opponent, but a shrewd and interesting man, and his non-controversial works, one of them an allegory in the style of " Pilgrim's Progress," deserve to be better known.

Far more important however was the advent of the Rev. John Robinson in 1604. He was born in Lincolnshire, possibly at Gainsborough, about 1576. Both Emmanuel and Christ's College have been claimed as his, but it seems certain that he entered Corpus Christi College in 1592. Cambridge was still a hot-bed of unorthodoxy ; only two years before this date, Francis Johnson had been obliged to resign his fellowship for directing his very considerable influence against the State Church ; William Perkins, Catechist at Christ's College, whom Robinson held in great esteem and often referred to, was giving offence to the authorities by his Puritan preaching, and controversies were going on between Peter Baro and the rigid Calvinists on such subjects as predestination and freewill ; subjects which Robinson was to deal with fully in later life.

In 1598 he became a Fellow of Corpus, and presumably took orders at the same time, though it is possible that his scruples about vestments and ceremonies prevented the submission to the authorities necessary for obtaining full orders. He then probably came in touch with the Brownists and Dutch Protestants of Norfolk, for he took charge of a parish near Norwich, possibly Mundham, fourteen miles from Yarmouth, and this he held until 1603, when he was suspended for increasing nonconformity. For some time he tried to retain a connection with the Church by using a leased chapel, or through the mastership of some hospital, where conformity might be less strictly enforced, but in this he failed.  Bishop Hall maliciously suggests that it was chagrin at this failure which led to his final separation from the Church of England, but we know from Robinson's own words how anxious he was to avoid separation, and how small a licence with regard to observances would have contented his conscience at first.  Robbed of any such hope, he preached for a time to a small Separatist congregation in Norwich, and in 1604 went to Cambridge to resign his fellowship, and cast in his lot finally with those who could find no room in the English Church.

He stayed sadly on for a few days at Cambridge, and there heard two sermons, one by Chaderton, whose text was "Tell the Church," and who emphasized the responsibility of discipline which lay with every true Church; the other by Paul Baynes on the separation of the servants of God from the wicked.  Probably Robinson felt more strongly about self-purification, than about the harm that might come from contact with the wicked, intolerance being so far from his nature, but, confirmed in his resolve by the words he had heard, he went to join Clyfton.

It is not known when Clyfton resigned his living and definitely broke with the Established Church; his youngest child Eleazer was born at Babworth in 1598, but no doubt by this time he and his congregation had become alienated from it.  He must have been aged by much anxiety and persecution, for, though he was born only about 1553, Bradford describes him as "a grave and fatherly old man when he came first into Holland, having a great white beard." [1]

Brewster too had striven hard for reforms within the Church, but when the parish services were ill-conducted, or not conducted at all, and when any private attempt to fill the gap was forbidden and severely punished, he lost hope, and persecution drove him to separation.  Bradford

[1] Dialogue in Young's "Chronicles."

writes of him, " And in the end, by the Tyranny of the
Bishops against the godly preachers, and people, in
silencing the one, and persecuting the other; he, and
many more of those times, begane to look further into
things, and to see into the unlawfulness of their callings,
and the burthen of many anti-Christian corruptions, which
both he, and they, endeavoured to cast of; as they also
did, (as in the begining of this Treatis is to be seen).

So about 1606 the Church at Scrooby was formally
organised, "there was first one stood up and made a
covenant, and then another, and these two joined together,
and so a third, and these became a church."[1]

The ecclesiastical organisation of the Pilgrim Church
was never elaborate; it did not model itself strictly on
the lines of the Holy Discipline, but chose the best men
it could get for the absolutely necessary offices, and did
not insist on any others.  Indeed, it was put to such
shifts for many years, that it was far less rigid in its
organization than were other Separatist churches, and it
certainly does not lose in human interest on that account.

Clyfton became pastor, with Robinson as his assistant ;
they may have had one or more deacons, and in later
years at least, Brewster was their elder.

Under his roof they met to hold their simple services.
"After they were joyned togither in comunion he was a
spetiall stay and help unto them, they ordinarily mett at
his house on the Lord's Day, (which was a Manor of the
Bishops) and with great love he entertained them when
they came, making provission for them to his great charge ;
and continued so to doe whilst they could stay in
England."  Very little is known of the congregation
which gathered there.   They were poor, unimportant
people, farmers for the most part, for there was little else
to do around Scrooby ; their doings were not likely to
cause remark, and to have gained notoriety as Separatists
would have been suicidal.   James had told the Puritans

[1] Murton, " Description," p. 169.

at the Hampton Court Conference that, unless they conformed, he would harry them out of the land, or do worse, and he meant to keep his word.

A few, in spite of all precautions, became known to the authorities, and from the records of the Ecclesiastical court at York,[1] we have the names of Gervase Nevile of Scrooby, who had to answer a charge of Brownism on March 22nd 1608; Richard Jackson and Robert Rochester, who, with William Brewster, were fined £20 apiece for not appearing before the commissioners on April 22nd 1608; and Thomas Toller of Sheffield, who likewise failed to appear; Hugo Bromhead may have been another member,[2] and on July 26th 1608 John Drewe, Thomas Jessop, and Joan Helwys, accused of Brownism, were sent back to prison for refusing to answer questions upon oath; but as the husband of Joan Helwys was a prominent man in the Gainsborough church, these may have been members of the sister congregation.

A few more Scrooby names are to be found in the Leyden records; Elizabeth Neal, who was betrothed and married to Edward Buckram; Edward Southworth, who went to Leyden and died there; and whose widow became the second wife of Governor Bradford; Francis Jessop, a man of wealth and family, who married Frances White in Worksop in 1605, and became a citizen of Leyden in 1625; and George Morton, who married Juliana Carpenter in Leyden in 1622. If Morton belonged, as is supposed, to the Mortons of Bawtry, he was the only member of the Scrooby Church who could claim a noble ancestry. The family was more than locally important, and its members were zealous Roman Catholics long after the Reformation. Nicholas Morton was "a notable busy factor for the Pope in England"[3] and was much implicated in the intrigues which circled around Mary Queen of Scots; it was he too who brought over the Papal Bull

---

[1] Quoted in Waddington, p. 163.     [2] Harl. MSS., 360.
[3] Strype, "Annals," ii. 577-9.

denouncing Elizabeth in 1570. For a member of such a family to become a Separatist would be striking; but certainly one named George remains unaccounted for about this time. George Morton was a prominent man among the Pilgrims in Holland, and was more than once their ambassador to England. He had intended to go with the *Mayflower*, but stayed on a little while in England, and saw to the publication of the account of their first winter in America, to which he wrote an introduction, and which is known as "Mourt's Relation." He went to Plymouth in 1623, but died less than a year after.

But the member of the Scrooby Church who was to be of permanent importance to its fortunes was William Bradford. He was a very young man at this time, and not until the Pilgrims reached America, and the commercial and political side of their enterprise became of pressing importance, had he a chance to show his powers. From that moment he took the lead and was foremost in everything they did. He was not a scholar like John Robinson, nor a man of the world like Brewster; he knew little of Courts and Universities; but he was a practical man of business, and had, besides, enough of both learning and statesmanship to rule over the simple little community. Above all, he was tolerant, public-spirited, and a shrewd judge of men, and the success of the colony was the best tribute to his gifts.

Already, however, he was recognised as an important member of the little band, partly through his position, but much more through his force of character and mental ability. He was born in 1588 at Austerfield in Yorkshire, a little village close to the borders of Nottinghamshire, only three miles from Scrooby. There is a record of his baptism at Austerfield Church in 1589, and the old baptismal font, which had come to base use as a drinking trough for cattle, has been lately rescued and reinstated, through American influence. Little is known of the

5

Bradford family, save the records of their births and deaths; they belonged to the yeoman class, and were moderately well-to-do. The will left by Robert Bradford, William's uncle, committed his children to the care of the most considerable persons in the district, and the family seems to have shared the best of a very limited society. This same will vigorously declares the Christian faith of its author, and leaves 10s. to Austerfield Church; but according to Cotton Mather, the spiritual opportunities of the district were few, and the people "as unacquainted with the Bible as the Jews do seem to have been with part of it in the days of Josiah."[1] Fletcher, the incumbent about this time, was, however, a resident minister, for his large family of children were all baptised at Austerfield, so they were better off than many parishes in England.

William Bradford was a delicate child; "soon and long sickness kept him, as he would afterwards thankfully say, from the vanities of youth." His father died in 1591, and his uncles, in whose charge he was, had intended him to be a farmer, but his ill-health made this impossible, and no doubt the same cause gave him time and inclination for thoughtful pursuits. Silvester, a clergyman living at Alkley near by, who received a legacy under Robert Bradford's will, and who was made guardian of William's cousin Mary, had a library of English and Latin books, and it may have been here that the boy studied. Brewster would be another tutor to him, after they met, and would give him more than book-learning. When he was twelve or fourteen years old, the Scriptures made a deep impression on his mind, and, being practical, he tried to find some counterpart of their teaching in actual life. Babworth was only ten miles away, and Clyfton's "illuminating ministry" soon led him first to Puritanism, and then, after much struggle and deliberation, to separation; "although the provoked rage of his friends tried all the ways imaginable to reclaim him from it." Not unnaturally,

[1] Magnalia Christi Americana.

BIRTHPLACE OF WILLIAM BRADFORD

they were opposed to his indulging in such a very unpopular hobby as Nonconformity, and must have thought that he was wilfully endangering his prospects for a whim, and requiting very poorly their care for him. William, however, stood firm, lamenting the breach with his friends, but showing himself willing to suffer all things for the sake of a good conscience. He neither wished them to be angry with him nor to be sorry for him, and though "some lamented him, some derided him, all dissuaded him," he would not yield, and as the chief of his relations died soon after, he was convinced "what a folly it had been to have quitted his profession in expectation of any satisfaction from them," a touch of reasoning which helps one to understand the adamant stuff the Pilgrims were made of, and their perfect readiness to sacrifice themselves, and any one else, on the altar of principle.

When they reached Holland, Bradford, like every one else, had to take a trade for his livelihood, and in Amsterdam he apprenticed himself to a French Protestant to learn the art of silk-dyeing. Evidently he had brought little private means out of England, but his uncle, Robert Bradford, who died a few months later, had probably been trustee for some property which William would inherit from his grandparents, for in 1611, being of age, we are told that he converted his estates into money. He then set up in trade for himself, but was unsuccessful, and lost a great part of his substance. In the record of his marriage with Dorothy May, in 1613, he is called a fustian worker, and he probably learned this trade when his commercial enterprise failed. His wife was only sixteen, the daughter of Mrs May, who was a member of Johnson's church in Amsterdam, and sister of Jacomyne May, who married Jean de l'Ecluse; and she was drowned off the *Mayflower* before they landed at Plymouth.

Bradford made use of his time in Holland to learn Dutch and French, having a talent for languages; but he is mentioned very little in the records of this time. These were years of preparation, the full account of his work belongs to the life at Plymouth. But his words must be quoted so often that one part of his later work cannot be left unmentioned any longer—his invaluable histories. Without them our knowledge of the Pilgrim movement would be very thin and colourless; his "Dialogue" is practically a defence of Separatism, and gives vivid pictures of many of its leaders; his "Letter Book," or rather the fragment that remains of it, gives much of the early correspondence of the emigrants; and his "History of the Plimoth Plantation" is the first authority on the early life of the colony, and the sole source of information on many points. Although the "History" was written probably during the last years of his life (1644-50), the project was an old one; he mentions it as early as 1625-6, and no doubt he was then collecting his material. It is written in simple graphic style, sometimes with much detail, sometimes more scantily than we could wish, but always with moderation and a true sense of proportion, and its interest never flags. The language is quaint and biblical, and nothing in the book strikes one more than Bradford's sense of the high destiny of the Pilgrims. To him they were God's chosen people, working out His will towards them; although he was by no means a superstitious man, every success and every misfortune was interpreted as a sign that God's Providence was watching over them, to reward or to reprove.

Bradford was the last man who would have written an autobiography; he was so modest, so unwilling to draw attention to himself, that private matters of the greatest importance to him are hardly mentioned. Even the death of his wife is hardly recorded, and he evidently dislikes to mention his constant re-election as Governor. But a history of the colony in which he was the leading spirit must be autobiographical to some extent, and our best knowledge of him comes from it. Very plainly we can see his absolute absorption in the church and the colony, an absorption that would have made him narrow, but for his warm heart and tolerant mind. Not more marked than this devotion is the capacity which made it effectual ; his courage amidst difficulties, his many-sided qualities, his unfailing grasp of the most complicated situation. Lastly the book throws beautiful lights upon his personal character ; the high-principled austerity which yet never became narrow or harsh ; the generous affection which made all the orphans of the community his children ; the utter lack of selfishness which made him count his private interests as nothing before the good of the State ; the sense of humour which was not a very common attribute among men of his way of thinking.

These are the qualities of a leader. Bradford found his opportunity, and no one who reads his works can be surprised at the place he took amongst the Pilgrims, nor at the success of a colony which had him at its head.

# CHAPTER IV

## THE MIGRATION TO AMSTERDAM

THE Scrooby Church had been organised; the scattered seeds of Separatism had once more sprung into life, but it was impossible that they could bear much fruit in England. The plant had too many enemies; it was hardly an English growth as yet, and it needed to grow strong in a more congenial soil and air.

So in the early years of James I. the members of the church felt that they must, as the king had said, "dispose of themselves and their families some other waies." Excommunication, fines, prolonged imprisonment, almost any penalty the Bishops chose to inflict, was the result of any breach of the law against holding religious meetings in private houses. A Papist imprisoned on this charge could gain release by taking the oath of allegiance, and a Separatist was sometimes liberated on the same condition if he were tried by judges or justices, but never if he fell into the hands of the Bishops, and a petition from some Brownists for like privileges with the Popish recusants is endorsed "read and rejected."[1]

The citations to Brewster and others have already been mentioned; Bradford writes that the Scrooby people were "hunted and persecuted on every side; so as their former afflictions were but as flea-bitings in comparison of these which now came upon them. For some were taken and clapt up in prison, others had their houses besett and watcht night and day, and hardly escaped

---

[1] Waddington, p. 167.

their hands; and y<sup>e</sup> most were faine to flie and leave their houses and habitations and the means of their livelehood."

It was impossible that the church could exist under these conditions, and the congregation, clinging to its newly-found beliefs, determined on flight. There could have been little question as to where they should go. In Holland alone could they hope for liberty of conscience; it was the home of the other churches which had fled from persecution; Brewster at least knew something of the place and the people; and they were willing to brave the isolation from their friends and their country, the difference of language and occupation which would await them. When one considers the hardships of travel in those days, the little knowledge these country folk could have had of foreign life, and the deep roots which such people strike in their native soil, this migration seems little less heroic than the one that carried them on a longer voyage to their final home in America.

It is very hard now to realise the difficulties of their journey. To begin with, the law forbade any persons, not soldiers or merchants, to leave the kingdom without the King's licence, excepting at Dover or Plymouth, and licences were not always to be had for the asking. There are many letters to Burghley and Walsingham extant, from noblemen and others, acknowledging, with what seems excessive gratitude, their help in obtaining them; and Edward Leigh, in his "Hints for Travellers, 1571-1671," says that "If any came heretofore to the Lords of the Council for a licence to travel, the old Lord Treasurer Burghley would examine him of England. If he found him ignorant, he would bid him stay at home, and know his own country first."

A further paragraph suggests the perils which hovered around a traveller in those days. "Before his voyage, he should make his peace with God; receive the Lord's Supper; satisfy his creditors, if he be in debt; pray earnestly to God to prosper him in his voyage and to keep him from danger ; and—if he be *sui juris*—he should make his last will, and wisely order all his affairs; since many that go far abroad return not home."

To take French leave and travel without a licence was an almost unpardonable offence.  Henry, Lord Morley, in 1575, wrote from Spain lamenting that both he and his wife had been compelled to do this, and that nothing would countervail against such a departure to lessen the Queen's indignation.[1]  But probably the Pilgrims could neither afford licences nor dare to apply for them, and all the ordinary difficulties of travel were increased a hundred-fold by the opposition which they encountered on every hand, which enforced secrecy, and left them at the mercy of any unscrupulous agent.

The first attempt to leave England of which we have an account was in the autumn of 1607.  They hired a ship from an English captain at Boston in Lincolnshire ; a day was fixed, and they awaited the ship in all readiness, but no ship appeared, and when it did come, and the captain took them on board by night, harassed with expense and weary of waiting, no sooner were they in his power, than he betrayed them deliberately to the officers of the law.  They were put into open boats, robbed of all that they had, and carried back to be a spectacle to the town of Boston.  Boston was strongly Puritan, as future events proved, and the Magistrates before whom they were brought pitied them, and used them well, feeling probably the unreasonableness of hindering the escape of Separatists who were liable to be banished by law, and for whom England was an impossible home ; but not until an order came from the Privy Council could they dismiss them.  When the order did come, most of them were sent back to their native place, but seven of them, Brewster being one, and Bradford possibly another, were kept in prison and bound over to the Assizes.  The winter of 1607-8 was a bitter one ; the Thames was frozen over for

[1] S. P. Dom., Oct. 31st, 1575, vol. xxiv., no. 43.

many weeks; the whole country suffered greatly, and the privations of these homeless people must have been terrible.

Another attempt took place in the spring of 1608. Somewhere between Grimsby and Hull, on the edge of a large common, a good way distant from any town, the Pilgrims waited for the coming of a Dutch shipmaster of Hull, who was to take them and their goods on board his ship to Holland, for having been so basely betrayed by an English captain, they hoped now to find more honesty in the Dutchman, and "he bade them not fear, for he would do well enough." Once more, therefore, a day had been appointed; the women and children with the goods were sent to the place in a small barque, the men came to meet them by land. But again they were there before the ship, the sea was rough and the women very sick, and so they prevailed upon the seamen to run the barque into a little creek hard by, where it would lie on ground at low water, and so when the ship came next morning, they were fast and could not move till noon.

The ship master, knowing the need for haste and secrecy, sent his boat to fetch off some of the men, who were walking about the shore. One boatload was got aboard; the boat was putting off for a second time, when the master saw an armed company on foot and on horseback, and realised that the whole district was roused to take these unfortunate people, who were neither allowed to stay in the kingdom nor to leave it in peace. Seeing this he "swore his countries oath 'Sacramente'! and hauing yᵉ wind faire, waighed |his ancor, hoysed sayles and away!"

So those on board were carried away without so much as a change of clothing; those on shore were left at the mercy of the troops. A few men stayed to help the women; the rest escaped, knowing that on them the heaviest penalties would fall, and that their apprehension would do more harm than good to the others. Sad were the lamentations of those unfortunate prisoners ; they were hurried from one place to the other, and the Justices were at their wits' end what to do with them. They could not imprison so many innocent women and children ; to send them home was still more impossible, for they had sold their houses and livings, and had no longer any homes to go to. Sir Walter Raleigh had asked who, if the Separatists were banished, should maintain their wives and children, and the predicament he had foreseen had now to be dealt with. Finally, both captives and constables were worn out, "necessity forced a way for them," and in spite of all their hindrances and discouragements, all got over to Holland at last. And so great and public had been their troubles, that by them their cause became more known, their conduct excited esteem, and their following was increased.

Those who had been carried off in the ship had a terrible voyage, taking fourteen days to reach their port, during seven of which they saw neither sun, moon, nor stars, and were driven near the coast of Norway. The mariners cried "we sinke, we sinke!" but the Pilgrims never lost their faith, and even with the water running into their mouths and ears they cried, " Yet, Lord, Thou canst saue! Yet, Lord, Thou canst saue." And saved indeed they were, for the storm ceased and they came safely into port, to the astonishment of all beholders.

Under the best circumstances the crossing to Holland then took several days, which might lengthen to weeks in bad weather. When William III. of England visited the country in 1690, his ship took three days to come from Gravesend within sight of the coast, after which he spent ten hours exposed to the wind and waves in a shallop, attempting to land on the island of Goree, and prevented by the fogs and ice, and this was no doubt considered a successful voyage.[1]

Even before getting aboard their ship, the Pilgrims

[1] Harl. Misc., vol. ii. p. 596.

must have encountered many hardships and difficulties. Cross roads hardly existed in England at this time, and the journey from Scrooby to the coast was a serious undertaking. On the tower of Boston Church, at York, at Bow Church in Cheapside, and on many other churches in the country, were placed lanterns which were lighted at night as marks for travellers to aim at in their journeys through woods and morasses, and the precaution was a very necessary one. The men, going to meet their families by land, must have walked over forty miles across country ; the women and children with their goods probably started from Scrooby by water on the river Idle, and travelling in flat-bottomed boats to the junction with the Trent, were there put into the barque, sailed in it to Hull, and thence to the point of embarkation between Hull and Great Grimsby, a tedious journey of some seventy miles. Once on board, after 200 miles of ocean voyage, the vessel had to skirt the Dutch coast for another fifty miles, and then, having entered the Zuyder Zee, to wind along narrow and crooked channels to the mouth of the Y and Amsterdam.

These are the only accounts we have of the many efforts by which the Pilgrim Church finally reached Holland, and for them William Bradford is the sole authority. No doubt he took part in both attempts. Mather's history of his life [1] states that he was one of those imprisoned at Boston, but that being a young man, only about eighteen years old, he was dismissed sooner than the rest. His account of the storm leaves no doubt that he was one of the men on board the Dutch ship, and he had not been long on land when he was falsely accused by an envious passenger of having fled out of England for crime. He was arrested, but the truth was soon known, and Bradford went to join his brethren. An entry in Zachary Clyfton's Bible states that his father, the Rev. Richard Clyfton, came into Amsterdam in Holland in

[1] In Magnalia Christi.

August 1608, and as he was probably one of the principal members whom Bradford says stayed to the last to help the weakest over before them, the whole congregation was by that time most likely assembled there.

Holland was at this time the resort of the persecuted of all nations, and no part of it so much so as Amsterdam. An English traveller about 1690 writes of it, " The great care of this state has ever been to favour no particular or curious inquisition into the Faith or Religious Principles of any peaceable man, who came to live under the Protection of their laws, and to suffer no violence or Oppression upon any man's conscience, whose opinions broke not out into expressions or actions of ill consequence to the State. A free form of Government, either making way for more Freedom in Religion, or else, having contended so far themselves for liberty in this Point, they thought it the more unreasonable for them to oppress others." [1]

Their independence and love of self-government had for centuries prevented any union between the seventeen provinces of the Low Countries, and had, moreover, made them claim very decided rights in return for their oath of allegiance to Spain. The charter which secured these rights was the most valued possession of any town. This spirit of independence, and their constant intercourse with strangers, had tended to break down uniformity of opinion on any point, and so the Provinces were excellent ground for the seed of the reformed religion. And there were plenty of hands to scatter the seed, for the foreigners who were attracted to the Low Countries by their wealth and trade, brought in new religious ideas, and the young nobles who went to study at Geneva came back full of the teaching of Calvin.

Not all the torments which Charles V. and Philip II. devised for the punishment of heresy could succeed in driving it out; instead, they did succeed in welding the

[1] Harl. Misc., ii. 600.

Protestant States together, and in teaching them through suffering a measure of toleration before unheard of. William of Orange was among the first to urge the use-lessness and barbarity of religious persecution ; and when, about 1573, the reformed religion as taught at Geneva was admitted into the public churches, the rest of the sects that endeavoured to promote the Reformation were like-wise permitted the exercise of their religion in private meetings.  If any sect became so numerous as to desire a public place of meeting, and was willing to bear the charge of a pastor and teacher, it might procure this privilege on paying for it to the public treasury, with the approval of the Magistrates, and on condition that one or more commissioners should have free admission to all its meetings.  At first an exception was made of Roman Catholics, seeing that their allegiance to a foreign power might make bad subjects of them ; they were allowed to exercise their religion in private, but might hold no public meetings ; but they had fought with the Protestants in the siege of Leyden, they had proved good citizens and loyal comrades, and they were connived at, so that the Roman Catholic religion was " as free and easy, tho' not so cheap and so avowed, as the rest." [1] Holland persistently refused a truce with Spain which made liberty to the Catholic religion a condition, but this was on political grounds.   To have accepted it would have been to make every Catholic in the country look to the Spanish king as his benefactor, and the Dutch were far too wise to risk a divided allegiance of this kind.   They would grant the boon themselves, but it should not be owed to any foreign power.

Great was the scorn poured upon Amsterdam by more exclusive neighbours, on account of her hospitality to all creeds; she was the Staple of sects, the Mint of schism, the Bank of conscience, where no opinion was so strange that it would not find credit.   But men found when

[1] Harl. Misc., ii. 600.

persecution was no more, that the venom and sting of their differences was marvellously removed; and this same traveller of 1690 concludes, "However it is, religion may possibly do more good in other places, but it does less hurt here; and wherever the invisible effects of it are greatest and most advantageous, I am sure the visible are so in this Country."[1]  All the writers of the time marvel that whereas most countries after long wars are ruined for many generations, Holland, both during her terrible struggle with Spain, and after it, had been steadily growing more populous and wealthy.  Fynes Moryson frankly gives up the puzzle, and says, after mentioning the fall of Antwerp and the waterways of Holland as possible reasons, "If any man require truer and greater reasons of these Prouinces growing richer by warre, let him make curious search thereof, for it is besides my purpose."[2]

No very lengthy search is needed; the ultimate cause was the sea, which, as Guicciardini said, was not only a neighbour, but a member of these Low Countries.

Nothing could have seemed more unpromising than the geographical conditions of Holland; the sea apparently was her greatest enemy, threatening constantly to flood and engulf her, and to make health impossible in this half-swamped land.  But the Dutch were determined to master their conditions, and the sea became their friend, providing them with means for the traffic which was life and wealth to them, and training their characters until they became the most remarkable nation of the age.  Their country was such, that only with extreme care could they preserve a foothold on it at all; looking as if "after a long contention between land and water, which it should belong to, it had been at length divided between them."

It is not to be wondered at that such conditions stimu-

[1] Harl. Misc., ii. 601.
[2] Itinerary, Part III., Bk. IV., Chap. vi., p. 287.

lated engineering enterprise, so that land was wrested from the very jaws of the ocean, the most untenable positions were held and defended, and the natural waterways, which were Holland's one and only geographical advantage, were so extended and utilised by the people, that rivers and canals ran to every town and every village, and almost as many people lived in boats as in houses.

Agricultural science was as important as that of engineering; to produce the maximum returns from their restricted lands, no effort of research or skill could be neglected, and the Dutch became the first agriculturalists of the world; their cattle the most famous, their produce in vegetables and flowers the most profuse.

But they did not content themselves with fighting the sea; they made it their friend and partner, and never was there such a nation of explorers, merchants and fishermen. "Sailors are as common with them as beggars with us," wrote an English observer; they had enormous fleets, both for fishing and commerce, and they became the carriers for every nation; their ships were to be found in every quarter of the globe. In this great shipping trade, Holland owed nothing to the excellence of her havens; Amsterdam, the best of them, was on such shallow waters that ordinary ships had to await the tide to come in, and great ones had to unlade at any time. But it is "not a Haven that draws trade, but Trade that fills an Haven and brings it into vogue."

They were not merely carriers, but great manufacturers and merchants at home. Theirs was the best cloth, the finest linen which could be obtained; and besides these home products, the markets of Holland teemed with the produce of other lands, and the country came to be the greatest storehouse of merchandise in Europe.

The art of finance the Dutch learnt from the Lombards and the Jews, and when the Bank of Amsterdam was founded in 1609, they were as prominent as financiers as they were as merchants. They never missed an opportunity ; every opening afforded by the discovery of the New World, and the consequent expansion of trade, they utilised to the full; and after the fall of Antwerp, when its great trade was diverted to Amsterdam, the population of that city was so enormously increased that it had to be practically rebuilt to accommodate it. And having got their opportunities, the Hollanders knew how to make use of them. They were extremely industrious. Fynes Moryson, writing at the end of the sixteenth century, ascribes most of the industry to the women, and says that while the husbands " snort idly at home," their wives for traffic sail to Hamburg, and manage most part of the business at home and in neighbouring cities.[1]

They were as frugal as they were industrious. With so much wealth in the country, the people were not luxurious, they lived well and with refinement, but there was little display, and an enormous proportion (as we should think) of their incomes went in taxes and contributions to the public works. The institutions and buildings of their country reaped the benefit ; but such heavy taxation could only have been possible where frugality was the order of life, and also where there was no possible suspicion of corruption in the administration. The people practically taxed themselves, and did it generously, knowing that their money went to enrich the country and not a set of officials. They spent their lives, as well as their money, for the State; great men educated and trained their children for public service, and a large number of offices were unpaid, and practically compulsory.

It was the sea that had been their tutor; it had taught them constant watchfulness and untiring industry ; it had taught them public-spiritedness, for in that long struggle every man knew that to save himself he must save his country; only by high intellectual and moral

[1] Itinerary, III., II. iv. p. 97.

qualities had they conquered it, and these qualities lay at the root of all their other successes.

To Amsterdam, perhaps the busiest town in all that busy country, thronged with people of every nation, so crowded that men lived in tents and hovels in the suburbs, waiting till houses could be built to receive them, came the poor storm-tossed congregation from Scrooby.

Governor Bradford describes their amazement when they arrived and saw the walled and fortified cities, guarded by armed men, the different customs of the people, their strange dress and uncouth language, so that it seemed they were come into a new world. A new world indeed it was, after Scrooby, but they had little time to speculate on these things, for they saw the " grimme and grisly face of powertie coming upon them like an armed man," and against him they must fight. How they fought him we do not know; coming as they did from an agricultural district, few of them could have known any trade ; but Bradford tells us that, after great hardships, they were fairly successful during the year they spent in Amsterdam, enough so, no doubt, to make the prospect of another move unwelcome.

When all the principal members had arrived, the affairs of the church were organised, Robinson now apparently becoming pastor, and Clyfton teacher. Probably the congregation numbered from 100 to 150 persons ; one marriage at least is recorded amongst them, but the church does not seem to have applied for a public meeting-house.

The life of the Pilgrims in Amsterdam seems to have been transitory and unsettled, and very little is known about it. It has been suggested that they never intended to settle permanently there, but Bradford's language does not give this impression. According to him, it is in the history of the other churches exiled from England that the explanation of their speedy removal is to be found, " Seeing how Master John Smith and his companie was

6

already fallen into contention with the church that was ther before them, and no means they could use, would doe any good to cure the same, and also that the flames of contention were like to break out in the Anciente Church itselfe, (as afterwards lamentably came to pass,) which things they prudently foreseeing, thought it was best to remove, before they were any way engaged with the same: though they well knew it would be much to the prejudice of their outward estats, both at presente and in likelyhood in the future, as indeed it proved to be. For these and some other reasons, they removed to Leyden." [1]

[1] Bradford MS., p. 12.

# CHAPTER V

## THE CHURCHES IN AMSTERDAM

THE story of the other churches in Amsterdam is a
very melancholy one, full of disaster and humiliation. When one finds good men who had given
up everything to do what they thought right squabbling
over details, so carried away in anger as to disgrace, not
only their own high profession but the common charity
of human beings, and others covering their ambitions and
spiteful actions with a cloak of religion, one would like
to pass it over as briefly as possible.

To tell the story simply as a background for the
brighter history of the Pilgrim Church would be cruelty,
but it must be told, not only to show the difficulties which
these early congregations had to meet, but because, out
of the fire of hatred and enmity, came new ideas, new
principles, which cooled and hardened into distinct and
permanent forms. Separatism in England, in spite of the
works of Browne and Barrow, was rather indefinite, and
only the general principles common to all free churches
had been fixed. They had declared the need for a new
visible Church on earth, its necessary independence of
higher ecclesiastical powers, and its right to keep itself
pure and well disciplined; all men who desired these
things, and left the Church of England to find them,
became Separatists, but naturally there were many different opinions among them, many different views as to how
the reform scheme could best be carried out. It was the
clash of these conflicting views that made life in Holland
turbulent, but, at the end of it, the Separatists were formed

into distinct and definite churches, which, in many cases, have kept their characteristics to this day.

Of the several British churches which found a haven in Amsterdam, the Barrowist church from Southwark was the first to settle there for any length of time, and to it was given the title of the "Ancient exiled English Church." Before Penry died in 1593, in one of his last letters, he had counselled flight, urging the stronger members of the church to help the weaker ones to a safe place of refuge, and pleading that his own "mess of fatherless and friendless orphans" should be taken with them. Most of the church members who were free at the time took his advice; they were followed by others, as they were liberated from prison, and though some few remained in London, and possibly formed the nucleus of a future church, the greater part of the congregation and all its officers settled in Amsterdam.

Their pastor, Francis Johnson, was a very remarkable man, who had already had a sufficiently varied experience. He was born about 1562, probably at Richmond in Yorkshire. We hear of him first at Christ's College, Cambridge, where he seems to have been a trouble to the authorities, for in 1589 he preached a sermon at St Mary's Church, exalting the system of government by elders, and on being called to account for this, he frankly avowed his liking for the new Presbyterian system. This was too much, even for Cambridge; Johnson was imprisoned, expelled, and, as he would not leave, imprisoned again. He seems to have had a following in the University, for a number of its members petitioned in his favour; but finally he resigned his fellowship and departed in 1590, after having caused a ferment on all sides.

Though he favoured innovations in church government, he was not as yet a Separatist, and he became preacher to the Company of English merchants of the Staple at Middelburg, an office which Cartwright and Jenner had held before him, and for which he received the comfortable salary of £200 a year. He also employed himself in trying to detect those Separatist treatises which were often sent over to Holland to be printed, and was finally commissioned by the English Ambassador to keep a watch on the secret press known to exist in the city.

About this time, Barrow and Greenwood were having printed their "Plaine Refutation of Mr Giffard's Booke," which was to defend their cause against the many slanders heaped upon it. This was a second attempt at publication, the first edition having been seized by Whitgift's agents at Flushing and Brill in 1591. The second had no better fortune; Johnson got wind of the matter, and, first allowing the book to be completely finished, he seized the whole edition, burning all but two copies, one of which he kept to look at himself and the other to give to a friend.[1]

But the book avenged itself. Johnson in his study first glanced at it, then read it through and through, and was finally so convinced of its truth, that he had no peace of mind until he had crossed the sea to confer with its authors. The interview confirmed him in his new opinions; he threw up his appointment in Middelburg, and joined the Barrowist society in London, which met in woods and fields and gravel pits; or in winter in some friendly house under cover of darkness. Fourteen years later he had printed at his own expense, a new edition of the book which had led him to leave the Church of England.

As we have seen already, when the church was re-organised in 1592, during Greenwood's temporary release from prison, Johnson became its pastor, and paid dearly for his promotion, for he speedily found himself in prison, with most of the important members of the company. Here he wrote a petition to Burghley, complaining of his treatment; here, too, he received a visit from Henry Jacob, a Puritan minister of Kent, who hoped to convince him of his errors, but who ended by being convinced himself and joining the Separatists.

[1] Bradford, Dialogue in Young's "Chronicles."

The executions of Barrow, Greenwood and Penry, and the sufferings of the Separatists in prison, had excited some sympathy in the country, and not a little indignation against the Bishops for their cruelty. The Privy Council therefore determined in future to banish the offenders instead of punishing them with death. A petition was received by the Council about 1593 from some subjects "falsely called Brownists" for leave to emigrate to Canada, where they might worship God according to their consciences, and serve Her Majesty,[1] and in 1597 certain merchants, who were undertaking an expedition to Rainea (near Newfoundland) made suit to the Queen "to transport out of this realm divers artificers and others, persons that are noted to be sectaries, whose minds are continually in an ecclesiastical ferment, whereof four shall at this present sail thither in those ships that go this present voyage." Leave was given to Francis Johnson, his brother George, Daniel Studley and John Clark, to join the expedition, and on the understanding that they were not to return, unless they would conform. The voyage was a failure; they were attacked by French pirates, and one ship was wrecked; the four exiles returned secretly to London, and thence to Amsterdam, where most of their church, after sojourning first at Campen, and then at Naarden, had by this time assembled. They were very, very poor. George Johnson writes that many weeks he had not above six, seven, or eight pence the week to live upon, and Ainsworth their teacher, was for some time porter to a bookseller, and lived upon "nine pence per week with roots boiled."[2] But Amsterdam was a busy and growing town, and when they were familiarised with its language and customs, they found trades by which to live.

Barrow had left most of his substance to the church, and they were helped too by contributions from friends

[1] S.P. Dom., Vol. ccxlvi., no. 56, 1593?
[2] Williams, "Answer to Mr Cotton's Letter," p. 39.

in London and in the Separatist church at Middelburg;
possibly also from the charities of Amsterdam.

As soon as they were somewhat settled, the church
issued anew its Confession of Faith and the reasons for
its separation from the English Church.  It also tried
to justify its position to its Dutch neighbours, in a
correspondence with Junius, divinity reader in the
University of Leyden, but these overtures were coldly
received, and Junius evidently thought that the less
attention they drew upon themselves the better.  "Having
found a place of rest, by the mercy of God, where ye
may be quiet," he wrote, "pity yourselves, your flock, your
entertainers, the whole church.  Ye shall do wisely if ye
do not stir," etc.[1]  Not until 1607 did they have any
regular church building, and before their first chapel was
finished it was burnt down, and the work had to begin
again.  Clyfton gives a description[2] of their service after
he joined them, first prayer and giving thanks by the
pastor or teacher, then the reading of the Scriptures with
explanations, then a sermon on some passage of Scripture,
the administration of the Sacraments, and finally a
collection for the support of the church and the poor.
The Psalms were sung, and prophecy was allowed when
the spirit moved, but it had no formal place in the service.

As to the conduct of the Ancient Church there are two
very different views.  Bradford praises both pastor and
people, describing Johnson as a grave man and an able
teacher, performing the duties of his office with dignity
and reverence; an excellent and convincing disputant.
He couples the church with that of the Pilgrims at Leyden
in his praises, "If you had seen them in their beauty and
order as we have done, you would have been very much
affected therewith we dare say."  He says that, when
united, the church numbered about three hundred com-
municants, with pastor and teacher, four ruling elders, three
deacons, and one ancient widow for a deaconess.  "She

[1] Waddington, p. 120.          [2] Clyfton's "Advertisement."

honoured her place, and was an ornament to the congregation. She usually sat in a convenient place in the congregation, with a little birchen rod in her hand, and kept little children in great awe from disturbing the congregation." [1]

This deaconess had much authority; through her, alms were dispensed; she looked after the sick; and although more than sixty years of age when chosen, she did them service many years.

Bradford was certainly in a position to know all about the Ancient Church, and here is a picture of a most orderly and reverent congregation, ruled over by a man of wisdom and intellect.

But in face of this eulogy, we have some very ugly evidence both as to the personal character of the pastor and the scandals and disorders of the church, and it has been argued that it was owing to these troubles that the Pilgrims so soon left Amsterdam for Leyden.

The charges are mainly contained in four books—one by George Johnson, one by the Rev. Thomas White, and two by Christopher Lawne and others, and it is fair to say that these persons had all either been excommunicated or had left the church under unpleasant circumstances.

The first dark shadow on the character of the pastor came from his relations with his own family. In 1594, whilst still in the Clink prison, Francis Johnson had married a widow named Mrs Thomasine Boys, whose first husband, Edward Boys, a haberdasher, had been a strong supporter of the Separatists. At his house at Fleet Street the meeting had been held at which Johnson was arrested [2]; he himself underwent many imprisonments, and finally died in the Clink.

George Johnson had tried hard to dissuade his brother from the marriage, urging that Mrs Boys was much noted for pride, and that it would give great offence to the brethren. But it was in vain, and all George could do

---

[1] Dialogue in Young's "Chronicles."     [2] Harl MSS., 7042.

was to obtain a promise from the widow that, if she married Francis, she would "do as became his estate."[1] Instead, she became more garish and proud in apparel than before; the church was deeply offended, but left it to George to deal with her. He wrote to Francis, protesting against her gold rings, her busks and her whalebones, which were so manifest that "many of ye saints were greeued"; he begged that her schowish hat might be exchanged for a sober taffety or felt; and he even offered to raise money to provide her with more suitable garments should the question of expense stand in her way. She did reform a little; her hat was not "so topishly set," and George was encouraged to hope for further reforms; but when members of the congregation urged him on to more complaints, the pastor's wife became "very peert and coppet."

Naturally Francis bitterly resented these criticisms on his bride; her clothes were all provided out of her own money, and Bradford says they were perfectly suitable to her rank. The quarrel, however, was patched up, and more friendly feeling existed between the brothers on their voyage and journey to Amsterdam. But once there, George felt himself slighted and meanly treated by his brother, who did not invite him to share his large house; and thinking, perhaps, that the pastor's wife was to blame for this neglect, his criticisms on her broke out once more.

Before a church council, George was called upon to answer for this criticism; he had charged her amongst other things with sin in the using of musk, and the wearing of a topish hat, and he was not inclined to withdraw his charges. The poor lady seems to have been unfortunate in her choice of headgear, for a "veluet hood" was also a cause of contention. The church, after deliberation, declared the hat to be "not topish in nature," whereupon a lengthy discussion ensued as to whether a hat not topish in nature could, under any circumstances, be

[1] George Johnson's "Discourse," p. 94.

considered topish, it having been particularly condemned in her as the pastor's wife. George, who was not very bright, asked to have this problem reduced to writing, and he made further accusations of flightiness and sloth. He had other disagreements with his brother, about the appointment of elders and the government of the church; and after vain endeavours to keep him quiet by bribes of office, Francis finally excommunicated him publicly in 1599. In 1603 was published an unfinished " Discourse " by George Johnson relating the story.

One is not surprised that poor Mrs Thomasine was overheard to say that she wished she were a widow again, but it is amazing that, considering the perils they had gone through, the straits they were in to earn a bare existence, the church should have been shaken by such trivial matters as these. The instinct to criticize and call to account was strong, as it had been in Browne's church, and equally fatal. The kindest explanation of George's conduct was that he had, as some said, " a crackt brain." He had suffered enough to account for it; in 1594 his father petitioned for the release of his two sons, saying that " the younger called George (in the Fleet) hath been kept sometimes two days and two nights together without any manner of sustenance; sometimes twenty nights together without any bedding save a straw mat; and as long without any change of linen; and all this sixteen months in the most dark and unwholesome rooms of the prison they could thrust them into; not suffering any of his friends to come unto him." [1]

His book shows that he was really conscientious and well-meaning, but his littleness and obstinacy must have been irritating in the extreme, and when Francis found that he was determined to disturb not only his domestic peace, but the peace of the church, he had some excuse for the excommunication. Robinson and Ainsworth, both just and moderate men, approved of it.

[1] Waddington, p. 105.

It is more difficult to excuse his treatment of their father. John Johnson came over to Amsterdam in 1602, in a vain attempt to make peace between his sons, and a letter written by him, and published by Lawne, in his " Prophane Schism," testifies to the gradual accumulation of neglect, slights, and indignities put upon him, ending in his public excommunication by his own son. Only the belief that he came not to make peace, but to awaken the old dispute after three years' slumber, can in any way modify the unpleasant impression which this letter gives. Francis had indeed shown that he was sincere, that he could sacrifice wealth and security for his convictions, but he was proving himself also to be proud, domineering and cruel, and this was a bad augury for his church.

Both White and Lawne make terrible accusations of immorality and misconduct of various kinds amongst the congregation. They were never satisfactorily refuted, but the charges are so indiscriminate and so violent that it is quite impossible to believe them as they stand. Francis Johnson wrote a reply to White's book, and two other members of the church brought a counter accusation of slander against him. But neither the Dutch church nor the Dutch magistrates had any desire to be mixed up in the quarrels of the Separatists; the case hardly received a fair hearing, White was discharged, and returned to England. Against Lawne no case was brought in the Courts, the attempt probably being considered futile and unwise; Clyfton, who joined the Ancient Church in 1609, wrote a reply, but it was not in itself a very complete defence, and it included an answer by Daniel Studley, who was the chief offender, and who was cast out of the church in 1612, actually admitting some of the charges, though professing sincere repentance. He was undoubtedly a bad character—a daring man, since he had helped to smuggle out Barrow's manuscripts from prison, but an unscrupulous man too. It was evidently very harmful to the church to retain such a man in office, and it gave some justice to Lawne's taunt that to separate from other churches on account of their ungodly members, and to hold communion with Studley, was to strain at a gnat and swallow a camel. The second of Lawne's books, " Brownism, etc.," is very unconvincing ; it consists of a contrast between the profession and practice of the Brownists, in parallel columns, and the temptation to make it complete at all costs has evidently proved irresistible. The profession is practically Barrow's " True Description."

Robinson, writing in 1614, speaks strongly of Lawne's libel and the falsity of many of the accusations it contained,[1] but some grains of truth lay at the bottom of them, and it seems certain that many things went on in the Ancient Church which the Pilgrims would be anxious to shun.

No doubt, too, they dreaded to be involved in the discord which began about 1609 between Johnson and his teacher Ainsworth, with regard to the government of the church, and the proportion of power which was to lie with the elders and with the congregation.

It may be that Elder Studley was the origin of this difficulty too ; complaints had been made of him by members of the church, who wished to depose him, and this naturally inclined him to deny any such rights on the part of the congregation. Johnson, however, had begun his career as a Presbyterian, and though Studley's influence may have had some effect, it is likely that the recent disputes and troubles had given him a distaste for popular government, and had led him to think kindly of an autocracy of elders which would have made very short work of such disturbances.

Ainsworth watched with alarm these Presbyterian tendencies, for, though far from advocating the democratic government of Browne's Church, he thought, as Barrow

[1] Works, iii. 96 and 99.

had done, that the congregation as a whole had certain very real powers, notably with regard to the choosing or deposing of its officers, and the receiving or excommunication of members.

But the middle course between government by the people and government by elders was a vague, if not impossible one, and so Ainsworth found each time he tried to define it, a true balance being impossible without the goodwill of both parties.

Leaning more and more towards Presbyterianism, Johnson at last conceded to a local church only the power to elect elders, not even to ordain them; it could not " cast out an offending member or depose an erring elder." His views were certainly an innovation on the original Confession and Articles of the Church published in 1596, 1598 and 1607; and he seems to have supported them with great narrowness and want of consideration.

Ainsworth, on the other hand, was very moderate and reasonable, anxious always for peace, but feeling that the issue involved the very principles of a Congregational Church. He was far the most cultured man and the finest character in the congregation—in fact, his nobility and uprightness are the strongest arguments against Lawne's wholesale attacks on the church, and one is led to believe that, if evil existed. it was confined to a very small number of his following.

Very little is known of his early life; he was born about 1579, probably at Swanton near Norwich, though some say in Lancashire, and his father was a yeoman. Roger Williams says of him that " he scarce set foot in colledge walls," [1] but this is probably a mistake, for he seems to have been for a time at St John's College Cambridge, and afterwards at Gonville and Caius. But though he was at the University four years in all, he did not graduate. No doubt he fell under the Puritan influences so rife in Cambridge, for it seems that, on leaving,

[1] " Bloudy Tenent," etc., 1644, p. 174.

he joined the half-formed Barrowist Church in London. Later he went to Ireland, but being persecuted for dissent he returned to London, and went on to join the emigrants in Amsterdam. When he came out of Ireland he was very poor, a single man, and content with very little, living on his 9d. a week, without letting anyone know of his poverty. But presently people found it out and helped him, and when, in 1607, he married a widow from Ipswich named Marjorie Appleby, he and his family had all that they needed.

Paget, a Puritan Minister of Amsterdam, and one of those who attacked most fiercely the Ancient Church, accused Ainsworth of having turned his coat and changed his religion five several times, and Lawne said he was "spotted again and again with apostasy," but according to Bradford, all that this vacillation amounted to was that he occasionally, after having separated, attended services in the Church of England. ｛In Amsterdam he became Teacher in the place of John Greenwood, and as the elders and pastor were still imprisoned in London, he apparently directed this branch of the congregation until the church was reconstituted in 1597, when he still retained his office.

He was also their chief scribe, and undertook the translation of their confession into Latin, and probably the preparation of their petition to King James; he may, too, have been one of those sent to England to present it. Besides being a very good linguist, he was a notable Hebrew scholar, and has left commentaries which are still of value. Bradford writes: "A very learned man he was, and a close student, which much impaired his health. We have heard some, eminent in the knowledge of the tongues of the University of Leyden, say that they thought he had not his better for the Hebrew tongue in the University, nor scarce in Europe. . . . He was powerful and profound in doctrine, although his voice was not strong; and had this excellency above many, that he was ready and pregnant in the Scriptures, as if the Book of God had been written in his heart." [1]

When the dispute about the power of the elders became very heated, Ainsworth at first urged that the two parties should remain united, adhering to their original Confession of Faith, and that no change should be made in the working of the church. This was of course refused. Then he proposed that they should part peaceably, and form two distinct congregations. This was also refused, unless his party would leave Amsterdam; and this was not a thing to be lightly done, seeing that they were, after a time of great poverty, established in trades and business in the city. Then Ainsworth proposed a conference with the Pilgrims,[2] who were already settled in Leyden, but Johnson was now going against another article of their Confession, and he disliked to ask counsel of any other church. They did, however, confer, and Robinson was one of the deputation sent from Leyden. His view was, that power belonged to the whole church under Christ, and that to its officers belonged only the government and guidance of the church in the use of this power, and he advised that matters should first be discussed by the elders and then submitted to the whole congregation. But no conclusion could be reached, and finally, in spite of Ainsworth's desire for peace, Johnson took the violent measure of deposing him and excommunicating his following.

The Ancient Church thus split asunder; Ainsworth's people withdrew, and worshipped in a Jews' Synagogue, only one door from the old meeting-house. But later, it was decided that to them this meeting-house belonged, as it had been owned by two men and a widow of their party.

Ainsworth was loth to bring any quarrel before the magistrates, but these persons felt that they could not brook their unjust loss, and made good their claim, although the land on which the building stood had been held in trust by a member of Johnson's party.

---

[1] "Dialogue."                [2] See Robinson's Works, iii. 460-84.

In 1613, deprived of their meeting-house, Johnson and his followers went to Emden, returning, however, to Amsterdam before 1617. Probably some, including Clyfton, had never left the city. Here, in 1618, Johnson died. "A Christian Plea," written in the last year of his life, shows how far he had strayed from the teaching of Barrow. He was still, as he had always been, a Calvinist in doctrine; but in polity he had become rather a Presbyterian than a Separatist, save on the one central point, the right of a particular church to regulate its affairs without the interference of any other ecclesiastical body. But he allowed great authority over the church to princes and magistrates, and looked to them to help in its maintenance, should the contributions of the members not suffice. His view of the eldership was entirely Presbyterian; "tell the church" meant "tell the elders." Unlike Barrow, he would permit the teachers of the church to teach outside their own congregations in schools and universities, and so submit to the approval of alien authorities; and would advocate suspension, or the withholding of the Sacraments, from the unrepentant, as an alternative punishment to excommunication. The marriage ceremony he considered to be a civil matter, but he would not forbid its performance by a minister, and whereas he, like Barrow,[1] had once insisted that even the buildings in which Popish worship had been held should be destroyed, he now thought that images, vestments, and temples need neither be done away with nor made a cause of separation.

One of the elders of his church, Francis Blackwell, prepared to lead the remnant of the flock to Virginia. They were arrested in London, and only by treachery and denial of their principles did they escape from the hands of the Bishops to continue their journey. It was a fatal journey to most. They had won the blessing of the Archbishop

---

[1] See Confession of Faith of the Ancient Church, and Barrow's "Brief Discovery," p. 133.

by ill means; they were so disunited that they cursed one another in the streets of Gravesend; they were packed like herrings in the ship, and most of them died of disease and starvation before ever they saw Virginia.

The other section of the Ancient Church under Ainsworth, lived uneventfully, as far as we know, until their pastor's death in 1623. They were officerless for a time, until John Canne became their pastor, and disorders seem to have quickly broken out, for John Robinson writes sternly to them in 1624. It is said that Canne suffered excommunication at the hands of his congregation, but the church lived on until 1701, when it was finally absorbed in the Scotch Presbyterian Church, founded in Amsterdam in 1607.

It was not, however, only the troubles in the Ancient Church existing and foreseen, which convinced the Pilgrims that Amsterdam was not a good place to settle in. The Rev. John Smyth and his Gainsborough church were involving themselves in considerable difficulties, both in their relations to Johnson's church and in the development of their own creed and polity.

This would no doubt be a great disappointment to the Scrooby people, for though apparently, during their stay in Amsterdam, they maintained a separate church organization, there must have been some practical intercourse; they would probably be obliged to worship occasionally in each other's meeting places, and it was to Smyth's church that the new-comers would chiefly look for fellowship and help. It had come over most recently, its members were from the same part of England; they may at one time have been a single congregation, and it was hard to find that it would prove, not a guide, but a stumbling-block in their way.

Even supposing that the Gainsborough church had been distinct from that of Scrooby from its earliest foundation, its pastor, the Rev. John Smyth, must have been very well known to Robinson and his fellows.

7

His commonplace name has made his history difficult to trace, but he was born probably about 1572, and was educated at Christ's College, Cambridge, 1586-93, where the Rev. Francis Johnson was his tutor.   Here no doubt he absorbed some heterodox ideas, but he took his M.A. in 1593, was ordained by William Wickham, and was a conforming minister at Lincoln probably as late as 1605, a book published in that year, called " A Pattern of true Prayer" by John Smyth of Lincoln, having been identified as his work.

John Cotton, an eminent New England divine, tells us that "the tyranny of the Ecclesiastical Courts was harsh towards him, and the yokes put upon him in the ministry too grievous to be borne."   Anxious to find some place where he could exercise his ministry with fewer restrictions, he heard of the " forward" people at Gainsborough, and came amongst them.   But separation from the Church of England was a violent measure, and he spent nine months in doubt before finally joining the Gainsborough church. In 1606 he became its pastor, and the church may have migrated to Holland soon after, but it is much more likely that it remained in England almost as long as the Pilgrims did.   Bishop Hall in 1608 addresses a letter to Smyth and Robinson as " Ringleaders of the late separation" and Robinson mentions Helwys, a prominent member of Smyth's church, as one who more than any other had furthered the passage of his congregation into strange countries.   " If any brought oars," he writes, " he brought sails."[1]

However this might be, Smyth was in Amsterdam in 1608, and seems for a short time to have united with the Ancient Church.   But he did not long remain with them. He was a little like Robert Browne in his eagerness to find the true way, and in his complete indifference as to how far it would lead him.   He was accused by his fellow-Separatists of much innovation and inconstancy

[1] Works, iii. 159.

but to an outsider he seems merely to have worked out the theories which they all held, to an extreme point. He was morbidly conscientious ; anxious to follow any course which seemed right, regardless of expediency, but at the same time lacking in stability and sense of proportion, so that, for the slightest flaw discovered in that course, he would abandon it, and in all sincerity seek for more light elsewhere. He says of himself, " Now I have in all my writings hitherto received instruction of others, and professed my readiness to be taught by others, and therefore I have so oftentimes been accused of inconstancy, well, let them think of me as they please, I profess I have changed, and shall be ready still to change for the better, and if it be their glory to be peremptory and immutable in their articles of religion, they may enjoy that glory without my envy, though not without the grief of my heart for them." [1]

His very openness of mind, admirable in itself, made him a difficult leader for the times. It was so necessary for the Separatists to find a foothold somewhere, to establish some rule to which they might cling, and they felt that Smyth exposed them to a charge of mere vagary.

As soon as he reached Amsterdam, he began to publish Separatist literature, and it is by his books alone that the rapid development of his opinions can be traced.

His early views on separation, and his relation to the Church of England, are given in " Principles and Inferences concerning the Visible Church " (1607 or 1608), and in "Parallels," an answer to an attack by Bernard. But within a year he had separated from the Ancient Church, and had published a pamphlet declaring " The Differences of the Churches of the Separation." They disagreed, first, because Smyth refused to permit the English Bible to be used in worship, holding that a written translation of the Scriptures was apocryphal

[1] " Retractation " in Barclay, Appendix to chap. vi.

and unlawful, and that teachers should translate verbally
from the Greek or Hebrew. Gradually he came to forbid the use of any book in divine service, either for
reading or singing.

The next difficulty arose when Smyth decided that
lay elders were anti-Christian, and that all elders should
be pastors.

Naturally Johnson, who was at this moment exalting
the power of the lay eldership, could not agree here.
Smyth's views about elders were the very reverse of
Presbyterian ; he held that "Whatsoever the eldership hath
it hath from Christ through the body of the Church, and
by the Church's disposition," and that "When the Church
hath chosen and ordained herself elders, then she loseth
none of her former power, but still retaineth it entire to
herself, to use when occasion ariseth." The difference
between the two views was characteristic of the men ;
Johnson, rather hard and domineering, bent on forcing
men to be good with all the machinery he could use ;
Smyth, warm-hearted and impetuous, trusting all his
reform schemes to impulses within the human heart,
and so only anxious to place his followers in the closest
relations possible with Christ.

There were some further difficulties, because Smyth
thought, as indeed Barrow and Johnson had done, that
contributions to the church treasury should be "a separation from them that are without," and being an act of
worship should be accompanied by prayer and thanks-
giving. And finally, he objected to infant baptism,
even when confined, as it was by the Separatists, to
the seed of the faithful. The rite had been connected
for ages with the false churches; it was impossible that
the child should make any confession of faith, or
understand the meaning of its privileges. Possibly, too,
he foresaw the confusion which actually came to pass in
later generations, when the seed of the faithful might be
no longer faithful themselves, and the church would come

to contain as many unregenerates as the Church of England had done.

These were the differences between Smyth and the Ancient Church in matters of government, but there were some doctrinal points of difference too.    As early as 1591, James Arminius had begun to teach his system of theology in Amsterdam.    Calvin's theory had been, that every soul was predestined to salvation or everlasting torment, and that the saints could not fall from grace.  Arminius taught in opposition to this, that Christ's atonement had placed the means of salvation within reach of all, but that only by individual belief and effort, constantly renewed, could it be grasped.    Smyth espoused his beliefs, as an unprejudiced man of his temperament naturally would, whilst the Ancient Church clung, as the Puritans, and most of the Separatists did, to Calvin's harsher doctrine.

Smyth determined to form a separate church organization, and he was followed by a number of people from the Ancient Church.    He was at once confronted with the problem which Barrow had puzzled over ; he held that their former baptism was false, and yet believed that only those truly baptized could set about the formation of a church estate.    Braving, as Barrow could not bring himself to do, the charge of Anabaptism, Smyth baptized first himself, then Helwys and his other followers, each making his confession of faith.    In 1609, in "The Character of the Beast," he published his views on baptism

Smyth's church was erected ; the "second English Church of the Separation."    Its service, in the original form, began with prayer, then came the reading and expounding of one or two chapters of the Bible, the successive prophesyings by different speakers on some text, followed by prayer and collection, the services lasting the formidable space of four hours in the morning, and three to four hours in the afternoon, with no singing. Smyth did, indeed, permit the "singing such psalms as the spirit declares to any person immediately without book," but this does not seem to have happened very often among his disciples.

He quickly repented of his se-baptism. At the time he had believed that no true Church existed with which he could join, and from which baptism might be had, but he came to see that the Mennonite or Baptist churches of Holland were true churches, and felt that this being so, it was not right that persons should baptize themselves, and set up new churches, without trying to join those already existing. "It was not lawful" for everyone that seeketh the truth to baptize, for then there might be as many churches as couples in the world. Always ready to act upon his convictions, Smyth and thirty-one members of his church applied in March 1610 to the Waterlander Mennonite Church for admission. But Helwys and a few of his followers held staunchly to the old views. To their minds, Smyth was admitting the old heresy of apostolic succession in denying their right to baptize themselves, and they felt very bitterly towards him. Although they too, apparently, agreed in all essentials with the Mennonite Church, which rejected infant baptism and held many of the views afterwards advocated by George Fox and the Quakers, they would not join it, and returning to London in 1611, they formed there under Helwys the first general Arminian Baptist Church in England.

Two very interesting works were issued by this church in the succeeding years; one by Helwys condemning flight from persecution, and one by Murton condemning persecution for religious views. In the latter, Murton entirely separated spiritual and civil authority, giving the magistrate no right of interference whatever in the church. "Earthly authority," he declared, "belongeth to earthly kings; but spiritual authority belongeth to that one spiritual king who is King of Kings."

Neither of these books were quite in accordance with the Pilgrims' views. Robinson thought [1] that men were

[1] Works, iii. 155-164.

free to fly or to abide, as seemed best to God's truth ; and that the magistrate might " use his lawful power lawfully, for the furtherance of Christ's kingdom and laws."

Smyth's application to the Mennonite Church was not immediately successful ; and with a few followers he found refuge in a bakehouse belonging to a kind-hearted Waterlander. These bakehouses were often attached to churches, to bake bread for the poor, and perhaps to shelter poor members. Here Smyth, far gone in consumption, and unchurched altogether now, remained until his death in 1612. In 1615 the remainder of his company was admitted to one of the Mennonite churches, and though for a short time they had a separate English service in the bakehouse, they were finally absorbed among the Dutch.

Smyth's Arminian and Baptist tendencies were so abhorred by his fellow Separatists, that he got very scant justice from them, and they are harder on him than we can quite understand. He had been a cause of reproach, and Robinson answering Bernard speaks sternly of him, " his instability and want of wit, is his sin and our cross." [1] Bradford too reproaches him, " his inconstancy and unstable judgment, and being so suddenly carried away with things, did soon overthrow him." [2]

Yet he had many noble qualities. He was a learned man, as even his enemies allow ; he was one of the first to realise the stupidity of persecution for religious opinions, and to assert the freedom of man's conscience from earthly control ; the " Confession " of his church shows a broad tolerance and kindliness of spirit which one can only admire.

In his last and most beautiful book, the " Retractation " of his errors, written when the light of another world was very near him, illuminating and putting into perspective all that had been dim and distorted before, Smyth writes with great sweetness and humility of his past mistakes of judgment, and laments the harshness and narrowness which may have blotted his former utterances. " My

[1] Works, i. 62.    [2] " Dialogue," p. 450.

desire is to end controversies among Christians, rather than to make and maintain them, especially in matters of the outward Church and ceremonies; and it is the grief of my heart that I have so long cumbered myself and spent my time therein, and I profess that difference in judgment for matter of circumstance, as are all things of the outward Church, shall not cause me to refuse the brotherhood of any penitent and faithful Christian whatsoever. And now from this day forward do I put an end to all controversies and questions about the outward Church and ceremonies with all men, and resolve to spend my time in the main matters wherein consisteth salvation. Without repentance, faith, remission of sin, and the new creature, there is no salvation, but there is salvation without the truth of all the outward ceremonies of the outward church." Smyth was a very lovable man, and had a great power of attracting friendship and affection. The very members of his church who separated from him, speak with the deepest feeling of their love and devotion to him, and the good cause they had for it, so that all their love was too little and not worthy of him. He was unselfish and kind-hearted, without any trace of self-seeking; he had no salary from the church, supporting himself as a doctor, and from the sick poor he took no fees, and from the richer sort only one-half as much as other doctors did. Rather than that any should want, he would neglect himself and his family, so careful was he of the poor. "Upon a time, seeing one slenderly apparelled, he sent them his gown, to make them clothes," thinking it but his duty "according to that speech in the Gospel, 'He that hath two coats, let him part with him that hath none,' so that he was well beloved of most men, and hated of none save a few of our English nation, who had nothing against him, but that he differed from them in some points of religion,"[1]

It must be admitted that the Separatist churches so far

[1] Barclay, Appendix to chap. vi.

had not covered themselves with glory.   The churches of
Browne, Johnson, and Smyth had each been devastated
by disputes and disagreements, and in each case their
leaders had very greatly modified their early opinions
about Separatism.   Disunion was perhaps inevitable,
"they only, who enjoy liberty," wrote Robinson, "know
how hard a thing it is to use aright   And when I see
them in England wondering at the dissensions in this
way, methinks I see two prisoners, being themselves fast
chained and manacled together by feet and hands, wondering to see that other men, at liberty, walk not closer
together than they do.   Their thraldom makes them
unequal censurers of the abuse of our liberty." [1]

The whole movement too was a reaction, and though
reaction has a certain strength of its own, it has one very
great weakness, that it is apt to go to extremes.   Moreover, this was a reaction directed by foreign influences ;
the leaders were not carrying out ideas which they had
gradually grown up to, but ideas which they had adopted,
sometimes rather hastily.   Eager for some new system,
they had copied that of the Calvinists, or the Anabaptists,
and it was some years before they learnt to modify
their ideas, and to make them part of themselves.

But if the leaders suffered from this kind of mental
indigestion, the body of the church was worse off still.
It followed its pastor often with surprising docility, only
accountable in a people long accustomed to priestly rule,
but it followed in reality far behind.   And for this reason
the men who, like Browne and Smyth, saw abstract truth
most clearly, and announced it most boldly, were not
necessarily the best leaders ; they were too far ahead of
their times, their light dazzled people and made them
blinder than before.   They wanted complete religious
freedom, they aimed at a spiritual church, and they forgot
that freedom to most men only meant supremacy, and that
human nature was frail and faulty.   The very qualities

[1] Works, iii. 100.

which made men Separatists, made it hard for them to agree; those who would not give way under such pressure as the Church of England put upon them, were likely to retain their rigidity, and moreover, the principle of separation from the ungodly itself fostered a pharisaical and critical spirit.

So their leaders had a difficult task, enough so to excuse some harshness; the soft and amiable side of their nature had not much play. Like the Socialists of to-day, they were fighting with their backs against the wall; in their deadly earnestness they could not afford to take things lightly. Like the Socialists, too, they had a great constructive work before them. The ultimate principle of separation was, that a church is a means, and not an end; an agency for the salvation of men, and that where a church does not fulfil its office thoroughly, other agencies will spring up. These men had rebelled against the existing order because they could not bear things as they were; to find new and effective methods of dealing with the problem was more difficult than to criticize and to denounce. It is interesting to note that those leaders who were most extreme in their Separatism were those who found later that they must modify their programme; to note, too, how under this burden of construction, they grew less ready to condemn, and drew gradually nearer to the churches they had once despised.

Amsterdam, too, was an unsettling place for churches in such an undeveloped stage of polity; there was a lack of stability in the very air. The complete freedom which it gave to all opinions at a time where uniformity was everywhere else enforced, the variety of nationalities, religion and politics to be found there, naturally attracted extreme men of every kind, and the barriers of tradition were all broken down.

But although the life of the churches there reads like a failure, it was not fruitless. The great questions of adult or infant baptism, of the limit of civil and spiritual authority, of the power of the elders, which ultimately caused the distinction between Baptist, Independent, and Presbyterian churches, had found exponents on either side. Moreover, the influence of Mennonite ideas, carried over to England by Helwys and Murton, paved the way for the foundation of another great Society, that of the Friends, and explains ths rapid growth of that body in later days. Much remained to be done, and it was probably Robinson's knowledge of the great work which still lay before the churches of the Separation, which led him away from the turbulent atmosphere of Amsterdam to seek some quiet refuge where his church might grow strong in peace.

There is still extant amongst the Court records of the city of Leyden for February 12th, 1609, the following application :—

"To the honourable the burgomasters and court of the city of Leyden, With due submission and respect, Ian Robarthse, Minister of the Divine Word, and some of the members of the Christian Reformed Religion, born in the Kingdom of Great Britain, to the number of one hundred persons or thereabouts, men and women, represent that they desire to come and live in this city, by the first day of May (N.S.) next ; and to have the freedom thereof in carrying on their trades, without being a burden in the least to anyone. They therefore address themselves to your Honours, humbly praying that your Honours will be pleased to grant them free consent to betake themselves as aforesaid. This doing," etc.

The court replied that "they refuse no honest persons free ingress to come and have their residence in this city ; provided that such persons behave themselves, and submit to the laws and ordinances ; and therefore the coming of the Memorialists will be agreeable and welcome.

" Thus done by the Burgomasters in their session at the Council House the 12th day of February 1609 (N.S.).

(Signed) "J. VAN HOUT, *Secretarius*." [1]

[1] Dexter, "England and Holland of the Pilgrims," p. 468.

# CHAPTER VI

## LIFE IN LEYDEN

HERE and there, underlying the story of Separatism in England, traces of Netherland influence have shone out, like sparks of electricity that betray the motive force. It could not be a coincidence that so many of its leaders were men who had been in contact with Dutch ideas; nor that the districts in which the Netherlanders had lived and worked, the towns in which they thronged, should have been those which found, first followers for Wyclif, then opponents of the luke-warm Episcopal reformation, and in days to come the strongest supporters of Puritanism and the Commonwealth. It might have been coincidence, but that this active spirit of freedom has so exact a counterpart in the history of the Dutch at home. It is said now that cobbling and dissent go hand in hand, and that the smell of shoe leather breeds Socialism, and certainly there seemed to be something about the manufacture of cloth, the chief Netherland industry, which was just as incompatible with subjection in those days. Cecil declared in 1559 that "those who depend on the making of cloths are of worse condition to be quietly governed than the husband-men,"[1] which shows that he realized the effects of the Dutch occupation, though not perhaps their cause.

But the influence had been vague. It had filtered in by means of friends and neighbours, and by hearsay evidence of a successful fight for liberty elsewhere, and it had created a powerful disturbance, but so far it had not enabled any one to make *his* particular cause a success.

[1] Froude, viii. p. 442.

Now, however, after long catching at the fringe of Dutch ideas, the English Separatists had a chance of grasping them completely. The most important of all their churches, the one which contained the best material, the finest instruments for the play of new ideas, had come to make its home in the heart of Netherland life and thought.

It is this which makes the twelve years spent by the Pilgrims in Holland of such immense importance. All we know of the facts of their stay there could be very briefly told, for neither their own writings nor the town records throw much light upon it. They did not belong to a class likely to write a great deal, and the few literary men among them were engaged in church controversy, and did not record much of their everyday life. The accounts of Bradford and Winslow were written many years after, when their minds were busy with the later development of the colony and church, when the years of their poverty and struggle in Leyden had faded into insignificance, and seemed a very small part of their life history. Again, the Pilgrims with one or two exceptions were not important enough to gain much notice in the town records, or contemporary documents. No labour has been spared by modern historians in trying to find out the true facts of their history, and every notice in the Leyden archives referring to persons known, or supposed to have belonged to Robinson's church, has been published,[1] but these are for the most part mere records of marriage or death ; admission to citizenship or membership of the University.

But the importance of their life there is altogether out of proportion with what we know of its facts. We judge of it first of all by the gradual development of opinion in the church at Leyden, tested by their decisions on various matters of dispute, and plainly to be seen in the writings of their pastor : again by the difference between the Pilgrims and later New England colonists in their

[1] Dexter, "The England and Holland of the Pilgrims."

methods of government, civil and religious, and in the spirit which they brought to bear on their problems: and finally, in the ultimate similarity between many American institutions and those of seventeenth-century Holland. This last point must not be pressed too far; for much of this similarity may be due to the Dutch colonies in America, and to the work of Penn and the Quakers, who were saturated with Dutch influence, but where Dutch institutions were at once adopted by Plymouth colony, and transmitted from the New England States to other parts of America, perhaps embodied in the constitution itself, it is fair to trace their origin to these quiet, formative years in Leyden.

From these years they emerged in a condition attained by no English Separatist church before them, able to use their freedom without instability, to exercise authority without tyranny: and to understand in any way the temper of the men who sailed in the *Mayflower*, who gave an example of wise government and religious charity to those who came after them, no circumstances of their environment can be lightly overlooked.

It is one of the difficulties of history that to understand anything one must know everything, and it seems as though before one can "place" the Pilgrim Fathers and their work, one must realize the whole of English civilization before them, the whole of American development after them, and above all, must do justice to the part which Holland played in both, and the history which prepared her for that part. But this is no place for a history of Holland, and a very rough idea of the principles which had guided her in her fight for freedom must suffice.

Centuries before she became a Republic, Holland had begun unconsciously to prepare for it. Her constitutional rights were very early secured, when in 1476 she bargained with Mary of Burgundy for her Magna Carta, the "Great Privilege" which, amongst other things, claimed that the

cities and estates should hold diets when they chose,
and that their consent should be necessary before war
was waged, or fresh taxes levied.   But Holland went
further than demanding that her people should be well
governed, she educated them to govern themselves.   At
a very early date the towns had become practical republics, appointing their own officials, and voting their
own taxes.   They were not democratic, quite the opposite
in fact, though the strict rules against the relationship of
officials, prevented the government from falling into the
hands of one family, as it did in Italian towns.   But this
system of city government, like the township system in
New England, had the great merit of training citizens for
rule and giving them insight into practical politics.   Bryce
writes that "The Town meeting has been not only the
source but the school of democracy,"[1] and the same may
be said of the City councils of Holland.   Above the city
government were the provincial estates in which deputies
from the towns and cities chosen by the people during
their pleasure met the nobles to decide their common
interests.   The clergy, unlike the custom in France and
England, never formed an estate in the Netherlands.
These provincial estates chose from amongst themselves
one, two, or three burgesses to represent each province in
the States-General.   "They are," writes Moryson, "wholly
in the power of the citizens who chose them."   An interesting point, having regard to future American history,
was their equality of voting.   The largest province,
however many representatives it might have, had only
one vote like the smallest, and the deputies of the nobles
had only one vote conjointly.   In the same way, when
the Federal Constitution of the United States was drawn
up it was decided that each State, without respect to size
or population, should be equally represented in the Senate,
whereas in the House of Representatives, the States should
have a number of deputies proportionate to their size.

[1] American Commonwealth, i. 621.

The idea was due to Connecticut, but the principle of the equality of States in matters concerning all had been recognized even in the confederation of the New England States in 1643, when each of the four plantations had (nominally at least) equal representation and equal power.

With their traditions and training, it was no wonder that, when unjust taxation and cruel persecution drove them to revolt, the Dutch were the first successful exponents of modern democracy. They had been educated in their local assemblies to govern themselves, and public spirit was the breath of their nostrils. When the crisis came they asserted a principle familiar enough now, but very daring at that time, namely, that government exists for the good of the people, and that where that is neglected all claim to allegiance is at an end. Still they clung to the name of a monarchy, they were asserting a principle, not attacking a system, and only when they were thwarted in their search for a King did they formally establish a republic. But, once established, there was none of the difficulty about working it that we find in England later, for the simple reason that it was not a reaction, but the natural outgrowth of generations of training. So too the success of the American Constitution is due largely to the fact that its framers "knew better than to commit the folly of breaking with the past. They were not seduced by the French fallacy that a new system of government could be ordered like a new suit of clothes."[1] It has proved most successful where it grew directly out of old institutions and habits of mind, least satisfactory where it was artificial and empiric.

One cannot cherish ideas of freedom in one direction and not in another, and the religious views of the Dutch were instinct with the same love of liberty. It is a question whether, as things were then, any monarch could have granted complete toleration without being considered a heathen, since the creed of his people was

[1] Lowell, Address, Oct. 1884. Quoted in Bryce, i. 34, note.

held to be his especial charge and care. The idea that
the subjects of a prince must take their creed from him
was a fixed one, and fatal to toleration, since it confused spiritual and temporal allegiance hopelessly, and a
difference in religious opinion was held to mean political
disaffection. Where the people were themselves the
rulers, there could be no such fear as this; the principle
of toleration is in itself democratic, and so it is not
strange that it was the Republic of Holland which first
felt able to uphold it. Calvinism contains some elements
of democracy, being hostile to the theories of divine right
which led to such an infinite deal of oppression and bad
government; still more democratic were the many sects,
such as the Anabaptists and Familists, which sprang up
for the most part in Germany, and whose members,
persecuted everywhere else, were unmolested, and even
admitted to rights of citizenship in Holland.

The real strength of Dutch democracy lay in the fact
that it was not only a theory of government. Nothing
which had gone to make up the civilization of the
Netherlands had belonged to a single class, or had been
unshared by the people, and so there was a genuine
equality long before it was politically recognized.

Since the battle of Courtrai in 1302, when the burghers
defeated a feudal army, the nobility of the Northern
Netherlands had never had an overweening importance.
There were great families even in Holland, and they had
their share of influence, but neither in political importance
nor in social estimation could they equal the men of the
cities, and so many of them had been driven to take
refuge in the fortified towns, that they almost ceased to
be a class apart. "They marry their children," writes
Guicciardini,[1] "into strange towns, yea and Forraine
Countreys, and marry noble with ignoble, yoong with
olde, maister and servant, which is not commendable,"
and Moryson says that "those who come to greatest

---

[1] "Low Countries," 1593, p. 15.

8

honour in this Commonwealth, are either advocates of
the Law, or Sonnes of Merchants," and that " The vulgar
sort so despise Gentlemen, or any superior if he affect
greatnesse, as upon like occasions they proverbially use
to say 'If he be rich, let him dine twice'." [1]  So that
class distinctions were probably less marked there, than
in any other country of the world. The people of
Holland, too, had all that sense of responsibility towards
their fellow-citizens which should be the strength of a
democracy.  Guicciardini tells us that there were no
beggars; the poor were amply provided for, eight
thousand poor children were annually kept and taught;
the families of soldiers and sailors were well looked after.
In every town were hospitals and asylums for the poor,
the sick and the insane, not only of their own nation, but
of strangers.  " Poverty and madness," writes an observer,
"do both inhabit handsomely."

Nor were art and learning the exclusive privilege of
a small class as in England.  Education was universal.
Guicciardini notes that all had "some smackering of
their Gra͠mer"; every one, even the husbandmen, could
write and read, and many who had never been out of
their own country could speak French, German, Italian,
Spanish and English.  As soon as printing (an invention
in which Holland played a large part) became general,
it was determined that all should learn to read and write,
and schools were established in every town and village.
At first the teachers were paid by the pupils, but by 1609
the schools were the common property of the people,
paid for out of the municipal rates. [2]  The Protestants
of the Netherlands saw the immense importance of
education to their cause, based as it was upon a
study of the Scriptures, and the general education of
the people, and the wide diffusion of printed books,
especially the Bible, had much to do with the *reality* of

[1] " Shakespeare's Europe," p. 289.
[2] Motley, " United Netherlands," iv. 567.

THE COURT OF A DUTCH HOUSE

DE HOOCH

the Dutch Reformation, and with its popular character.
As well as state schools, there were greater facilities for
higher education than in other countries. The University
of Leyden was famous throughout Europe, and Franeker
in Friesland, established eleven years later, was free to
all. When the Hollanders despoiled the Roman Catholic
churches, there was no loot, and their wealth, instead of
enriching private persons, was used to support the clergy,
and to carry on charities, and also to endow schools and
Universities. They met the challenge of the Jesuit
College at Douai by rival foundations which attracted
Protestants from all countries.

The art of Holland belonged to the people, as much as
its learning. Good architecture was to be found not only
in churches and palaces, but in municipal buildings, and
even private houses. Every house, too, had its pictures
and decorations. "The lining of their houses is more
rich than the outside, not in hangings, but in pictures,
which even the poorest of the boors are there furnished
with; not a cobler but has his toys for ornament." [1]

Guicciardini ascribes to the Netherlanders the invention
of oil-painting, and their genuine love of art was proved
by the rapid spread of wood-engraving, which enabled
every one to obtain cheaply a reproduction more or less
artistic. This diffusion of artistic sense and taste, even
among the poorest, was remarkable at a time when in
England there was little real comfort or refinement for
any class, when splendour and show was reserved for the
great, and when the lot of the common people was
unutterly sordid and mean, and it had its effect on the
development of the Reformation. Whereas in England,
all that was beautiful was associated with the Church which
the Puritans condemned, or with the Court, which they
knew to be frivolous and bad, in Holland there was
beauty in the things of everyday life, in what they knew
to be good and wholesome, and so they never felt that

[1] Harl. Misc. ii. 596.

perverted hatred of the beautiful which has done so much to harm the reputation of Puritanism. Here again, as in their rational and cheerful views on Sabbath-keeping, they were saved because there was no reaction. The only form of art which they seemed unable to square with their Puritan convictions, was unfortunately music. Guicciardini says the people were all natural musicians; they had done much to restore the art of music, and had invented many musical instruments, but after the Reformation this was all given up.

All the legal and social features of Dutch life are of the greatest interest, showing as they do a very remarkable degree of civilization, but only a few points can be touched upon which seem to have influenced American life directly through the Pilgrims.

First of all, perhaps, comes the high position of women. In Holland, boys and girls were educated alike, the same schools being open to both, and the woman was almost the more important factor in family and business life. Her equality in business matters was so clearly recognized, that in most cities husband and wife were equally bound for each other's debts. Naturally the English writers of the time do not admire this characteristic; according to Moryson, the husbands were in absolute bondage, and he mentions one wife who said that her husband " had newly asked her leave to goe abroade," " I may boldly say," he adds, " that the women of these parts, are above all others truly taxed with this unnatural domineering over their Husbands "; [1] and even Guicciardini writes, " The Women governe all, both within doores and without, and make all bargaines, which joyned with the naturall desire that Women have to bear rule, maketh them too too imperious and troublesome."

Within the family, the rights of the wife and children were very carefully guarded. A wife could not only dispose by will of her own dowry as she liked, but could

"Shakespeare's Europe," 28.

if she had no children, bequeath to her kinsmen, after her
husband's death, half of any of his goods which he had
acquired since marriage. Should husbands " either
break in lifetime, or be found banckerouts at death the
wives are preferred to all debtors in the recovery of their
dowry." [1] So also it was enacted in Plymouth in 1636
that lands might be seized to pay the debts of a deceased
man, but that the portion reserved for the support of his
wife and family was to be untouched. And in 1646 the
consent of the wife became necessary to the sale of lands
or houses.

A second interesting point was their manner of
inheritance. There was far greater equality amongst
members of the family than in England. In Holland,
the father's estate was usually left to all his children
equally, so that few could live on their inheritance, but
must learn a trade to support themselves. A son might
only be disinherited for certain causes approved by the
law, and a father might only leave two-thirds of his
estate away from his children. Moreover, after their
mother's death, the children could compel their father to
divide his goods with them, lest he should waste all.
Moryson, himself a younger son, is lost in admiration of
this plan of equal inheritance, and is never tired of
inveighing against the English law of primogeniture,
which leaves the eldest son lying sluggishly at home, and
thrusts the younger out into wars and foreign travel in a
state of penury which (he implies) makes decent behaviour
impossible. This injustice alone, he thinks, is enough to
account for the bad name which the English have abroad.
In 1627, when De Rasières visited Plymouth, he found
that " In the inheritance they place all the children in one
degree, only the eldest son has an acknowledgment for
his seniority of birth." [2]

---

[1] Moryson's " Itinerary," III. II. iv. 97.
[2] De Rasières' letter, quoted in Palfrey i. 227, note. See also " Plymouth
Records " (iii. 207, 1660).

Not less important was the law respecting the transfer of land.   No land in Holland could be bought or mortgaged but by writings before one of the Eschevins (Municipal Officers) and one secretary of the town, who enrolled it in the public registers : after fifteen or sixteen months the title could not be disputed.[1]   A law was passed in Plymouth to the same effect in 1636, and was later adopted by the Court of Massachusetts and by other States, and the system has done much to give simplicity and security to legal transfers.

It is not necessary to press the analogy, or to insist too much on the resemblance between Dutch and American institutions.   No one can fail to see that the principle of equality in political and religious matters, which is the basis of American life, their ideas on education and philanthropy, and much of their legal procedure, had some origin other than English, but this belongs to a wider field of inquiry.   What one must insist upon is the share of Dutch influence in the broad liberal spirit of the Pilgrims, a spirit which waned sadly after the death of the first generation, and which was overshadowed, almost obscured by the narrower English Puritanism of Massachusetts.

The Pilgrims could have found no more beautiful and interesting home than Leyden.   It had been an important town ever since the thirteenth century, when the growth of the cloth trade necessitated the first great enlargement of the city.   The towns of the Netherlands were the chief market for English wool, and the skill of their weavers made the cloth trade one of their chief sources of wealth. Leyden was famous for its manufactures of woollen cloth and serge, and three times already had the city boundaries been extended, a fourth enlargement being commenced in 1610.   With all this growth, the town remained curiously unchanged in its older districts, the new sections forming outer shells or ramparts to the original city.

[1] Guicciardini, p. 31, verso.

LEYDEN

(FROM "DÉLICES DE LEIDE," 1712)

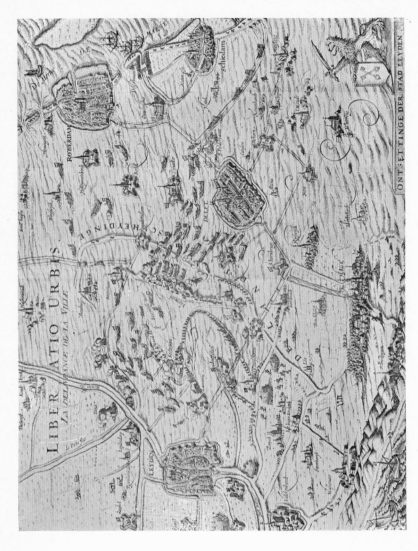

THE RELIEF OF LEYDEN

About the thirteenth century, too, Leyden became a municipality, and the citizens gradually gained a larger and larger share in self-government. In the sixteenth century it was one of six towns which sent deputies to the Assembly of States to consider taxation.

But important as the city had long been, it was the cruel siege by the Spaniards which gave it its final pre-eminence. From October 1573 to March 1574 it was besieged by Valdez, and when his troops were called off to intercept Count Louis of Nassau, the citizens actually neglected to revictual the place. So when, after the defeat of Louis, and the patriots at Mookeheyde, Valdez returned and opened a second siege, their sufferings were terrible. They endured them staunchly, though to famine was added pestilence, and when a few grew fainthearted and reproached the burgomaster Van der Werf, he offered them his body for bread rather than that they should yield. "I can die but once," he said, "whether by your hands, the enemy's, or by the hand of God. . . . Your menaces move me not; my life is at your disposal; here is my sword, plunge it into my breast and divide my flesh among you. Take my body to appease your hunger, but expect no surrender so long as I remain alive."

His courage put new heart into the defenders, and they hurled defiance at the Spaniards. "Ye call us rat-eaters," they cried, "and it is true. So long, then, as ye hear dog bark or cat mew within the walls, ye may know that the city holds out, and when all has perished but ourselves, be sure that we will each devour our left arms, retaining our right to defend our women, our liberty, and our religion against the foreign tyrant."[1] When finally the dykes were cut, and at the beginning of October a fleet slowly floated in, relieved the town, and drove off the Spaniards, Leyden was famous for ever. She had proved to the Spaniards the mettle of the men they were fighting against, she had proved to her own countrymen that they

[1] Motley, "Dutch Republic," p. 576.

could defy their powerful enemy with success; moreover, she had proved that men of different creeds could fight and suffer side by side against a common oppressor, and so the groundwork of a future toleration was laid.

A series of pictures in the Leyden town-hall represent the most notable events of the siege. There too, were placed after death, fastened up by the wings, the pigeons which had been sent into the town to announce the coming relief.

To commemorate their triumph, an annual fair was established lasting ten days. It was the event of the year in Leyden ; on October 3rd the bells pealed, the civic guard marched through the city, armed and in gala dress, a solemn review took place, then the corporation chose their magistrates for the year, and a great banquet was held. It was a general holiday, because, as Moryson says, "that day Leyden was besegged by the Spaniards, in memory whereof they have publike playes, poorely representing the Actions and Crueltyes of that siege."[1] Moryson, coming from Shakespeare's England, is always scornful of the dramatic efforts of the Dutch. But the real reward which Leyden received for her service to the States, was the establishment of the University. She chose it in preference to exemption from taxation, and it was founded by Charter in 1575, established first in the cloister of St Barbe, and then transferred to the chapel of the Jacobins, and endowed with property formerly belonging to the Roman Catholic churches. By a polite fiction, the charter was supposed to be granted by Philip of Spain "after ripely deliberating with our dear cousin, William, Prince of Orange," and he was thus represented as founding a University to reward Leyden for rebellion against himself.

The object was by no means only to do honour to Leyden. There had been very famous Dutch scholars, and some of the world's most valuable inventions are

[1] "Shakespeare's Europe," 376.

due to them,[1] but so far they had had no university of
their own, but had depended on the Roman Catholic
Universities of Flanders. Now they were cut off from
these by their difference in religion. Even had they
wished it, they could no longer safely attend them; the
eldest son of the Prince of Orange, who was a student at
Louvain, was carried off by the Spaniards during the war,
and kept prisoner in Spain for twenty years.[2] It was
felt necessary to have some University of their own,
where Protestant clergy and scholars could be trained.
The University of Leyden was under the general control
of William of Orange, its real founder, and he had power
to name the Rector. Later, this duty devolved upon the
States, who also paid the stipends and elected the three
curators who, together with four burgomasters, controlled
the officers and support of the University. Its establishment filled such a crying need, and it was conducted on
such liberal lines, that some of the greatest men of the
day were at once associated with it; such men as Junius,
Justus Lipsius, Scaliger, Vossius, Hugo, Grotius, Spinoza,
Cheverius and Peter Paaw. There were Professors in
divinity, medicine (including anatomy, chemistry, and
botany), classics, civil law, logic, mathematics, and oriental
languages, their stipends varying from 200 guldens to
1200, the highest being paid to Francis Junius, professor
of divinity. In addition to this, all professors had houses
allotted to them by the States, save two, who had instead the rent of some lands. The divines disputed twice
a week, other professors occasionally, not on set days,
but each in his special auditory. As the authorities were
extremely broad-minded in their appointments, and introduced men of very varying shades of belief, these
disputes were sometimes heated. Gomar and Arminus
were joint-professors of theology when the Pilgrims
first arrived in Leyden, and all through their stay fierce

[1] See Guicciardini and Motley, iv. 569-71.
[2] Fynes Moryson, "Itinerary," III. IV. vi. 279.

warfare was going on between the representatives of different schools of thought, Arminians and Calvinists, Remonstrants and Counter-Remonstrants.

At the time of Moryson's visit (1598), there were about four hundred students in the University; he talks of seeing the "Professors and Studients, partly in gownes, partly in Cloakes, all wearing hatts (for I never sawe any cornered Capps worne by Graduates in any University beyonde the Seas)." As time went on, they had many foreign students, English especially, and never so many perhaps as in the eighteenth century, when the religious tests at the English Universities closed their doors to all dissenters.

Besides the University proper, a special college of theology was founded in Leyden in 1591 for divinity students. It was in the convent of the "Cell-brothers," and admitted two students from each city, who were supported by scholarships from these cities. It is this college which Moryson refers to, when he speaks of some poor scholars maintained in a ruinous college, each having only Thirty Flemish pounds yearly, and being given only six years to take their degrees; but in spite of his scorn, this college had some very famous professors, and it met the needs of those unable to afford the cost of education at the University.

So henceforth, Leyden was not only important for commerce, but also for learning, and the population grew by leaps and bounds. The students lived for the most part in the houses of the citizens, and the burghers with whom they lived shared in the privileges which the University gave to her members, so the two elements of manufacturing and student life could never have been very distinct and separate, much less antagonistic.

Besides the interest and variety of its life, Leyden had great natural beauties. Polyander, a member of the University in 1610, thought it the loveliest city in the world, and all contemporaries admire it. Moryson speaks of it as a city of much beauty, with houses fairly

THE OLD LIBRARY, LEYDEN UNIVERSITY
(FROM "DÉLICES DE LEIDE," 1712)

built and uniform ; and one street much fairer than the
rest, in the midst of which was a piece of ground railed
in, where the merchants used to meet.  The imposing
buildings, the spacious streets and squares, all gave an
idea of prosperity and order, and the city regulations
show how much importance was given to the care of the
town.  If a cry of fire were raised, the owner of the
house had to pay six guldens as the penalty of his care-
lessness ; a night watch paraded the streets to guard
against accident or evildoing ; and each time the clock
struck, a trumpet in the steeple assured the citizens that
they might sleep again securely, for all was well.

Another writer [1] calls Leyden the neatest and cleanest
of all Dutch towns.  As the Rhine water surrounded
much of the city, and passed through it in many streams,
shaded by limes, poplars, and willows, small canals
making almost every house accessible by water, the
moist atmosphere compelled the inhabitants to be very
careful lest the air should become unwholesome.  This
was the more necessary, because about Leyden the waters
were not easily renewed, and were, as Moryson says of
those at Haarlem, subject to stinking.  Haarlem Meer,
the great lake of fresh water, refreshed the town, and
helped to renew the canals, and so Leyden long refused
consent to the draining of this inland sea.  The general
moisture compelled them to have very well-paved streets,
and to make long causeways between towns, and so
careful were they of these, that at the gates of Leyden
the men dismounted from their waggons, and only women
might be carried into the city, lest the wheels of the loaded
waggons should break the brick pavements of the streets. [2]

Much of their traffic was, of course, done by boat, and
at a set hour every day boats passed from Leyden to all
the next cities.  Probably the Pilgrims made all their
journey from Amsterdam by water, along the Haarlem
canal to the entrance of Haarlem Meer, where their boats

[1] Harl. Misc. ii. 598.        [2] Moryson's "Itinerary," I. I. iv. 45.

would have to be lifted by force of hands over the dam
into the lake. Then, after travelling about five miles
along its waters they would pass through one canal after
another into one of the channels of the Rhine, and so to
Leyden. It was a privilege granted to the people of
Haarlem that all boats should be lifted by hand over the
dam, so that heavy freights could not go that way, and
the merchants, travelling by land, might be forced to
pass through their town.

Not splendour, but comfort, and comfort widely diffused,
was the keynote of Dutch life. The houses were as well
kept within as without, and ornamented with shining
vessels of brass and copper. The house linen was a
marvel of purity and fineness, and bed was a luxury,
though hard to attain, for it was generally like a berth on
board ship; high enough up to need a ladder or stairs,
and walled in with wainscot.

As for the dress of the people, the men wore modest
attire suited to their rank as merchants, without much
lace or ornament. Generally they had short cloaks of
English cloth, with one small lace to cover the seams,
and a narrow facing of silk or velvet. Their doublets
were made close to the body, their breeches were long
and fastened under the knees, and made mostly of cloth
or thin stuff, occasionally of silk or velvet. The women
were beginning to imitate the English and French
fashions, both married and unmarried covered their heads
with a coif of fine Holland linen; they wore gowns of
some light stuff, mostly black, with little or no lace, and
small but fine neck ruffs. All their linen indeed was of
the finest. When going out, the women put on a veil
over their heads hanging down behind, below the waist,
with a kind of horn rising over the forehead. Most
foreign observers seemed to think that their mode of
dress disfigured their natural beauty, especially the
custom of wearing earwires, which pinched in the cheeks
and gave a curious appearance to the face. According

to one "Unless it be themselves, they let none of God's creatures lose anything of their natural beauty."

For their diet, Moryson tells us, that butter was the first and last dish at table. "Men of butter," Alva had called them in derision. On their frequent journeys by boat from town to town, they would carry with them cheese and boxes of butter for their food. They lived well though simply ; all, even the servants, had four meals in the day, but two of them were of butter and cheese only. They also fed much upon roots, and used fresh meats almost entirely, keeping salted food only to pro voke drinking. It was, indeed, due to the extensive cultivation of winter roots by the Dutch, and the possibility through this of keeping cattle alive through the winter, that scurvy and leprosy ceased to be the awful and unavoidable scourges they had formerly been.

Life in Leyden was simple enough, but gay, and perhaps too free to suit an ultra-Puritan conscience. The people were by no means ostentatiously religious; there were three Reformed Churches in Leyden, but Moryson did not consider it at all a religious city, observing that at the time of divine service there were far more people in the market-place than in the church. But their religion was of a practical kind, not kept for Sunday, or for church; their moral standard was high, and their commercial integrity a byword. "They will not," writes Moryson "cozen a chylde or a stranger in changing a peece of gold, nor in the price or quality of thinges they buy." [1] He thought them hard to persuade, and seldom deceived, for they trusted nobody, paid no compliments, and expected none.

They were indeed not much given to observances of any kind. Holland in general had few ceremonies, shows or feasts At the opening of the University, Leyden permitted herself a dignified and classic pageant. Following the burgher Militia and five companies of infantry,

[1] Shakespeare's " Europe," 369.

came a female figure representing the Holy Gospel, clad in snowy garments, on a triumphal car, attended by the four Evangelists.   Then came Justice riding blindfold upon a unicorn, with four learned doctors of classic times in her train.   Then the goddess of medicine on horseback, with four ancient physicians, and finally Minerva, with Aristotle, Cicero, Plato, and Virgil, fully attended.   After these came the city band, the officers of the town and University, and the body of the citizens, and when the procession reached the Nuns' Bridge, Apollo and the nine muses floated down the Rhine, stepped from their barge, and greeted each Professor in turn with a kiss.

There were certain ceremonies, too, when new doctors were admitted to the University, and at the annual fair there was amusement of a less dignified kind, mountebanks and players, and general festivity.   But the chief rejoicings were at the time of a wedding.   Most of the people were betrothed or married very young ; sometimes the betrothal was a long one, and great liberty was allowed to the betrothed pair.   Often a girl would go for long voyages with her sailor lover, and where the master of the ship was a wooer, a garland of roses would be hung from the top of the main mast.   At the time Moryson was in Holland (1598), marriage was solemnized in church, though somewhat privately, but within ten years it had become almost entirely a civil ceremony, taking place before the magistrates.   The wedding festivities lasted for several days, and friends of all ages were entertained. For two or three evenings, friends and strangers came in to dance ; the elders went to bed, and the young men and maids "danced all night and at the twilight in the morning they danced about some of the next streets, and so taking theire leaves went home."

Such were the surroundings to which the Pilgrims came in May 1609, and amongst which they were to make their home for almost a dozen years.   We know little as to how far they joined in the everyday life of Leyden and

adopted its customs. Probably from the reasons given
for their final departure, they tried to live a life of their
own in religious and social matters, but in the two main
occupations of the town, its commerce, and its student
life, they certainly shared; in the first, through their
necessities, in the second, through the tastes of some of
their number, and on account of the privileges which
membership of the University conferred. Many became
citizens for business purposes, for only a citizen could
gain admittance into the trade guilds. Many became
members of the University, which gave them, besides
literary opportunities, immunity from the jurisdiction of
the city police, from the billeting of soldiers and military
duties and levies, besides obtaining them a fixed amount
of wine and beer free of duty. This last was a consideration; it was held to be a great hardship to drink water in
those days, and probably was, and except at Middelburg,
the staple for French wines, and Dort, the staple for
Rhenish, the impost was as great as the price of the wine.

But these admissions came later; the first necessity on
arriving in the city was to be housed, and to find some
employment which would bring them daily bread, and
neither of these things was easy. Leyden was full to over-
flowing, as the need for enlargement in 1610 proved; some
may have found shelter in the small houses often built on
convent ground, which would now be in the hands of the
State; some may even have gone to the numerous
hospitals founded by the charity of the Dutch in every
city for the sick, poor and aged of their own and other
nations. The fact that many families are known to have
changed their dwellings very soon, shows that their first
abodes were often temporary and unsatisfactory; Brewster
for instance, lived first in a street with the unpleasant
name of Stinksteeg, there he lost a child, and quickly
moved to a better house in St Ursula's Lane, and finally
to Choir Alley near to St Peter's Church. Gradually
most of the people collected in the neighbourhood of St

Peter's, which was near to the University, and on the whole the best part of the town. As to their work, they were forced to be content with very humble trades. The records of marriage usually give the employment of each of the people contracting or witnessing, and most of the trades mentioned are unskilled. They were poor, few of them had experience in anything but agriculture, in which they would be entirely outclassed by the Dutch, and Leyden gave less scope for untrained work than did a seaport town like Amsterdam, which must have afforded plenty of miscellaneous employment. Many of them became say or serge weavers, wool-combers and carders; the record of the marriage of William Bradford with Dorothy May in 1613 calls him a fustian worker. Brewster set up a printing press, of which we shall hear more later, and Winslow probably helped him. Some few became merchants, some made bombazine, and some made hats.

There are twenty-two sets of records in Leyden in which traces of the Pilgrims may be found; but the names are often indistinct and ill-spelt, and it is difficult to be sure of the identity. Chief amongst these records are those of betrothal, marriage, and burial, of people to be taxed, tenants and property owners, of admissions to citizenship and to the University, and of the doings of the Court. None of the notices found can be without interest to those who trace their descent from members of the Leyden Church, but the one of the greatest general interest is the record of the purchase of Robinson's house in Bell Alley in 1611. Where he lived, and where the church assembled before this time, is quite unknown. They did not apply on arrival (as did the Presbyterian Church under Durie) for a place of worship, either because they were too poor to bear the necessary charges, or because they feared to make *any* demands, and courted peace in obscurity.

The " house of the Green Door," as the new purchase was called, had a garden, and a large piece of ground adjoining, and was nearly opposite the belfry of St Peter's Church. It was bought in the names of John Robinson, William Jepson, Henry Wood, and Ralph Tickens (brother-in-law to Robinson), and the price paid was equivalent to £1400 then, £350 being paid down, and the remainder to be paid in annual instalments of £87, 10s. The seller reserved to himself the room over the door, which seems generally to have belonged to the master of the house, for an English traveller a few years later writes, "It is sure his fear that renders him suspicious ; that he may therefore certainly see who enters, you shall ever find his window over his door." In the house of the Green Door Robinson lived. Winslow says that before the departure for America "they, I say, that stayed at Leyden feasted us that were to goe, at our Pastor's house being large."[1] Apparently Robinson and his family were the sole occupants of it, and the share borne in the charge by the three other men makes it seem likely that it was a church investment. The house was probably enlarged and used as a meeting-house, or possibly a separate chapel was built, and the size of the piece of land would permit not only of such enlargement, but also of the building of some smaller houses and workshops for the use of other members of the church. After Robinson's death, Jepson bought out the interest of the others, and the house was pulled down and rebuilt in 1683. A tablet has been placed on the present building to mark the site of the labours of John Robinson and his fellows, the sole landmark of their life in the city.

Though poor and humble, the Pilgrims had a good character in Leyden, they were trusted by all, and the magistrates recognized them as law abiding citizens. They had many valuable additions to their number, so many in fact that the personnel of the church from which the *Mayflower* passengers were drawn, was probably very different from that of the Scrooby church. Some of the

---

[1] Hypocrisie Unmasked, p. 90.

9

men who were to be the backbone of the new colony joined them during these years in Leyden. Edward Winslow, a native of Droitwich in England, was travelling on the continent, and learning something of the Leyden church, was so attracted by it that he joined it about 1617. He went with the colonists to America, was governor for several years, and being a literary man, is, after Bradford, the chief source of our information about their early life there. He is the only one among the Pilgrims of whom any portrait is known to exist ; and the only one who attained any eminence outside the colony, for much of his later life was spent in England. He conducted many of the negotiations between Plymouth and the English government, not always unscathed, for in 1635, whilst on a mission to England, he was imprisoned on the charge of having taught in church, although a layman, and of having married people in his capacity of magistrate. He was always foremost in any dealings with the Indians, and in 1649 founded a corporation for propagating the gospel among the Indians of New England, probably the earliest of English foreign missions. Under Cromwell he held several important appointments abroad, and died at sea in 1655.

Miles Standish was another who cast in his lot with the Pilgrims at this time, though he never joined their church. Born at Duxbury Hall in Lancashire, of good family, he was in some way deprived of his inheritance, and became a soldier of fortune in the Netherlands. His name will always be associated with the romantic story of his court-ship of Priscilla Mullins, but it is a prosaic fact that, in spite of its unsuccess, he was twice married. His kind heart and fiery temper, his absolute intrepidity and un-bounded resource, make his name stand out in all accounts of their life in America. The Dutch army had been reorganized by Prince Maurice on democratic principles ; rank was given according to merit, not birth ; the pay was high and regular, the discipline of the strictest, and Standish probably learnt military lessons from it, as did

Cromwell's future leaders. He was not only an excellent military leader, but prominent in the government of the colony, and acted as governor's assistant for nineteen years. In 1631, when the colony grew and scattered, he settled on Captain's Hill in Duxbury, named after his birthplace, and there he died in 1656.

Amongst others who probably joined the church in Leyden, were Samuel Fuller, a physician of London, who became deacon both there and at Plymouth, and was one of the chief men of the colony; John Carver, also a deacon in Leyden and the first governor of Plymouth; Robert Cushman, who, with Carver, made most of the arrangements for their voyage; Isaac Allerton, who married Brewster's daughter Fear; and was the commercial agent of the colony, until he proved untrustworthy; and many others of lesser importance.

It may be thought that the Pilgrims lived so obscurely in Leyden, so aloof from the life around them, that they could not have been influenced by it so deeply as had been represented. This may be true of some, though they probably learnt more than they knew. But the new colony, mere handful as it was, would be moulded by the ideas of its chief men; its leaders were men of parts, able to profit by experience, to discriminate between good and bad precedent, and the share they had taken in Dutch life was not really so small: Robinson disputing with divines and studying their views; Brewster teaching English to " Great men's sons " and learning from them ideas of government and policy unknown in England; Standish serving in the Dutch army, observing its discipline and efficiency; others, in the university and in commerce, were each fitting themselves to transmit to their new home the best and most vital elements of the civilization around them. They did not do it unaided, for direct Dutch influence on America was not wanting, but they did their share, and not only America, but England through America, has felt its lasting power.

# CHAPTER VII

## THE CHURCH IN LEYDEN

THESE years in Leyden, important as they were in affecting the social and political future of New England and America, had an influence just as great, and much more immediate, on the history of Congregationalism. The free churches were, so to speak, in the making; the process of differentiation amongst the Separatists, begun with such unhappy quarrels at Amsterdam, was still going on; and in Leyden, where the church was neither persecuted nor bewildered by too much variety of opinion, the main principles of congregational rule were established. So far as we know, the work was done peaceably; there seem to have been none of the quarrels and recriminations there that had caused such scandal in Amsterdam. Difficulties arose, as they must in all human societies, but they vanished before Robinson's judgment and charity. "And if at any time," wrote Bradford, "any differences arose or offences broak out (as it cannot be but some time ther will, even among the best of men), they were ever so mete with and nipt in the head betimes, or otherwise so well composed; as still love, peace, and communion were continued; Or els the Church purged of those that were yncurable and yncorrigible; when after which patience used, no other means would serve; which seldom came to pass."[1]

After the troubles and disasters of the earlier churches, it is a relief to come upon this happier history, and there is no doubt that the peace and kindliness in the church,

[1] Bradford MS. p. 13.

on which both Winslow and Robinson are eloquent, was
very largely the work of the latter.  As Brewster had
been the central figure at Scrooby, as Bradford was to be
the leader in the early days in America, so John Robinson
was the very soul of the life in Leyden, and his influence
impressed itself not only on the men he knew, but on
generations to come.  The churches of the Separation in
their earliest days depended on the pastor for more than
ordinary teaching and guidance; he held the reins,
whatever the theory of rule might be, and he must hold
them tightly lest his people should be scattered, and fail
to tread out a straight path for themselves.  They had to
work out now the same problem that had faced the Church
of England fifty years before, the finding and keeping of
a new rule where the old one had been abandoned.  It
was a hard task, and probably nothing but the character
and personal influence of Robinson saved his church from
a fate like that of the earlier ones.  Browne, Johnson, and
Smyth, men with great qualifications and real religious
aspiration, had each made shipwreck of his cause.  There
were indeed other men of great power in the Leyden
church, but the piety and learning of Harrison, the saint-
liness and moderation of Ainsworth, the staunchness and
affection of Smyth's followers, had availed little when
their pastor's judgment was at fault.  To Robinson, therefore, must be given all honour for the happier lot of the
Pilgrim Church, and his people were the first to acknowledge their debt to him.

The importance of the character of the Leyden church,
and the development of its religious views was very
great.  Congregationalism, in fact the free church system
altogether, was on its trial, and the respect won by the
church among the citizens of Leyden, the reputation
gained by John Robinson amongst scholars and divines,
established its credit once and for all.  It was by no
means a barren credit either.  The good name of the
church decided the kind of recruits likely to be attracted

by it. It has already been noticed, that many of those who were afterwards to be leaders, joined the Pilgrims in Leyden. Such men as Winslow, Carver and Cushman, did not cast in their lot with these poor people for any worldly advantage, in fact we hear that the hardships of their life frightened many away. It was the sanity of their religious views, and the goodness of their lives, that gained them such valuable support, and so caused New Plymouth to be peopled by a picked body of men. The Leyden church too had other friends, men who later influenced the religious thought of England, and the chief of these was perhaps Henry Jacob. Being sent to argue with Francis Johnson in prison, he had himself been converted to Separatism, and taking refuge at Middelburg, had long corresponded with John Robinson on church matters. In 1609 he came to live in Leyden; and in 1616, moved perhaps by the picture Helwys had drawn of the neglected people in England, and the cowardice of the Separatists who fled from persecution, instead of ministering to them, he returned to London, collected the scattered remnants of Southwark congregation, and established the first permanent Independent church in England. Thus the principles of the Leyden church were transferred, with little modification, to England and America, and practically decided the form of Congregationalism in both countries.

The history of the growth of thought in the church, the modifications of its position due to practical experience, and the influence of the life around, are of course best studied in the writings of Robinson himself. "Only God," he once wrote, "is not taught by experience," and they show a gradual broadening of principle and a growing liberality, in all matters of government and external policy, together with the most rigid conservatism in doctrine.

Like most reformers of his day, whether Church of England, Puritan or Separatist, Robinson was a Calvinist in doctrine, and he never saw any need to modify his

views on this point.   In Calvinism, he saw the greatest
possibilities of practical reform, and he was unaffected
alike by the Arminian doctrine of freewill, and the
Anabaptist doctrines of inner light and personal revelation.
All he heard of these ideas in Leyden, seems only to have
intensified his views, for his theology became more rigidly
Calvinistic as years went on.

Arminianism, in particular, had gained much ground in
Holland, and many were the discussions of it in the University of Leyden, for one of the Professors of Divinity
preached for it, and the other against it, and each had a
following amongst the students.   Robinson listened both
to the one and to the other, and gained such a mastery of
the subject, that he was asked by John Polyander and
the Calvinist preachers of the town, to dispute against
Episcopius, the Arminian Professor, who was putting
forth his best strength, both in writing and debate.
Robinson was unwilling at first, being a stranger, but
when it was urged upon him that he alone was able to
uphold and defend the truth, he consented, and not only
once, but three times, he defeated the great Professor in
argument.   He had become a member of the University
in 1615, and now its Professors would have willingly
given him some preferment out of gratitude, but that
they feared to offend the English government.   James I.
recognized and feared the power of Leyden University ; he
claimed a very decided right to interfere in their appointments, and had strongly objected to Vorstius, an
Arminian Professor, threatening " to forbid all the youth
of our subjects to frequent a university that is so infected
as Leyden," unless he were removed ; and he was not
likely to approve of any honour done to one of the hated
English Separatists.

So long as Arminianism remained only the subject of
theological discussion in the schools, the tolerant Dutch
were not likely to interfere with it, but unfortunately it
became identified with a political party which demanded

a national church controlled by the state, and a prolonged truce with Spain. The Calvinists, on the other hand, wanted a free church in a free state, and sided with Prince Maurice in favouring war with Spain. The question was a very complicated one, involving not only the relations of Church and State, but the choice between State rights, advocated by John of Barneveldt, and a united Holland. To settle it the Synod of Dort was held in 1618; as a result of it the Arminians were declared heretics and schismatics; Episcopius and many others were banished; and the Remonstrants, as the Arminian followers of John of Barneveldt were called, were forbidden to hold office in church or university. The verdict was a blot on the Hollanders' reputation for tolerance, but it was aimed at the political, rather than the religious views of the Arminians. Their theological arguments were hardly listened to at the Synod; the deposed ministers were paid and supplied with funds; many of them were allowed to return within a few years, and other sects, holding identical religious beliefs, were left in peace.

As Robinson had sided with the Calvinist party at the University, so he upheld the decrees of the Synod on every point. In a controversy with Murton in 1624, called "A Defence of the Doctrine propounded by the Synod of Dort," he supports its Calvinism unflinchingly on the five points of predestination, election, falling away, free will, and the original state of man.

In matters of polity, however, he was far more flexible; his views on separation show very striking modifications, and all in the direction of tolerance and fraternity. He could not fail to be influenced by the tolerance around him; by the practical demonstration of different forms of church government living side by side in peace. In his earliest treatise, "An answer to a censorious Epistle," written in reply to Hall and published at Amsterdam in 1608, he defends separation as the first step towards communion with God, and is proud to be a "ringleader"

Fort qui à été sur le Breestraat.

FORTIFICATION OF LEYDEN DURING THE ARMINIAN TROUBLES

(FROM "DÉLICES DE LEIDE," 1712)

in so good a thing. He claimed to have separated, not
from the ceremonies or the corruptions of the Church, but
from the Church itself, since whilst it was so composed
and governed, it could never cease to be corrupt, and
could not be a true church. It was the system which
could permit such corruption, that he objected to. Briefly,
his position was this, that the Church of England must
be false, because by the nature of its organization it could
not be purified, and because its government was un-
scriptural. (This consideration, as with Browne, came
later than the practical one to Robinson.) From such a
church, separation was a duty, first because no Christian
could remain in a false church, and also because to remain
in communion with corrupt members would constitute
connivancy in their sin. From this position, Robinson
never definitely receded, but he grew to interpret the
meaning of communion much more broadly than at first.
In his earliest works he permits of no intercourse whatever with members of a false church, even if personal
relations with Christ could be discerned in them. In 1612,
after a controversy with Mr Ames, he allowed communion
in private prayer and other exercises with the godly
members of the Established Church, but no share must
be taken in their church communion, or in any service
authorised by the church power and ministry. With the
reformed churches of France and Holland, however, he
now permitted full communion. Later came a tract "Of
the lawfulness of hearing Ministers in the Church of
England," which shows a still further advance. He speaks
in it of the many in that Church who belong to the true
faith, just as he had done himself before separating, and
shows that it is useful, and even necessary, to hear their
teaching on occasions ; and when his advice was asked
by Jacob, he upheld a member of his congregation who
had attended Anglican worship. "Men must not," he
said, "lose the benefit of that which is good, because it is
mingled with what is erroneous."

By the two distinctions he made, on the one hand between private and church action, and on the other between communion in that which was lawful in church order, and that which was unlawful, Robinson was able to modify greatly the position of the Separatists. In speaking of his private life, Bradford says, " And none did more offend him than those that were close and cleaving to themselves, and retired from the common good ; as also shuch as would be stiffe and rigid in matters of outward order, and ynvey against the evils of others, and yet be remisse in themselves, and not so carefull to express a virtuous conversation." [1]   The same views guided his conduct in the relations of churches.   Others emphasized differences ; he dwelt on likenesses, and found more and more as he grew older.   His broad mind and strong sense of proportion led him to ignore surface differences where there was an underlying sameness of principle, and wherever his very real convictions permitted it, he aimed not at isolation, but at union and brotherhood.

It was not a matter only of temperament, but of policy. Robinson knew that, for his church to gain credit, not only must the personal character of the members be as immaculate as possible, but also the church must establish some satisfactory relations with other reformed churches. He knew perfectly well, and had always admitted that there were scores of excellent men in churches which he considered false ones, and he knew too that if this fact were not recognized and acted upon, first the usefulness, and afterwards the very existence of his church, would be threatened.   An entirely isolated position was neither wholesome nor possible for any length of time, and so we hear from Bradford that Robinson always urged communion with the French and Dutch reformed churches, and with the Scotch.   With the Church of England, only private communion was allowed ; there could be no official communion, for episcopal government, the liturgy and

[1] Bradford MS. p. 13.

stinted prayers, and the confusion of the corrupt with the worthy in the Lord's Supper, Robinson testified against to the day of his death. Nevertheless, he allowed none to boast of their separation from the Church of England, and if any new-comers gloried in it, they were reproved and told "That we required no such things at their hands." [1]

With regard to the independence of each church, Robinson admitted no ecclesiastical power superior to the congregation. Each congregation, he claimed, had complete powers of self-organization, it could and must call and ordain its own officers. To Synods he allowed no great authority, though he thought them helpful; but he did allow the interference of lay authority, and never completely severed the functions of Church and State. The magistrates, according to him, could make no law forcing an unholy person to church, or forcing a church to receive him; union with the true church must be purely voluntary. But he could repress idolatry, and use the civil sword against it; he could ensure the right preaching of the Gospel in his own domain, and force the people to hear it, and even punish them if they persisted in preferring the false to the true church. In short, the magistrate could not compel any man to join the church, but he could punish him for his obstinacy in refusing to do so voluntarily. This narrow view of spiritual liberty, joined with the still narrower views of the Massachusetts Puritans, accounted for many of the mistakes and difficulties in the religious history of New England.

Within the church, Robinson's ideas of government were democratic. A church, he thought, could exist without its officers, and whilst they were obviously necessary for orderly government, the elders were to be in no sense "the church." They merely prepared, instead of transacting business in their private consistory; and the people were responsible for their good government; to give the rule entirely into their hands, he thought,

[1] Hypocrisie Unmasked, p. 99.

would be like enclosing commons on the plea that they were badly kept. The leadership of the elder in the Pilgrim Church was mostly moral and non-official; his function was to instruct and guide the people into concurrence with his views, and where such a man as Brewster held the position, this became practicable and worked for the general good. Moreover, Robinson acknowledged no merely "governing" elder; he was to be "apt to teach," and so entirely unlike the Presbyterian elders who were concerned with discipline only. For some time after the Pilgrims reached America, Brewster was more like their pastor than their elder; he conducted all the services of their church, save that Robinson, when consulted in 1623, denied his right to administer Sacraments, and they were forced to forego these privileges of the church for many years. Lay preaching was also encouraged, and came to be a necessary preliminary to a call to office; but he restricted it to those only who were qualified, thinking that it came "within the compasse but of a few of the multitude," two or three perhaps in each church.

If his views on the eldership were Brownist, Robinson was very much at one with Barrow on the subject of Baptism. He saw no necessity, as Smyth and the Anabaptists did, for repudiating baptism, even when administered by a false church. Such a false order could not vitiate the sacrament itself; by faith and the spirit it was sanctified to those who received it rightly. It was a covenant between God and man, originated in a true church, and unimpaired by any later intervention of false orders; a covenant, too, which comprehended the children of the righteous in their fathers as branches in the roots. He agreed with Barrow, too, that the ceremonies of marriage and burial, being common to all men, whether christian or heathen, were no part of the services of the church, and should be performed not by the pastor, but by a civil magistrate.

Hardly less interesting than the controversial side of Robinson's writings, is the light which they throw on his personal character. His "Observations Divine and Moral," possibly the abstracts of the many sermons preached to his people, show a man eminently practical in all that he thought and did, a man to whom a merely intellectual view of religion would be impossible. Religion to him was "the secret relationship which the soul bears to God," a relationship which must mould the entire life of a man, and find expression in everything he did. "We must take heed," he wrote, "of a shadowish love of goodness and piety only in the abstract, and must love it in the concrete." And again, "God is not partial, as men are ; nor regards that church and chamber religion towards Him, which is not accompanied in the house and streets with loving kindness and mercy and all goodness towards men."

To such a man the position of condemnation into which his Separatism forced him, could not fail to be painful, and indeed the suspicion of schism was one of the sorrows of his life. He saw all its evils, the harm done by leaving a former course of religion lightly, the danger of religious disputes, however necessary, the fear lest men should be driven to wish their adversaries worse than they were, that they might be the more justified. But if his people had been forced as a church to condemn others, he gave them no encouragement to do so in private life, constantly urging charity, kindliness towards everyone, and patience with the evil-doer. The cord of friendship with such a one would be rather untwined than broken, in sorrow rather than in anger, and a disposition always shown to resume the friendship.

His was a serious turn of mind, seeing little purpose in mirth, possessed of a passion for truth and sincerity which made him suspicious of flattery or flowery speech. Such words seemed to him mere wantonness ; "As a woman over curiously trimmed is to be suspected, so is a speech."

But though serious, he was very far from being morbid or gloomy, never exalting self-sacrifice for its own sake, never making a bugbear of conscience. A large conscience he thought good, but an over-large use of conscience was not ; crosses were not to be desired simply because they were natural evils, for by no means all the crosses which Christians took up were really the crosses of Christ. He was still further from any tinge of fanaticism, or any blind belief in prayer without effort, marvelling that men should neglect the help of physicians in illness, trusting to God's special help ; and saying that " For us to ask anything at the hands of the Lord which withal we do not offer ourselves ready instruments to effect and bring to pass, is to tempt God's power and to abuse his goodness."

Nor was he superstitious. The belief in witchcraft, responsible for so much cruelty elsewhere, had no hold amongst the Dutch, nor amongst the Leyden church, and not until the death of Bradford and the early settlers were any witches put to death in Plymouth.

None of Robinson's utterances, however, are more expressive of his moderation, sound sense, and charity, than his farewell address to those leaving for America, and his letter sent after them to Southampton. A sketch of the farewell address was preserved by Winslow in his account of the Leyden church ; in it, he exhorted all to follow him no farther than he followed Christ, and to be ready for any truth and light which should break forth out of the Holy Word. For that here was more light to come he was convinced. He begged his people to shake off the name of Brownist, and lamented the rigidness of Lutheranism, and Calvinism, whose followers would move not one step further than Luther and Calvin had done. Bradford says in his " Dialogue " that " the Devil getteth great advantage by names amongst Christians," and evidently Robinson had the same feeling, and dreaded a form of religion which should take its name and characteristics from one man, however good, feeling that it would thereby become cramped and incapable of growth. He begged his flock to study union, rather than division ; and to close as far as possible with the non-conforming Puritans of the English Church, prophesying that there would be little difference between them when they came to the practice of the Ordinances out of the Kingdom, which indeed proved true. Amongst these, he thought that they might find a pastor, and they were not to hesitate out of loyalty to him, for a flock with two Shepherds " is not indangered, but secured by it."

Controversy has raged round the command to receive more light. It has been taken on the one hand to imply a certain vagueness and indecision in Robinson's theological views, and has been used as ground of justification for many departures from the original creed. Others read a different meaning into the words, and take them to refer, not to the dogma of the church, but to its polity, and this is far more consistent with what we know of the speaker. He never showed signs of wavering from the theology of Calvin, but the form of church government was to him, in the first place, a matter of practical expediency, and it could be modified to suit the time and circumstance. It would be in keeping with his character to sacrifice the letter to the spirit, and to throw down the training walls when the river had worn out a safe channel for itself.

The letter of farewell to Southampton is full of sound sense and practical advice. He urged his people to peace with God and man, for they were coming amongst unknown dangers and perils. They must be careful neither to give or take offence readily, for they would have great provocation to it through circumstances ; and they must be more than usually thoughtful for the common good, and wise in choosing their leaders and obeying them. That this advice, and the teaching that had gone before it, bore good fruit, no one who reads an account of the early years of the settlement can doubt.

Of Robinson's private life very little is known. He

moved into the Bell Alley house in May 1612, and in 1622 was living there with his wife (Bridget White), six children and a maid-servant. He lost three children during his lifetime, in 1618, 1621, and 1623, and on March 1st, 1625, he died himself, not of the plague which was then raging, but of a sort of inward ague. His friends were all with him in his short illness ; Roger White wrote full of grief to the Pilgrims in America, " If 'either prayers, tears, or means would have saved his life, he had not gone hence," and much as he had been loved in his lifetime, not until he died did they realise how irreparable was their loss. He was buried in a humble grave at St Peters, the small sum of nine florins giving a right to it only for seven years, when all bodies were removed. Most of the graves so rented, just below the pavement, were tenanted by very lowly artisans, journeymen, and weavers, and the church must indeed have been poor which could afford no better burying place for its beloved pastor. But the University and Ministers of the City did all honour to him who was to rest there, and followed him to the grave with all their accustomed ceremonies, bewailing the loss not only to his own church, but saying " That all the churches of Christ sustained a loss by the death of that worthy Instrument of the Gospel."

He was a man for whom even his adversaries had a good word ; slanderer Lawne respects his judgment and honesty : Baillie calls him " the most learned, polished and modest spirit " that ever separated from the Church of England." [1] His widow and children went to New England in 1629. It had been the great hope of his church, both in Holland and America, that they might be united once more under their pastor's rule, but it was not to be. Robinson never saw the triumph of the men he had trained, he shared all their trials, and died before success came. As he himself wrote, " Religion is not always sown and reaped in " one age. One soweth and another reapeth." [2]

[1] Dissuasive, p. 17.                    [2] Works, ii. 66.

At his death the Leyden church stood out clearly distinct from the other churches of the separation. It advocated a milder form of separatism than that of Browne and Barrow, a semi-separatism which Baillie calls "a fair bridge, at least a fair arch of a bridge, for union." It acknowledged a limited power of the magistrate in ecclesiastical matters, and claimed the right to flee from persecution, and so differed from the followers of Helwys and Murton, whose views on these two points were derived from the Anabaptists, and were curiously similar to those later held by the Quakers. It differed, too, from them and from Smyth on the subject of Baptism, for it denied the necessity of rebaptism, and administered the rite to all infants who were the seed of the faithful. Finally, it differed from the Ancient Church in its popular view of church government, and in its insistence on a teaching, and not merely a governing, eldership. In America, this position underwent certain modifications largely through the influence of Massachusetts. The confusion of the functions of Church and State grew until the church ruled the state; the whole power of the church came to be embodied in its officers, often in the pastor alone, conditions of church membership became so strict that the "Half way covenant" (1662) was devised to procure baptism for the children of good and orthodox people, who yet could not obtain full church privileges, and these changes led to laxity and decay in religious life. Every remedy tried was in the direction of Presbyterianism; the power of church officers, the authority of Synods, were exalted until all the churches, even that of Plymouth, lost for a time their true congregational and democratic character. But the work of John Wise and Nathaniel Emmons restored them to their old position, and modern Congregationalism still owes its main features to the work of the church in Leyden, and John Robinson.

10

# CHAPTER VIII

## THE PILGRIM PRESS

THERE was one weapon of democracy which the Separatists had learned to value long before they went to Holland, namely, a free press. Perhaps we appreciate this advantage rather reluctantly nowadays, when its abuses are so glaring, and its good work taken as a matter of course, but according to all authorities, it has done more to secure freedom and justice than any other single agent. The very efforts made to strangle it were a testimonial; as an organ of public opinion it was a thing impossible, save in a free country, free both in politics and religion, and Elizabeth, always quick to see where things were leading to, recognized this from the first.

In England, where education was confined to a very small class, comparatively few books were issued in the early years of printing, and these for the most part were aristocratic in nature; but so soon as the Reformation movement began to take hold, and its tendency to make people think for themselves was perceived, the press was placed under censorship. Elizabeth did not approve of people thinking for themselves, and if any of her subjects had acquired the bad habit, she was determined that the outcome of their thoughts should have as little influence as possible.

Censorship of the press had in pre-Reformation days belonged to the Church; afterwards it became part of the prerogative of the Crown. A monopoly of printing was granted to the Stationers' Company; presses were allowed only in London, Edinburgh and Dublin, and at each of the Universities, and even there, the number of them was strictly limited. By the injuctions of 1559, all publications were to be licensed either by the Queen, or by six of the Privy Council, the Archbishops, the Bishop of London, the Chancellors of the Universities, or the Bishop and Archdeacon of the place at which they were printed. In 1576 the Stationers' Company was ordered to make a weekly search to prevent the printing of any unlicensed books, and the control of the press was at this time largely in their hands. But with all their precautions, many books of which Elizabeth strongly disapproved, saw the light of day; the very number of her proclamations against the publishing of "seditious libels," show that they were not very effective; in June 1583 Bishop Aylmer complained to Burghley of one Thomas, who had issued books under the pretence of being a printer of the University of Cambridge; [1] and the heavy penalties for possessing a private printing press did not deter some bold spirits. As most of the offending publications were on religious matters, censorship of the press became the affair of the Bishops; in 1584 came a decree of the Star Chamber against unlicensed printing, and two years later, under the influence of Whitgift, a second decree made such publication liable to the severest penalties. Under these decrees Barrow, Greenwood, Penry, and Udall were condemned. It was a question whether the Star Chamber had not exceeded its powers, and Selden, years later, maintained that no just law of England restrained the liberty of the press, but James and Charles feared it as much as Elizabeth had done, and Prynne, Bastwick, Burton and others, suffered under decrees of the same body. The restrictions on the press did not end with the downfall of the Star Chamber, and only in 1695 was direct censorship exchanged for the indirect control of the libel laws.

[1] S. P. Dom., June 1583, vol. clxi. no. 1.

What the actual dangers and difficulties of unlicensed printing were, we know from the story of the printing of the Marprelate tracts, which came out at the trial of some of those concerned.[1] How the first Martin was printed at Mistress Crane's house at Moulsey, Kingston on Thames, where Waldegrave, a Puritan printer, had a press and a basket or two of letters ; how the implements were fetched from there in a cart to Sir Richard Knightley's house at Fawsley in Northamptonshire, where a second tract was issued ; and how, from there, they were taken in another cart to "The Friary" at Coventry, where a tenant of Sir Richard's hid them and the workmen, until a third and fourth were printed.  The search grew hot then, and Waldegrave retired from the business, taking with him the "Dutch letters" or German black letter type, but the press and some letters which remained were taken to Newton Lane, near Manchester, and another printer found, who was hard at work when their lair was surprised, the press and letters seized, and the sheets destroyed.  Still the work went on ; the printer escaped, obtained a second lot of letters, and issued the final tracts from a "low parlour" in Mr Weekston's house at Wolston, kept there under the name of "an Embroyderer."  Chased from one end of the country to the other, in the utmost danger, one does not know whether to admire the printers most for the pertinacity which managed to produce the tracts, or for the fidelity which kept the name of their author secret.

The Marprelate tracts might fairly be open to objection, but even a harmless publication was not easy to procure. In 1607, Sir T. Wilson writing to Sir Thomas Lake, asks for privilege for the printing of certain books, and begs that the bill should "have reference to none but the King's Counsel, for if I have to do with Bishops or others, I shall never have an end."  He offers in return for the

---

[1] Harleian MSS., 6849 and 7042, and Arber's introduction to the "Marprelate Controversy."

favour, a gratuity of forty or fifty angels "to buy my lady a velvet gown, and a most devoted and thankful heart!"[1]

These restrictions on printing were peculiarly hard on the Separatists. Not only were they personally injured and attacked, but the cause to which they were sacrificing everything was open to every kind of slander and misrepresentation, and neither by preaching nor writing had they any chance to defend themselves. As they themselves complained in a petition to the Queen in 1593, "The followers of Reformation lack liberty to answer in their own cause. If they speak they be silenced; if they write, they want printers. They be shut up in close prisons; their hands as it were bound, and then buffeted."

Private printing in England was too great a risk, and we should have known very little of the Separatist churches had there been as severe restrictions elsewhere.

But in Holland, the press was practically free, the only proviso being that private character and public morals were not to be attacked. So far as their own country was concerned, the Hollanders' plan was quite safe and worked well, for where the government was controlled by the nation, and no form of religion was interfered with, there was no outcry from oppressed people to be feared; but their printers were far too obliging in printing foreign books, to suit the autocrats of other countries. If provided with some English type, and a manuscript, they would print it off as a matter of business, no matter what it contained. Protests were made from time to time, and when it was realized that religous exiles from England meant to flood their country with separatist literature, the emigration which had been encouraged before was looked upon in quite a different light. Probably to this was due the hostility which the Pilgrims encountered in their attempt to sail from Boston. As a matter of fact, all the earliest separatist books were

[1] S. P. Dom., Ap. 12th, 1607, vol. xxxix.

printed in Holland; the first thing which every exiled community did on reaching its shores, was to publish some justification or explanation of its conduct, or to rush into wordy warfare with opponents across the Channel. Browne's chief works were printed in Middelburg; Barrow and Greenwood, as we have seen, sent their manuscripts over to Dort, or to that secret press in Middelburg which Francis Johnson helped to destroy; at Amsterdam Giles Thorpe, first deacon and then elder in Ainsworth's church, had set up a press of his own, and there printed many important works by Ainsworth, Clyfton, and others, among them probably Robinson's "Justification of separation." And now Leyden was to become another such centre, and to send across the seas some of those literary bombshells so much dreaded by James and his Bishops. The city was very famous for its printing; the Elzevir press, whose works were within the precincts of the Academy, printed in exquisite form all the theses of the University, and the great books of every country, but so far as we know no English controversial works had been printed in Leyden. When Brewster settled there, like all the rest of the church, he had to earn his living, for although it was the custom in later days for the elder of a church to receive a salary, the Leyden congregation was probably too poor now to support any officer besides the pastor. Bradford tells us that he taught English "and also had means to set up printing, by the help of some freinds; and so had imployment ynough; and by reason of many books which would not be alowed to be printed in England, they might have had more than they could doe." From other sources we know more about this printing concern. With Brewster was associated Thomas Brewer, a man of means and position, who had settled in Leyden, and who spent his life in furthering the Puritan cause. Apparently he did not take an active part in the business, but supplied the funds, and on him fell the penalties when

King James discovered what was going on. Edward
Winslow was possibly in it too, though his name is
not mentioned, as in the notice of his marriage at Leyden
in 1618 he is described as a printer. No mention is anywhere made of a press, and it is possible that they simply
set up types, and had them printed off by some Dutch
printer in the city. The first books were issued by the
firm in the autumn of 1616, and were entirely non-com-
mittal; Thomas Cartwright's "Commentarii in Proverbia
Salomonis," with a preface by Polyander, and Dr
William Ames' "Rescriptio Contracta." Unlike the
works which followed, these two were marked with
Brewster's name, and that of the place where they were
printed, but this was dangerous, for the similarity of type
led to the identification of other less innocent publications. About a dozen other books, which may with
tolerable certainty be ascribed to the Pilgrim Press, were
issued in 1617, 1618, and 1619; all strongly Puritan, if
not separatist in character.

In 1619 the partners brought a hornet's nest about their
ears by printing two books of David Calderwood's; "De
regimine Ecclesiæ Scoticanæ Brevis Relatio," and "Perth
Assembly." At this time, James I. was trying to force
Episcopacy down the throats of his Scotch subjects, and
they resisted it with an obstinacy equal to his own. The
General Assembly, held at Perth in 1618, had nominally
accepted the "Five Articles" which James urged upon
them, and which enforced certain ceremonies distasteful to
the Presbyterian mind, but the people were in reality as far
from accepting them, as from accepting the Bishops who
nominally ruled over them, and David Calderwood was
sure of sympathy when he wrote his version of the "Perth
Assembly." But he could not get it printed. There was
no chance for it in Great Britain, and finally it was done
by Brewster at Leyden, and the copies smuggled over to
Scotland in vats as if they had been wine and spirits.
The Archbishop of St Andrew's passed them by without

suspicion on the landing-place at Leith, but once they were unpacked, wine and spirits could not have had a more exciting effect. The King and the Bishops were furious; Calderwood was at once suspected of being the author, and he was hunted from house to house and town to town till finally, financed by the women of Edinburgh, he reached Holland in safety.

On Cathkin, a printer of Edinburgh, fell the first suspicion of having published this notorious work, and he was examined and bullied by the King himself; but was set at liberty after three weeks, having proved that he had had no hand in the matter. Naturally enough, they looked next to Holland, and Sir Dudley Carleton, Ambassador to the Hague, was deputed to find the offenders. He at first thought the book had come from Middelburg, and one Richard Schinders of that city was examined, but managed to prove his innocence.[1]

Then Carleton, having seen so many copies of "Perth Assembly" in Leyden, became suspicious of some press in that city, and when he discovered there Calderwood's earlier book also, and heard that Brewster was the printer, the thing became a certainty. Nothing could have enraged the King more than any help given to the Presbyterians whom he was trying to subdue, and when the Pilgrim Press was found to be the guilty one, a long correspondence took place between Sir Dudley Carleton and Sir Robert Naunton, Secretary of State, who wrote on behalf of the King urging that every effort should be made to bring the partners to justice. It was not altogether a simple matter. The States wanted to stand well with King James, and would probably have been willing to hand over Brewster, the active partner and an insignificant man, if he had really committed an offence against England, but Brewer was a member of the University, entitled to special privileges, and there was some delay in getting permission from the town and

[1] Carleton Letters, p. 353.

University authorities to make a search. Finally it was given, and officers were appointed to examine Brewster's library for any unauthorised works. In an attic in his house in Bell Alley were found the books and printing materials; the types were seized, the garret door was nailed in two places, the seal of the officer, impressed in green wax over paper, was placed upon the lock and nails, a catalogue was made of the books, and the chamber door where they were found was sealed with the aforesaid seal upon the lock and nails. This was all very well, but what James wanted was the persons of the offenders, and Brewster, the chief of them, had disappeared. They thought they had him in Leyden, but the officer was " a dull drunken fellow, " and took the wrong man. He was heard of in London, in Leyden, in London again ; they searched for him vigorously in both these places, in Leiderdorp and in Amsterdam, but where he spent the year before sailing from Delfshaven in July 1620, is a secret which has been kept up to the present day. He was certainly in London part of the time, arranging for the voyage to America, and was pursued there by the Bishop of London. He had removed his family and belongings from Leyden, and whilst in England his son conformed and went to church.[1] An attempt was made to discover Brewster's hiding place by means of an intercepted letter from him to his son, but though the messenger was imprisoned he would not reveal it.

Brewer was less fortunate ; possibly he relied on the fact that he had been a sleeping partner only, and took fewer precautions. He was examined, and detained in the place assigned for members of the University, and when James understood that Brewster had escaped him, he wanted to have Brewer over in England, that he might examine him, and try to gain some admissions about his partner. There were difficulties about this, as there had been about his imprisonment, for the University was

[1] S. P. Dom., Aug. 3rd, 1619, vol. cx. no. 7.

jealous of its privileges; but although it liked to protect its many foreign students, it also liked to be in favour with foreign princes, and a compromise was at last effected. The University got from Brewer a statement that he went of his own free will, and in return, Brewer got from Carleton very exact promises as to the kind of treatment he should receive, and finally he set out; not as a prisoner, but escorted first by officers of the University, and then from Rotterdam by Sir William Zouche, who was travelling that way. They were long delayed at Flushing by a storm, so great "as the streets, in some places, have run with salt water that hath scaled the walls, and in other, it hath made pools and lakes, and kept the people within their own doors"; and Carleton writes that Sir William had scandalized the Brownists by teaching Brewer to drink healths.[1]  Not for nearly three weeks did they reach Whitehall, and James was ill-pleased with the delay; still more so with the conditions which made him powerless to injure Brewer by so much as a hair. He turned on his Ambassador, as Elizabeth might have done, but Carleton had never outstepped his authority, and further, he urged that any ill-treatment of Brewer would cause the Leyden University to refuse the King's demands another time. Altogether James got very little satisfaction out of the examination, and Brewer was allowed to return. He had escaped this danger, but shortly after Robinson's death he left Leyden for good, and went to live in England, where his separatist principles made him a suspected character. He was imprisoned in 1626 for a denunciation of the prelates, and being released in 1640 under the Long Parliament, lived only about a month to enjoy his freedom.

His types and papers remained in the keeping of the Leyden University; the Pilgrim Press was of course utterly at an end. Moreover, the States, who in 1618 had made some restrictions on libellous publication within

[1] Letters, p. 423.

their own country, probably as a result of the Arminian disturbances, at the urgent request of Sir Dudley Carleton enlarged the edict in January 1620 to forbid the licentious printing of libels and pamphlets, either in strange languages or their own, extending it to foreigners in amity with the State as well as themselves. So that it became much less easy to have printed in Holland books offensive to the English government.

But the work which had been done could not be undone; the Separatists had spoken, and it was Holland that had helped them to articulate. Here again, the Pilgrims had done their share on behalf of liberty; here again, it was the conditions of their life in Leyden which helped them to make themselves felt in England, to perpetuate and to carry over to America some of the monuments of their church history.

# CHAPTER IX

## THE DEPARTURE FOR AMERICA

AFTER about eight or nine years in Leyden, welcome refuge though it had been, the leaders of the Pilgrim Church began to realize that their settlement there was not satisfactory. No doubt they had hoped that it would be permanent, and had looked forward to a time when they could enjoy some rest from the grinding toil and poverty of the early days, and when they would have assured not only the existence, but the spread and growth of their denomination. Or they may have hoped that exile was only temporary; that a day might soon come when they could go back to England, and live in peace in their own land, amongst their own people.

But as the years passed by their hopes grew fainter and fainter; there was nothing in the state of affairs in England to encourage them, and meanwhile, evils which they had not foreseen in their present life made themselves felt.

They found the life in Holland very hard, and it did not grow much easier with time. Many spent all their means there, and failing to gain a livelihood, were forced to return to England; others, although they endured hardships bravely, grew old before their time, and threatened to sink under their burdens. The church had grown in numbers, but not so much as had been hoped; so hard was the life that few would join them from England, and fewer still would stay when they had experienced it. Even the prisons of England, terrible as they were in those days, seemed preferable.

156

Perhaps the strongest inducement to change was the thought of their children. It was difficult to educate them in a foreign country; and they, too, had to take their share of toil; those who were willing and industrious worked so hard for their parents that their strength was overtaxed, and their health injured with their heavy labours. Whether on account of the change of climate and diet, or the hardness of the life, the death-roll amongst infants and children was very heavy during these years in Holland.

Not only did they fear for the health of their children, but for what was even more precious in their eyes, their character. So much licence was allowed to young people among the Dutch, a licence indeed very seldom abused by them, but liable to be entirely misunderstood by people of different traditions. Then, too, the equality amongst members of a family, the different relations between young and old, were quite opposed to the more patriarchal English system, and so the chroniclers, Bradford and Winslow, are much too hard on the Dutch, and speak too strongly of the evil influence of their example. Not but what it may have done harm. Freedom may be harmless enough as a birthright, but dangerous at first to those accustomed to artificial restraints. Moreover, for the children to act in defiance of the accepted standards of their community would give them a sense of outlawry; conscience would be burdened, and self-respect would be injured almost as much as by actual wrong-doing.

Naturally the gaiety and freedom of the young Dutch people appealed to these poor children, who could have so few pleasures in their lives. Some of them left the close toil of the city, and became soldiers and sailors, beyond the reach of the influences which their parents craved for them; others revolted against the greyness of their lives, and fell into the many temptations which a great city offered, so that there was real fear that posterity would not carry on the high traditions of the Pilgrims.

The children were "getting ye raines off their neks, and departing from their parents." [1]

Dutch Sabbath keeping was also a great trial to them. Most of the Reformed Churches abroad kept Sunday as it had been kept in the Church of Rome, with religious services in the morning, and amusements in the afternoon ; but in England the Puritans had very early demanded stricter rules. In Holland, where the standard of morality and industry had always been high, no one saw anything to object to in innocent amusements on the one holiday of the week ; but Puritanism in England always went to extremes, because it was a protest. English society was so corrupt and frivolous, that a firm stand was perhaps necessary, and though the Puritans were unreasonable in their condemnation of all sports and amusements, there was something to be said on their side, for until they had made changes there was no day of rest in England, work went on, and Parliament sat as usual on every day of the seven.

The Pilgrims, too, felt that they could not live happily under a foreign government, however generous. They feared that in time they would lose their native language, and the very name of English, and there was some ground for this fear, for of the very considerable number who remained in Leyden, no subsequent history can be traced, and it has been said that there are not more than three names of families in Leyden now that bear any resemblance to the names of the exiles.

Apart from this, their position was bound to be unsatisfactory. A large and growing community, they yet had no real ties with the country in which they lived. To a limited extent they shared in its organizations, but they could feel no identity of interests with them, and they could find no scope for their own powers. They were in fact isolated, and their life was too narrow. Their religious interests held them together, but without those political and social duties which go to make up a

[1] Bradford MS., p. 16.

man's life, there was danger that these interests would become exaggerated; that all their unspent powers would be wasted on petty quarrels and futile arguments, and that the church would be shipwrecked like those of Amsterdam.  If they were to preserve their nationality and their religious principles beyond the first generation, they must have more room, a free space in which to grow.  And finally, beyond all these personal reasons, and illuminating the gloom and uncertainty of their position, was the great hope they had that they were not living for themselves alone, but to be a beacon to others.  They thought it might be their lot to lay the foundations of a great church, and to advance the Gospel of the Kingdom of Christ in some remote part of the world.  This was the hope that cheered them through all their difficulties : this was the great responsibility that decided their conduct towards each other, and towards all with whom they dealt; it forced self-interest into the background, and gave an extraordinary weight and solemnity to all that they did.  Their enterprise was, as it were, consecrated from the first, and though they say little about it, it is quite evident that, by the older leaders at least, the idea was never lost sight of.

They were grateful to the city which had sheltered them for so long, and anxious to prove that they left it on good terms with all men.  Amongst the many reproaches cast upon their church, it was said in later years that the departure for America was on account of their disagreements; that they could not live peaceably together, and that the Dutch were anxious to get rid of them, and both Bradford and Winslow write to disprove the charge, and to give the true reason for their going. They wanted a place where they might enjoy such liberty of religion as they then had, but under the protection of the King and State of England ; they wanted to show the way to other Englishmen to enlarge the Church of Christ.

After first Robinson and Brewster, and then some other chief members of the church had privately discussed and matured this idea of removal, it was made public, and the whole congregation joined in the great discussion. Some were at once in favour of a change, and did their best to arouse enthusiasm for it. But others were daunted by the dangers and difficulties which they saw and guessed at; they remembered the trials of their voyage to Holland and the early days there; they feared the longer voyage, the famine and nakedness, the sickness from unaccustomed climate and food, which might await them in a strange and uncivilized land. There, too, they would find no friendly help such as the Dutch had given them; instead, if they had neighbours at all, they would be fierce inhuman savages, the tales of whose cruelty caused the blood to curdle.

And besides these difficulties, and the chance that they might fail, as many other would-be colonists had done, how were they ever to start on this enterprise, since few of them had ever been rich, and those few had lost much of their estates? Not only would the voyage and necessary outfit be quite beyond their means, but they must be sure of reinforcements to be sent after them until they could find food for themselves.

Many of these drawbacks were very real; but finally the enthusiasts carried the day. They admitted the difficulties, though some of them were only conjectural, but they argued that all great actions were attended with great difficulties, and although the scheme would not be easy to carry out, they claimed that it was possible. Again, they were not undertaking it lightly, they had good and honourable reasons for the attempt, and might surely expect a blessing on it. They were poor and in exile, the years of the Truce between Spain and the States were out; if war began, the persecution of the Spaniards, and the pestilence and famine of an invaded country, might be as hard to endure as the hardships of

to sue to his majestie that he would be pleased to grant them freedome of Religion."[1]

At the beginning of the seventeenth century, the first romance of exploration and discovery was wearing off. These were not the days in which Drake came home loaded with Spanish treasure, and Sir Walter Raleigh sailed up the Orinoco in search of an El Dorado. Not that the importance of newly discovered lands had by any means waned in men's minds; but it had ceased to appeal to their imaginations only, and, instead, was appealing to their business instincts. They were no longer dazzled by the prospect of fabulous wealth to be had for the asking, but were settling down to a clear-sighted view of how, by diligence and hard work, these discoveries might be turned to account. Anyone who reads first a volume of Elizabethan travel, and then the practical words of Captain John Smith, will appreciate this change of spirit.

The usual method of starting a colony, and establishing trade relations, was by forming a Chartered Company. Virginia, since 1606, had been in the hands of two such companies; the London Virginia Company, to which was given land in America between 34° and 41° North Latitude, and the Plymouth Virginia Company (so called because most of its promoters were West of England men), to which was given land between 30° and 45° North Latitude. These companies had the right to grant patents, subletting portions of land to intending colonists under conditions to be agreed upon between themselves.

It was to the London Virginia Company that the Pilgrims determined to apply for a grant of land within their territory, encouraged no doubt by knowing that Brewster's old friend, Sir Edwin Sandys, was one of the Council.

Not only, however, would they need a patent from the Virginia Company to settle on their land, but they must

[1] Bradford MS., p. 18.

obtain from the King, through the Privy Council, permission to worship freely after their own fashion, and to conduct some form of government in the colony; and also they must, somehow, get financial help to pay for their passage and outfit, and to enable them to establish trade by which they could live.

It was in 1617 that the decision to leave Leyden was made, and in the autumn of that year two members of the church were sent over to England to open the three-fold negotiations. These two agents were John Carver and Robert Cushman, both of whom seem to have joined the church during its life in Holland. Carver was apparently in Leyden as early as 1609, for there is record that a child of his was buried at St Pancras Church in July of that year. He is also mentioned as being witness at weddings there in 1616, 1617, and 1618. He was a deacon in Robinson's church, and evidently an important member, for besides being trusted with these delicate negotiations, he was made governor of one of the ships for the voyage, and chosen governor of the new colony as soon as they reached Plymouth.

Of Cushman, little is known before this time, save that he was a wool-carder, that his home was at Canterbury in England, and that he married in Leyden, as his second wife, Mary Singleton in 1617.

With regard to the first point, the obtaining of a patent to colonize, Carver and Cushman made a good beginning. Sir Edwin Sandys befriended them from the first, and they found the Virginia Company very willing to grant them a patent with ample privileges, and to help them in any way possible. Robinson and Brewster received a letter from Sir Edwin Sandys giving them encouraging reports of their business, which was not to be finally settled until the agents had returned to Leyden, and had some conference with the church. They answered this letter, full of gratitude, and put forth some other inducements to convince their friend, as he might well be convinced, that

they were worthy of his help. They were undertaking
the work in the full belief that the Lord was with them,
and would prosper it according to the simplicity of their
hearts; they were "well weaned from y^e delicate milke
of our mother countrie," used to hardship, and patient to
overcome it. No more industrious nor frugal people could
be found, nor any more careful of each other's interest,
through the sacred Bond and Covenant of the Lord.
And finally, they were not men to be discouraged by
little things, nor daunted in their enterprise by small dis-
contents. They knew what life had to promise them,
both in England and in Holland; they knew that they
risked all by going away, and that, few as their comforts
were, should they fail and be forced to return, they could
never hope to regain them, nor indeed to attain to so
great ones in any other place.

Such brave and modest hopes courted no disappointment,
such quiet courage was their best claim to help and support.

As to the second point, permission to worship freely in
their new home, the agents brought back less cheering
news. Robinson had drawn up and sent over by them
the following Declaration of Faith and Church polity. It
is most skilfully worded, and without yielding any of the
essential points of difference, it draws the church as
closely as possible into line with the Church of England.

" Seven Articles which the Church of Leyden sent to the
Council of England to be considered of, in respect of their
Judgements: occasioned about their going to Virginia,
anno 1618, (really before November 1617).

" 1. To the Confession of Faith (39 Articles of 1562)
published in the name of the Church of England, and to
every Article thereof; we do (with the Reformed Churches
where we live and also elsewhere) assent wholly.

" 2. As we do acknowledge the Doctrine of Faith there
taught, so do we the fruits and effects of the same Doctrine,
to the begetting of saving faith in thousands in the land
(of England) Conformists and Reformists, as they are

called; with whom also, as with our brethren, we do desire to keep spiritual communion in peace; and will practice in our parts all lawful things.

" 3. The King's Majesty we acknowledge for Supreme Governor in his Dominions in all causes, and over all persons: and that none may decline or appeal from his authority or judgement in any cause whatsoever: but that in all things obedience is due unto him; either active, if the thing commanded be not against God's Word; or passive if it be, except pardon can be obtained.

" 4. We judge it lawful for His Majesty to appoint Bishops, Civil Overseers, or Officers in authority under him, in the several Provinces, Dioceses, Congregations, or Parishes, to oversee the Churches, and govern them civilly according to the laws of the land: unto whom they are, in all things, to give an account; and by them, to be ordered according to godliness.

" 5. The authority of the present Bishops in the land, we do acknowledge, so far forth as the same is derived from His Majesty unto them; and as they proceed in his name: whom we will also therein honour in all things; and him, in them.

" 6. We believe that no Synod, Classes, Convocation, or Assembly of Ecclesiastical Officers hath any power or authority at all, but as the same by the Magistrate given unto them.

" 7. Lastly, we desire to give unto all Superiors due honour, to preserve the unity of the Spirit with all that fear God, to have peace with all men what in us lieth, and wherein we err, to be instructed by any.

" Subscribed per John Robinson and William Brewster." [1]

This document seems to concede a great deal, but if it is closely examined, the main positions of the Separatists will be found inviolate. No official communion with the Church of England is admitted, only spiritual communion with the righteous of that Church; no power is recognized

[1] Arber's " Pilgrim Fathers," pp. 280-281.

in either the King or his magistrates against private
conscience, and the power of Bishops and Church officers
is not based upon the continuity of their order.

Sir Edwin Sandys tried to help them here too, and
had persuaded Sir Robert Naunton, one of the chief
Secretaries of State, to move the King in favour of them.
He represented that they could not live comfortably
under the government of another State, and desired to
enjoy their liberty of conscience under the King's protection in America, where they would both advance his
Majesty's dominions and the spread of the Gospel.

"This, His Majesty said, was a good and honest
motion: and asking, what profits might arise in the
part wee intended? (for our eye was upon the most
Northern parts of Virginia) 'twas answered 'Fishing.'
To which hee replyed, with his ordinary asseveration 'So
God have my soule 'tis an honest Trade, 'twas the
Apostles owne calling, etc.' But afterwards he told
Sir Robert Nawnton, (who took all occasions to further
it) that we should confer with the Bishops of Canterbury
and London etc. Whereupon wee were advised to persist
upon his first approbation, and not to entangle ourselves
with them." [1]

The church had hoped to have the right of liberty
of religion granted to them, and confirmed under the
King's broad seal, but all the messengers could obtain
was a qualified permission. The King promised that he
would connive at them, and would not molest them, if
they were peaceable; but he would not allow or tolerate
them by his public authority under his seal. This was
a great discouragement. Many felt that they would have
been better off if they had asked no leave at all, than
to have been answered thus; and they were ready to
abandon the whole enterprise. But some of the chief
men thought that the King meant well by them, although
he could not countenance them officially, and on the

[1] Winslow, "Hypocrisie Unmasked," p. 90.

other hand, they argued that if harm were intended against them, a seal as broad as the house floor would not protect them, for some means would be found to reverse or evade its privileges, " They must rest herein on God's Providence, as they had done in other things."

Early in 1618, letters were sent to Sir John Wolstenholme, a member of the Privy Council, and of the Virginia Company, further explaining their ecclesiastical position with regard to the ministry, the two Sacraments, and the Oath of Supremacy, and recommending themselves as reasonable Christians, and not sowers of dissension. " Who shall make your ministers ? " Sir John enquired ; and when they answered that the power of making was in the church, this reply put their cause in great danger, but Sabine Staresmore, the man whom Francis Blackwell betrayed into the hands of the Bishops a few months later, and who presented these letters, wrote to them that all was going well.

Nothing had been done by the first agents about the third point, the raising of funds for the enterprise. The next messengers sent were Cushman and Brewster ; when they started is not exactly known, but they had certainly been in England some time in May 1619.

They went to conclude with the Virginia Company about the patent, and to treat with any merchants who were favourably inclined to advance money for their adventure. Probably they expected that the business of the patent would be very straightforward, as most of the arrangements had been made beforehand ; but when Cushman and Brewster arrived, they found that the London Virginia Company was in such a state of dissension, that nothing could be settled. The Council had split into two factions about the appointment of a Treasurer and Governor, the real discord being one of principle, between royal nomination and popular election.

Sir Edwin Sandys led the popular party, and his election by them was disputed by the other faction, and

meanwhile no business could be done.   Cushman wrote
that Brewster was ill, and he himself weary of the long
delay; their supporters were fast falling away; but finally,
on the 19th of June 1619, a patent was granted to them,
and confirmed under the Company's seal.   By the advice
of their friends it was not taken in the name of their own
people, but in the name of Master John Whincop, a religious
gentleman of the household of the Dowager Countess
of Lincoln, who intended to go with them, although, as
things fell out, he never did.   This patent is not extant;
but it probably embraced a tract of territory near the
mouth of the Hudson River, and we have Bradford's
word for it that it cost them much in time and money.

There now remained only the financial problem.   The
Pilgrims wanted not only free shipping, but money for
their outfit, and trading goods to establish some way of
living in the new colony.   In this the Virginia Company
could not help them, for it was penniless, and, indeed,
became bankrupt a few years later (1624).   They had
had some offers of help in England, but these friends
had cooled off during the long delay; and now came an
offer from some Dutch merchants, who were willing to
transport them to the Hudson River, and to provide
them with cattle, if they would live under their Government.   From a petition made by the New Netherland
Company to the Prince of Orange, in which mention is
made of this plan, their object seems to have been to
use the Pilgrims in the foundation of a new commonwealth under the Dutch Government, and to forestall any
attempts to establish an English colony in the district.

Nothing but extreme necessity could have made the
Pilgrims listen for a moment to such an offer, since one
of their great anxieties was to preserve their nationality,
and to live under English government.   They did, however, consider it for a time, when fortunately another
opportunity came their way.

There came to Leyden about this time one Thomas

Weston, a merchant of London, who was to be an important factor in their lives for many years to come. He had known some of them previously, and had befriended them, though in what way is not known; and he came now to tell them that he and some Merchant Adventurers who were friends of his, and who had taken out a patent from the London Company in the name of John Pierce, would advance money to supplement what the Pilgrims had, and would provide them with shipping and all that was necessary. Articles of agreement were to be drawn up, showing the terms of the contract, to assure his friends that they would have some return for their money. Weston's offer was accepted, negotiations with the Dutch were broken off, and the terms with the Adventurers drawn up and agreed to.

Captain John Smith says that these Adventurers were about seventy in number, some gentlemen, some merchants, some handicraftsmen; they adventured small sums or great, according to their condition. They lived mostly about London, and were not a corporation, but joined together voluntarily in a society aiming to do good and to plant religion. A President and Treasurer were elected annually; for ordinary business, the vote of the majority held good, but in weighty affairs all must consent.

One cannot help thinking, from their dealings with the Leyden people, that their motives were less purely philanthropic than Smith represents; they seemed to have talked religion and dragged it in the dust, making it a cloak for both greed and dishonesty.

Weston also told them that a patent was to be granted to certain lords for New England, the northerly portion of the land granted to the Plymouth Virginia Company, which was to be distinct from the Virginia Government, and he afterwards advised them to obtain a patent for land there, thinking that the fishing would be more profitable, and perhaps that they would be less interfered with. They thought of doing so, but as the Council for New

England did not obtain its charter until November 1620, nothing was actually done, and they sailed under the earlier patent from the London Company.

And now they had received their patent from the Virginia Company ; they had gained a qualified permission to carry on their church in America, and they had the promise of financial support from the Adventurers.

Carver and Cushman were sent once more to England to receive the funds, and to provide for the shipping and other necessaries, with strict injunctions to depart in no way from the agreement already made. Active preparations began in Leyden ; some were appointed to make the necessary arrangements there ; those who were going made ready, sold their property, and put any money they could spare into the common stock. A public and solemn fast was held, and it was resolved that one part of the church should go at first, and the other remain behind ; that the youngest and strongest should go first ; that none should go but those that freely offered themselves, and that if the majority went, the pastor should go with them, if not, the elder only. If those who went were forced to return, their brethren should help them ; if they prospered, they should help the others to join them.

A small majority determined to remain behind for the present, though all but a very few intended to follow after. One hundred and fifty persons, with Brewster their elder, prepared to go, and it was decided that each part should be an absolute church of themselves, since they might never meet again ; but if they were once more joined together, they should all be accounted members of the same church, without any ceremony of readmission.

Meanwhile the preparations did not go altogether smoothly. The money was not easy to raise, for some of those who had promised withdrew altogether, some wanted them to go to Guiana, others to Virginia ; with others again Virginia found so little favour that they would not adventure a penny to send anyone there. The poor people in Leyden, who had sold their property, were in great straits, but finally a settlement was made, and the majority of the Adventurers agreed for Virginia.

But now came a still greater difficulty. Weston and some of the others insisted on altering the articles of agreement drawn up and agreed to in Leyden, making the conditions much harder for the colonists.

The new articles were as follows :—

" 1. The Adventurers and Planters do agree, That every person that goeth, being aged sixteen years and upwards, be rated at £10, and £10 to be accounted a single share.

" 2. That he that goeth in person and furnisheth himself out with £10, either in money or other provisions, be accounted as having £20 in Stock, and in the Division shall receive a Double Share.

" 3. The persons transported, and the Adventurers, shall continue their Joint Stock and Partnership together the space of seven years ; except some unexpected impediment do cause the whole Company to agree otherwise ; during which time, all profits and benefits that are got by trade, traffic, trucking, working, fishing, or any other means, of any person or persons, remain still in the Common Stock until the Division.

" 4. That at their coming there (Virginia), they choose out such a number of fit persons as may furnish their ships and boats for fishing upon the sea ; imploying the rest in their several faculties upon the land, as building houses, tilling and planting the ground, and making such commodities as shall be most useful for the Colony.

" 5. That at the end of the seven years, the Capital and Profits (viz : the houses, lands, goods and chattles) be equally divided betwixt the Adventurers and Planters, which done, every man shall be free from other of them, of any debt or detriment concerning this Adventure.

" 6. Whosoever cometh to the Colony hereafter, or putteth any into the Stock, shall, at the end of the seven years, be allowed proportionately to the time of his so doing.

" 7. He that shall carry his wife and children, or servants, shall be allowed for every person, now aged sixteen years and upwards, a single share in the Division; or, if he provide them with necessaries, a Double share: or if they be between ten years old and sixteen, then two of them to be reckoned for a person, both in Transportation and Division.

" 8. That such children as now go, and are under the age of ten years, have no other share in the Division but fifty acres of unmanured land.

" 9. That such persons as die before the seven years be expired, their Executors to have their part or Share at the Division, proportionately to the time of their life in the Colony.

" 10. That all such persons as are of this Colony are to have their meat, drink, apparel, and all provisions out of the Common Stock and goods of the said Colony." [1]

The chief difference between these and the original articles was in clause five, where it had formerly been agreed " That the houses and lands improved, especially gardens and home lots, should remain, undivided, wholly to the Planters, at the seven years end." And also there had been an eleventh clause: " That they should have two days in a week for their own private employment, for the more comfort of themselves and their families; especially such as had families"; and this was now left out.

The responsibility of accepting these conditions seems to belong to Robert Cushman. The agents had been expressly forbidden to make any new arrangement without permission from the church, but, harassed by the difficulties of his task, seeing that the Adventurers would give up the scheme on the slightest provocation, and knowing what would be the plight of those in Leyden, who had already abandoned their property and trades, Cushman felt forced to agree. Fearing that the news would cause dissension and further delay at Leyden, he

[1] Arber's " Pilgrim Fathers," pp. 305-6.

tried to keep the new conditions secret, but rumours travelled to some at least of the church, and a lengthy correspondence ensued; urgent protests from the planters and attempted self-justification on the part of Cushman.

First came a letter from four chief men of the church, Samuel Fuller, Edward Winslow, William Bradford, and Isaac Allerton, to Carver and Cushman, complaining that the rumoured conditions were unreasonable, and that the agents had no right to exceed their commission in any way, but evidently hoping that the report was false. More letters must have passed before Cushman's reply to the church in general on June 20th, 1620. In it he urged that, as the Leyden people complained that the conditions had been changed without their knowing them, so the Adventurers might complain that the original articles had been framed without the knowledge of any of them, save Mr Weston; and he based his whole justification on the fact that without the alterations, they would neither have had means for the voyage, nor supplies when they reached the new colony. Money had already been withdrawn on account of the fifth clause as it first stood; Sir George Farrer alone withdrew £500. He answered at length a paper of objections which had been sent to him, but his arguments are not very convincing; there was no blinking the fact that the new conditions were hard ones, and his best excuse was necessity. Robinson wrote also on the subject to Carver, lamenting that conditions should have been made which would be such a hardship to the planters, and would bring so little extra advantage to the Adventurers. Comparatively few of the colonists would work upon the land and in building, almost all at trading and fishing. " So as yᵉ land and house will be but a trifle for aduantage to yᵉ Aduenturers; and yet the deuission of it a great discouragmente to yᵉ Planters; who would with singuler care make it comfortable, with borowed houres from their sleep. The same consideration of comone ymploymente constantly by the most, is a good

reason not to have yᵉ 2 daies in a weeke deneyed yᵉ few
Planters for priuate use, which yet is subordinate to comōne
good. Consider also, how much unfite that you and your
liks, must serue a new prentishipe of 7 years ; and not a
daies·freedome from taske." [1]

Difficulties seemed to increase, both in England and
Leyden, as the preparations went on ; the confusion of
carrying on negotiations at a distance, and between so
many parties, threatened ruin to the scheme.

Besides the Leyden people, a number of colonists were
to go from London, Essex, and other places, and these
appointed an agent of their own, Christopher Martin, to
join with Carver and Cushman in making arrangements
and procuring supplies. Possibly some of Ainsworth's
people from Amsterdam thought of going too, for
Cushman speaks of troublesome negotiations with them,
and Weston was there early in June. Martin seems to
have been hard to work with, and would go his own way,
without counsel or advice. He and Carver were doing
the provisioning at Southampton, against the advice of
Weston and Cushman, who were in London, and thought
it would have been better done there ; salt and nets were
to be bought in Holland, the centre of the fishing trade.
It was difficult to make arrangements simultaneously
in three places ; money was not coming in so well as had
been expected ; Weston was growing weary of the whole
affair, and threatened to abandon it ; and meanwhile,
the summer was slipping by, and the most favourable
season for the voyage already past. Cushman's letters
sound positively distracted ; obviously, though well meaning, he was not the man to move calmly through this
turmoil. Robinson blamed himself for having employed
him, for though a good man, he was " most unfit to deal
for other men by reason of his singularity and too great
indifferency for any conditions." The Leyden people
thought of buying a ship for the voyage ; Weston made

[1] Bradford MS., p. 30.

merry over their idea, and advised hiring, but finally the *Speedwell*, of some sixty tons, was bought and fitted in Holland, the intention being to keep it in the colony for fishing and trading purposes. Another ship, the *Mayflower*, of one hundred and eighty tons, was hired in London to transport the remainder of the people. Strange to say, Bradford does not mention the names of either of these ships, calling them throughout "the bigger ship" and "the lesser ship," and this although he gives the name of almost every later ship that came to the colony. No authentic picture or model of the historic *Mayflower* is known to exist; judging by other vessels of that date, she was probably square rigged, with two or three masts, and a bowsprit pointing upwards; very high in the bow and stern, and broad in the beam; a slow, clumsy vessel, but very roomy. But the many pictures of her are all imaginary; even the name of the "bigger ship" is not mentioned by the chroniclers until 1623, when it occurs in a heading in the official records of the Old Colony. The name of the "lesser ship" was first given by Nathaniel Morton in his "New England's Memorial."

When all preparations were complete and the *Speedwell* ready to depart, a Day of Humiliation was appointed in the Leyden church. Robinson took as his text, "And there, at the river, by Ahava, I proclaimed a Fast, that we might humble ourselves before our God; and seek of him a right way for us, and for our children, and for all our substance." From this text he gave the famous "Farewell Address" which Winslow has recorded, and most of the day was spent in hearing his advice and in tearful prayers to God.

The time of departure came, and those of the church who were to stay behind went with their brethren to Delfshaven, a few miles away, where the ship was waiting to receive them. "So they lefte y^t goodly and pleasante citie, which had been ther resting place nere twelve years;

THE *MAYFLOWER* IN PLYMOUTH HARBOUR

but they knew they were pilgrimes, and looked not much on those things; but lift up their eyes to yᵉ heauens, their dearest cuntrie, and quieted their spirits." From Amsterdam, too, came others to take leave of them, and they spent the night in friendly discourse and farewells. The next day they went aboard with their friends; their pastor commended to the Lord and His blessing the people he was never to see again, then went ashore with the remainder of his flock, and the real parting took place. Even the Dutch strangers on the shore were moved by the sorrow of it, "but the tide, which stays for no man," called them away. From the ship a volley of small shot was fired, and three pieces of ordinance, and so they set sail for Southampton.

They had a prosperous voyage, and probably arrived on August 5th, to find that the *Mayflower* had already brought from London the rest of their company. There was no time to waste in Southampton, and any moment might bring danger to some of them from the hostile Bishops, but some business still remained to be done. The new articles of agreement with the Adventurers were not yet signed; the altered clauses now became known to all, and great was the discontent. Carver denied all responsibility for the changes, as he had been busy with other work; Cushman pleaded the consent of his fellow agents, and also the necessity for what he had done; Weston came down from London, and urged them to confirm the conditions; but, in spite of all that could be said, the people absolutely refused to abide by Cushman's promises, and would not sign the agreement. Weston departed in a rage, telling them "They must then looke to stand on their owne leggs." As they needed about £100 more to complete their arrangements, and no one would advance them a penny, they were obliged to sell off some of their butter, of which they had a large supply, before they could clear the port. A letter was written by the chief of the company to the Adventurers, regretting the

dispute which had arisen, explaining their objections, and
on what grounds they refused to sign the agreement.
They promised also " That if large profits should not
arise within yᵉ 7 years, yᵗ we will continue togeather longer
with you ; if yᵉ Lord giue a Blesing." Fortunately for
them, this was not accepted. They had been hard put to
it to clear their debts in Southampton, and were left with
little butter, no oil, not a sole to mend a shoe, nor every
man a sword to his side ; wanting muskets, armour, and
many other absolute necessaries.

But at last their business was completed, and a letter
of advice from Robinson having been read to all, the
company was divided between the two ships, a governor
and two or three assistants being chosen for each, to order
the people, and see to the disposing of the provisions.
This done, they put to sea, but their delays were not over
yet. Reynolds, the Captain of the *Speedwell*, soon complained that his ship was leaky, and they were forced to
put back, first into Dartmouth, then again into Plymouth,
and to have her overhauled. No special leak was discovered, and it seems probable that, through some error
in fitting the ship in Holland, she had been overmasted.
Reynolds discovered this, and as he and the crew had
been hired to stay a year in the colony, and as they feared,
that, if provisions ran short, those on the lesser ship would
come off the worst, they began to repent of their bargain,
and agreed to put on too much sail. This, in the overmasted condition of the ship, strained the hull in sailing,
and made it " leakie as a seiue." Some of them, later, confessed this stratagem, and after the ship was sold and put
into her old trim, she made many voyages in perfect
safety.

But this the Pilgrims did not know, and thinking that
the ship was too weak to bear the voyage, they resolved at
Plymouth to dismiss her and part of the company, and to
take all who could be accommodated on to the *Mayflower*.
So another parting took place ; those who went back

(eighteen or twenty) were either those who were weak and
burdened with children, and would make but poor
colonists, or those who began to fear the undertaking,
having had a taste of its difficulties.  Among these were
Robert Cushman and his family.  His " hart and courage
was gone from them before (as it seems), though his body
was with them, till now he departed."  Evidently the
hard work he had done, and the criticism and blame which
had fallen upon him, had damaged both his health and
his temper for a time ; his letters to Leyden show the
irritability of overwrought nerves, and in a letter written
during the delay at Dartmouth to Edward Southworth,
he complains of real illness, and is positively pessimistic
about the voyage.  He says that it had been as full of
crosses, as themselves had been of crookedness ; that the
*Speedwell* was leaky as a sieve, with a board two feet
long that a man might have pulled off with his fingers ;
where the water came in " as at a molehole."  The victuals
he thought would be half eaten up before they left the
coast of England, and would not last a month after they
came to America.  Moreover, there were disagreements
among the passengers.  Christopher Martin, who had
been made governor of the bigger ship, with Cushman as
assistant, did nothing but insult and abuse the people,
and dictate to the sailors of things he knew nothing about.
He absolutely refused to account for the money which had
been entrusted to him to spend at Southampton, and denied
all responsibility for the conditions, because it had not
fallen to his lot actually to negotiate with the Adventurers.

" Prepare for euill tidings of us, euery day," wrote
Cushman, but indeed his letter must be looked upon
rather as the outburst of an overwrought mind than as
any just statement of facts ; he himself ends with an
apology : " Pass by my weake maner, for my head is
weake, and my body feeble."

He soon recovered his courage, and came out with his

son in the *Fortune* in the following autumn, and did much good service for the colony until his death in 1625.

Finally, on the 16th of September, the *Mayflower* started on her real voyage. She was sixty-five days at sea, having at first a good wind and fair weather, so that, save for sea-sickness, all went well. They encountered some heavy storms later on, in one of which one of the main beams of the midships was bowed and cracked, so that they feared they might have to return. But they were almost half-way across, and after a consultation between the Master (Captain Jones) and other Officers, they decided that the ship was strong and able to continue ; the beam was raised by a great iron screw which the passengers had brought out of Holland, a post was put under it and securely bound, and the decks and upper works were caulked. "So they committed themselues to y^e will of God and resolued to proceede."

In some of the storms, they were forced to drift about without sails for days together, and no wonder that Captain Smith writes that "being pestered nine weeks in this leaking unwholesome ship, lying wet in their cabins ; most of them grew very weak, and weary of the sea."[1] Only one passenger died, towards the end of the voyage ; William Butten, a servant of Samuel Fuller. One, at least, of the sailors died too, a proud and profane young man, who had jeered and insulted over the poor seasick passengers, and promised that he would help to throw them overboard before their journey's end, and enjoy their property. But he himself was the first to be thrown overboard, and the Pilgrims saw the hand of God upon him, and believed that his curses had lighted on his own head.

Another young man had a narrow escape, being thrown overboard in a storm by the pitching of the ship ; but he caught hold of the topsail halliards, which hung overboard, and held on, though he was several fathoms under water, till he was hauled up by the rope, and pulled on board

[1] Arber's "Captain John Smith," p. 260.

again with a boat-hook, something the worse for his adventure, but alive.

On November 19th they saw land once more, and recognized it as Cape Cod.  Passengers and officers once more consulted together, and decided to sail southward in the direction of the Hudson River.  Their patent was for North Virginia; they had had favourable news of the Hudson River from the New Netherland Company, and no doubt they desired to be as near to some other colony as might be.  But they found the ship was becoming entangled with dangerous shoals and breakers, the wind dropped, and they resolved to bear up again for the Cape. The next day but one they got into the Cape Harbour, and rejoicing in their safety, fell upon their knees to thank God for His mercy, which had delivered them from the perils of the ocean, and brought them once more to land.

With the landing at Cape Cod, the Pilgrims entered upon the second phase of their work, and the character of their history changes.

Bradford's History, Mourt's Relation, and other documents in which the Pilgrims themselves tell of their early years in America, have very little to say of their church, or of their creed, and this for two great reasons. It was not that they lost sight for one moment of the cause for which they lived, but they were practical men, and knew that, until their material existence was assured, and until they were able in some tangible way to justify the effort that had been made to send them out, no credit, no honour would be reflected on their church.  In the second place, that church could claim now to be fairly established ; they were far away from the possibility of interference, and, when friction was at an end, it would have been mere folly to insist too much on differences with which their correspondents were not in sympathy.  But they were far from lowering their flag.  From the outset, every action among themselves, every dealing with the Indians, or with merchants at home, was dictated by the sense that they had come there to be an example, that no suspicion of self-interest or falsehood must rest on them as representatives of the true church. And, although they forebore to irritate their opponents by asserting their views unnecessarily, they stood firmly by their convictions when any attempt was made to violate them.

But they were no longer mainly occupied with the definition and defence of their creed and polity, which was by this time practically established on democratic lines. They were now to carry this principle of democracy into civil affairs, and their history becomes the history of a colonial adventure, and the establishment of a democratic state.

# APPENDIX TO PART I

## THE "MAYFLOWER" PASSENGERS AND THEIR FAMILIES

THE *Mayflower* passengers, from Bradford's Manuscript :—

"The names of those which came over first, in ye year 1620 and were (by the blesing of God) the first Beginers and (in a sort) the foundation, of all the plantations, and colonies, in New England (And their families)."

8   Mr John Caruer, Kathrine his wife. Desire Minter; and two man seruants, John Howland, Roger Wilder, William Latham, a boy, and a maidseruant, and a child y$^t$ was put to him called Jasper More.

6   Mr William Brewster, Mary his wife, with two sons, whose names were Loue and Wrasling, and a boy was put to him called Richard More; and another of his brothers; the rest of his children were left behind and came ouer afterwards.

5   Mr Edward Winslow, Elizabeth his wife, and two men seruants, caled Georg Sowle and Elias Story; also a little girl was put to him caled Ellen, the sister of Richard More.

2   William Bradford and Dorothy his wife, hauing but one child, a sone left behind, who came afterward.

6   Mr Isaack Allerton, and Mary his wife; with three children Bartholmew, Remember and Mary, and a seruant boy, John Hooke.

2   Mr Samuel Fuller: and a seruant caled William Butten. His wife was behind and a child, which came afterwards.

2   John Cradston, and his sone John Cradston.

2   Captain Myles Standish and Rose, his wife.

4   Mr Christopher Martin and his wife; and two seruants, Salomon Prower, and John Langemore.

5   Mr William Mullines, and his wife; and two children Joseph, and Priscilla; and a seruant Robart Carter.

6   Mr William White, and Susana his wife; and one sone caled Resolued, and one borne a ship-bord caled Peregriene, and two seruants, named William Holbeck and Edward Thomson.

8   Mr Steuen Hopkins, and Elizabeth his wife; and two children, caled Giles and Constanta a doughter, both by a former wife. And two more by this wife caled Damaris and Oceanus, the last was borne at sea. And two seruants caled Edward Doty and Edward Litster.

1   Mr Richard Warren, but his wife and children were left behind and came afterwards.

4   John Billinton, and Elen his wife; and two sones John and Francis.

4   Edward Tillie and Ann his wife, and two children that were their cossens; Henry Samson & Humility Coper.

3   John Tillie and his wife; and Eelizabeth their doughter.

2   Francis Cooke and his sone John; But his wife and other children came afterwards.

2   Thomas Rogers and Joseph his sone; his other children came afterwards.

2¹  Thomas Tinker, and his wife and a sone.

2   John Rigdale and Alice his wife.

3   James Chilton and his wife, and Mary their doughter; they had another doughter yᵗ was maried came afterward.

3   Edward Fuller, and his wife; and Samuell their sonne.

3   John Turner, and two sones; he had a doughter came some years after to Salem, wher she is now liuing.

3   Francis Eaton and Sarah his wife, and Samuell their sone, a young child.

¹ Three.

10  Moyses Fletcher, John Goodman, Thomas Williams, Digorie Preist, Edmond Margeson, Peter Browne, Richard Britterige, Richard Clarke, Richard Gardenar, Gilbart Winslow.

1  John Alden was hired for a cooper at South-Hampton wher the ship victuled ; and being a hopeful young man was much desired, but left to his owne liking to go, or stay when he came here, but he stayed, and maryed here.

2  John Allerton, and Thomas Enlish were both hired, the later goe master of a shalop here, and the other was reputed as one of ye company, but was to go back (being a seaman) for the help of others behind.  But they both dyed here, before the shipe returned.

2  There were allso other two seamen hired to stay a year here in the country, William Treuore ; and one Ely.  But when their time was out they both returned.

These being aboute a hundred souls came ouer in this first ship ; and began this worke, which God of his goodnes hath hithertoo blessed ; let his holy name haue y^e praise.  And seeing it hath pleased him to giue me to see thirty years completed since these beginnings.  And that the great works of his providence are to be obserued, I have thought it not unworthy my paines, to take a view of the decreasings and yncreasings of these persons, and such changs as hath pased over them, and theirs, in this thirty years.  It may be of some use to such as come after ; but howeuer, I shall rest in my owne benefite.

I will therefore take them in order as they lie.

Mr Caruer and his wife, dyed the first year, he in ye spring, she in ye somer ; also his man Roger, and ye little boy Jasper, dyed before either of them, of ye commone ynfection.

Desire Minter, returned to her freind and proued not very well and dyed in England.  His seruant boy Latham, after more than twenty years stay in the country, went into England ; and from thence to the Bahamy Islands in ye West Yndees ; and ther with some others was starued for want of food. His maid seruant maried, and dyed a year or too after here in this place. His seruant John Howland maried the doughter of John Tillie, Elizabeth and they are both now liuing; and haue ten children now all liuing, and their eldest doughter hath four childre.

15 And ther two doughter, one all liuing and other of their children maridgable, so fifteen are come of them.

Mr Brewster liued to very old age; about eighty years he was when he dyed, hauing liued some twenty three or twenty four years here in ye countrie, and though his wife dyed long before yet she dyed aged. His son Wrastle dyed a yonge man unmaried; his sone Loue liued till this year
4 1650, and dyed and left four children, now liuing. His daughters which came ouer after him, are dead, but haue left sundry children aliue; his eldst sone is still liuing, and hath nine or ten children, one maried who hath a child
2 or two. Richard More, his brother, dyed the first winter;
4 but his is maried, and hath four or five children all liuing.

Mr Edward Winslow, his wife dyed the first winter, and
2 he maried with the widow of Mr White, and hath two children liuing by her marigable, besides sundry that are dead. One of his seruants dyed, as also the little girle soone after the ships ariued. But his man Georg Sowle,
8 is still liuing and hath eight childre.

William Bradford, his wife dyed soone after ther arriuall,
4 and he maried againe; and hath four children, three whereof are maried. (who dyed 9th of May 1658).[1]

Mr Allerton his wife dyed with the first, and his seruant John Hooke, his sone Bartle is maried in England, but I know not how many children he hath. His doughter Remember is maried at Salem, and hath three or four children liuing. And his doughter Mary is maried here and hath four children. Him selfe maried againe with ye doughter of Mr Brewster, and hath one sone liuing by here, but she is long since dead. And he is maried againe, and hath left this place long agoe. So I account his yncrease
8 to be eight besids his sone in England.

[1] 9th of May 1657.

Mr Fuller, his seruant dyed at sea; and after his wife came
2 ouer, he had tow children by her; which are liuing and
grow up to yeares.   But he dyed some fifteen years agoe.
John Crakston dyed in the first mortality; and about some
o five or six years after his sone dyed, hauing lost himself in
ye woods, his feet became frozen, which put him into a
feauor, of which he dyed.

Captain Standish his wife dyed in the first sicknes; and
4 he maried againe, and hath four sones liueing, and some are
dead.   (Who dyed 3rd of Octob. 1655).

Mr Martin, he, and all his, dyed in the first ynfection; not
long after the ariuall.

Mr Molines, and his wife, his sone, and his seruant, dyed
the first winter.   Only his daughter Priscila suruiued, and
15 maried with John Alden, who are both liuing, and haue
eleven children.   And their eldest doughter is maried and
hath fiue children.   (See N.E. Memorial, p. 22.)

Mr White and his two seruants dyed soone after ther
landing.   His wife maried with Mr Winslow (as is before
noted).   His two sons are maried, and Resolued hath five
children;   Peregrine tow, all liuing, so their yncrease are
7 seven.

Mr Hopkins, and his wife are now both dead; but the liued
above twenty years in this place, and had one sone, and
four doughters borne here.   Ther sone became a seaman,
and dyed at Barbadoes, one doughter dyed here, and two
are maried, one of them hath two children, and one is yet
5 to mary.   So their yncrease, which still suruiue are five.
4 But his sone Giles is maried, and hath four children.   His
12 doughter Constanta, is also maried, and hath twelve
children, all of them liuing, and one of them maried.

Mr Richard Warren liued some four or fiue years, and had
his wife come over to him.   By whom he had two sons
before dyed; and one of them is maryed, and hath two
4 children, so his yncrease is four.   But he had five doughters
more came over with his wife, who are all maried; and
liuing, and haue many children.

And of the old stock (of one and other) ther are yet liuing this present year 1650 nere thirty persons. Let the Lord haue ye praise ; who is the High Preseruer of men.

(Twelfe persons liuing of the old stock this present yeare 1679.)

(Two persons liueing that come ouer in the first ship 1620, this present yeare 1690. Resolued White and Mary Chusman the daughter of Mr Alderton.)

(And John Cooke the sone of Francis Cooke that came in the first ship is still liuing this present yeare 1694.)

(And Mary Cushman is still liuing this present yeare 1698.)

(The sentences in brackets are not in the handwriting of the rest, and were added later.)

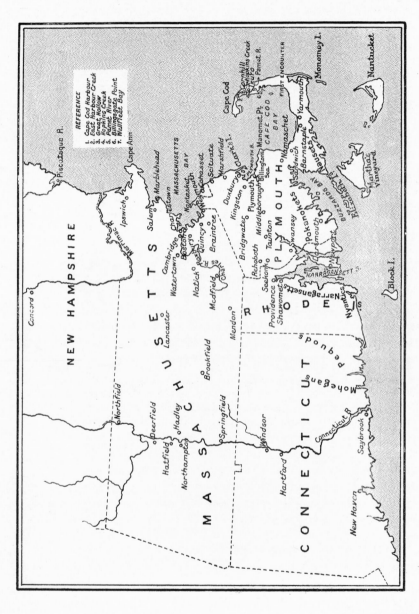

MAP OF PLYMOUTH AND SURROUNDING COLONIES

# PART II.—PLYMOUTH COLONY

## CHAPTER X

### THE FIRST WINTER

PLYMOUTH Colony, the home of the Pilgrims in America, existed as a separate state only from 1620 to 1691, and by far the most important part of its history is included in the years before 1660, when under such men as Bradford, Standish, Brewster and Winslow, it pursued a vigorous and independent policy.

In one sense, particularly in the early years, the story is one of adventure, of exploration in a strange country, where the forests seemed to murmur of lurking perils, and the smoke of a fire gave warning of dangerous neighbours; of precarious settlement where want and disease played havoc, and only a chance discovery of corn, or the timely coming of a fishing-boat, saved the lives of the planters; of hostility or rude hospitality from the native tribes. This is the picturesque side of the story, which the actors in it never realized at all. There was no Captain John Smith among them, to magnify their adventures and cast a glamour over their everyday affairs, and the narratives of Bradford and Winslow are wonderfully simple and unsensational. They had not gone out to seek adventures, but to make homes for themselves, and to earn their living, and when marvels arose and confronted them, the Pilgrims disposed of them as quickly and quietly as possible, and went on with the day's work.

In another sense, their story tells of the growth of a very remarkable state of society, so isolated from the ordinary influences of civilized life, that it grew simply out of the primitive needs of human beings, modified only by their religious convictions. Religious and moral considerations decided who should inhabit the colony, who should hold land, who should have special privileges, and how the brief times of rest and leisure should be used. No class instincts, no artistic desires, no merely intellectual theories could have any share in moulding the character of their society. And the isolation from outside influence, whether of foreign nations, of rank or culture, the adoption of religious opinion as the one standard by which all things were measured, led to an amount of concentration and repression which bears fruit in New England still.

But the main importance of their story is on its political side. At first sight, all that the Pilgrims did seems so provisional, so very much dictated by the needs of the moment, that it seems less the working out of a great principle, than obedience to necessity. But they did, either through example, or through their own personal dispositions, choose forms of government which have had permanent influence ; and beneath their disconnected tentative efforts lie two germs of later American history, the idea of self-government with all its influence on character and social life, and the tendency to federation, which in linking the colonies of New England, only foreshadowed the later union of the United States.

All the short history of Plymouth Colony is an explanation and illustration of these two things. Neither was deliberate, they were the natural result of the position of the settlers, geographical, political and religious. The Pilgrims found themselves on a solitary coast, where previous attempts at colonization had been brief and disastrous, hundreds of miles from their nearest white neighbours. They had no charter for this district, no political authority from the King or from the New

England Company, their only immediate relations were with the Adventurers, and these were purely mercantile. And yet, with all external authority removed, a strong government had never been so necessary, with disaffection amongst some of their people, with pioneers wanting a leader, settlers an arbitrator, and the whole colony in need of organized military defence against the Indians.

They took immediate steps to establish the necessary government, and though all that they did was done in the King's name, there could be no doubt that it would take a democratic form.   Dutch example was strong in their minds, their church teaching was largely democratic, their lives involved an almost absolute equality of condition.   For the present they were bound to a system of communism, which long left traces in their land laws, and even after this was less rigidly enforced, all were absolutely dependent on their own work, the poverty of the soil making it impossible for any to live on it in idleness.

For ten years they lived alone, gradually building up the machinery of their political independence; then came other colonies to the neighbourhood, and the similarity of their religious belief and aims, and the need for mutual help, led to the New England Confederation, which, however, affected this political independence only in matters of external policy.

The act by which they assumed powers of government was done before the Pilgrims came to harbour at Cape Cod.   Their outlook then was of the gloomiest, they were weak and ill from the voyage and the close crowded ship, and before them stretched an inhospitable coast, where the bitter winter weather and the savage natives would hinder every attempt at making a settlement.   Behind them was the ocean, cutting them off from their friends and country ; their only stronghold was the ship, and its master threatened to desert them, lest provisions should be too scanty for the return voyage.   So the past was full

13

of suffering, the present of uncertainty, whilst famine and sudden death loomed large in their vision of the future.

The leaders wisely determined that some source of authority must immediately be recognised, that their first acts might carry official weight. Faction was already showing itself on board ship, where the discontented ones said they had come out under a patent to Virginia, and not to these parts, and that they would acknowledge no allegiance to any one if they settled there. Such want of union would have been fatal, and it is was decided to bind the company together by a voluntary compact founding the government on the will of the people. The following document was drawn up and signed :—

"In the name of God, Amen. We whose names are underwriten, the loyall subjects of our dread Soveraigne Lord King James by the grace of God, of great Britaine, Franc, and Ireland king, defender of the faith, etc. Hauing undertaken, for the glorie of God, and aduancemente of the christian faith and honour of our king and countrie, a voyage to plant the first colonie in the Northerne parts of Virginia, Doe by these presents solemnly and mutually in the presence of God, and one of another ; couenant and combine ourselues togeather into a ciuill body politick ; for our better ordering and preseruation and furtherance of the ends aforesaid ; and by vertue hearof to enacte, constitute, and frame shuch just and equall lawes, ordinances, Acts, constitutions, and offices, from time to time, as shall be thought most meete and conuenient for the generall good of the Colonie : Unto which we promise all due submission and obedience. In witnes whereof we haue hereunder subscribed our names at Cap Codd the 11 of Nouember in the year of the raigne of our soueraigne Lord King James of England, France, and Ireland the eighteenth and of Scotland the fiftie fourth Anno Domini 1620." [1]

Forty-one out of the sixty-five male adult passengers

---

[1] Bradford MS., p. 54.  The date " 11th Nov. " is of course old style.

signed this compact. Thirteen more were sons, whose allegiance might be included in that of their fathers, and eight of the remaining eleven died very shortly after, and may have been too ill to sign. By this step, which recognized the settlers themselves as the real source of power, the Pilgrims had for all practical purposes made themselves politically independent, and as the colony was remote, and England for many years to come was occupied with troubles of her own, this independence and the forms of government which it dictated were never seriously interfered with. Whilst courts were held, and officers sworn in strictly in the King's name, a complete machinery of republican government was being built up.

Having settled the question of authority, the Pilgrims turned to their work of colonization. They had reached the coast, not of Virginia as they expected, but of New England, a more desolate region still. It had, indeed, been visited before. Gosnold, trying in 1602 to find a direct passage from England to America, had come upon a promontory which he called Cape Cod, and his sailors were the first Englishmen to set foot in New England. He sailed about the coast, and even prepared to found a colony on the Elizabeth Isles, but when his ship was ready to leave, the little band of settlers lost heart, and returned with it, fearing starvation and Indian treachery.

A year later, Martin Pring was sent out by the merchants of Bristol on a voyage of trade and discovery, and indeed the Council of the Plymouth Virginia Company, within whose grant this territory was supposed to lie, sent out many expeditions in the early years of the century, but though some were successful enough, no permanent plantation was made, and little was done besides fishing.

In 1614, at the sole charge of four merchants of London, Captain John Smith was sent there with two ships. With him he took six or seven different maps or " plots

[1] Arber's "Captain John Smith, p. 187.

of North Virginia and New England, which, though
costly, proved to be equally unlike each other and the
country.  So whilst his men were busy fishing, he took a
little boat and passing close along the shore, made a
draught of the coast from Penobscot to Cape Cod, and
called the country New England.  Hunt, the master of
the second ship, was an unprincipled scoundrel, who,
having failed to rob Smith of his plans and leave him to
starve on a desert island, kidnapped a party of Indians,
and sailed away to sell them into slavery in Spain.
Jealous of the fame which Smith must win for his knowledge of New England, Hunt tried to " drown that name
with the eccho of Cannaday,"[1] so Smith on his return
took his discourse and his map to Prince Charles, begging
him to confirm the name of New England, and to christen
the principal places discovered, so that it would be henceforth "an unmannerly presumption in any that doth alter
them without his leave."

Employed by Sir Ferdinand Gorges and other members
of the Plymouth Company, Smith attempted a second
voyage in 1615, with sixteen men who were to found a
colony.  But his ship was driven back by tempests, and
when it started once more, it was attacked by pirates ;
Smith himself was captured, and escaped alone in an open
boat from the harbour of Rochelle.  From this time forth
he devoted himself to the cause of colonization, travelling
over the country to tell men of the wonders and possibilities of New England life, minimising its hardships,
and exalting its riches and pleasures.  In words and
books he described the land between Penobscot and Cape
Cod, which must have been very different from the desola-
tion of to-day ; its good harbours, its coasts, overgrown
with timber of every kind, its rivers running from the
lakes where lived the beaver and the otter, its riches of
iron and steel and stone, its abundance of fish, fowl and
good fruits.  " Of all the foure parts of the world that I

---

[1] Arber's " Captain John Smith," p. 699.

have yet seene not inhabited," he wrote, "could I haue but meanes to transport a Colonie, I would rather live here than anywhere; and if it did not maintaine itselfe, were wee but once indifferently well fitted, let us starue." [1]

Of all the riches of the country, the chief was its fish, and the best part for fishing was around Cape Cod. Through its fisheries, Smith constantly urged, the country might become richer than Holland; cod, hake, mullet, sturgeon, and herring were to be had in abundance, and he ended his panegyrics with one invariable formula, " Therefore (honourable and worthy Countrymen) let not the meannesse of the word Fish distaste you, for it will afford as good gold as the mines of Guiana and Tumbatu, with lesse hazard and charge, and more certaintie and facilitie: and so I humbly rest." [2]

Smith states that he offered his help to the Pilgrims before their departure, but that they refused it, saying that his books and maps would be "better cheap" to teach them than himself, and to this false economy he attributes the misery of their early months in the country. A more obvious cause, and one which they had been unable to avoid, was the lateness of their voyage, for November was a terrible time to arrive, houseless and badly provisioned, in this unknown country. But delay could only make things worse, and having armed themselves against disaffection, and undertaken the burdens of government, the Pilgrim leaders determined that not a moment should be lost in proceeding to the work of actual settlement.

The *Mayflower* came to anchor in the Bay of Cape Cod on November 21st, and the same afternoon sixteen men, headed by Captain Standish, and well armed, went on shore to explore, and to fetch back wood to the ship.[3] The shore proved to be a small neck of land, partly sandhills, partly wooded; neither person nor habitation could they find, but they brought back stores of juniper,

---

[1] Arber's "Captain John Smith," p. 193-4.          [2] *Ibid.*, p. 277.
[3] For this account see "Mourt's Relation."

smelling very sweet and strong, which served them for fuel all the time the ship lay there. The next day was the Sabbath, an inviolable day of rest, but on Monday work began again in earnest. Unfortunately the shallop, in which they had hoped to make their explorations, was found to be in very bad repair, so the carpenter was set to work on it; many of the others went ashore in the long boat, and the women found fresh water to wash their clothes. The water of the bay was very shallow at the shore, and everyone was forced to wade "a bow shoot or two," and this exposure in the freezing weather led to the devastating illness which came upon them later.

Impatient of delay, on Wednesday the 25th November, a party of ten men gained a reluctant permission to explore by land with what provisions they could carry, without waiting for the shallop. The long boat set them on shore, and led by Standish, Bradford, Hopkins, and Tilley, each man with his musket, sword, and corslet, they had marched for about a mile when they saw coming towards them five savages with a dog. The Indians fled into a wood whistling their dog after them; the men followed them for about ten miles, when night fell, and after setting sentinels and building a fire, they made an encampment. Next morning they followed the track of the Indians again round the head of a long creek (East Harbour Creek), but could find neither the men nor their houses. Worse still, they could find no fresh water, and having with them only biscuit and cheese, and a little bottle of aqua vitae, they were overcome with thirst. Soon, however, they came to a deep valley (East Harbour in Truro) where they saw a deer, and were able to drink at a spring of fresh water. "We . . . sat us downe and drunke our first New England water with as much delight as ever we drunke drinke in all our liues." Then they marched south to the shore, built a fire as a signal of safety to the ship, and continued their journey.

They had seen from the ship, as they came into harbour, what looked like a river running into the land, and so they marched in that direction. In another valley they found a fresh water pond and traces of an Indian plantation, and then they came at last upon some heaps of sand (Great Hollow) covered with mats, and knew that they were among the haunts of the red men. They digged, and found a bow and arrows and other things, but guessed that it was a grave, and so covered it up and left it "because we thought it would be odious unto them to ransacke their sepulchers."

Soon after came a more important discovery, the remains of a house (Cornhill, Hopkin's Creek): a ship's kettle, which had evidently been brought out of Europe ; and under a newly made heap of sand two baskets, full of fresh Indian corn, both loose and on the ear. The basket held three or four bushels, and was as much as two of them could lift up from the ground, and they were already laden with armour, but as much as they could carry they took away in the kettle, determining to pay for it when they could meet with any of the owners. The rest they buried again. Near the same place they found the remains of a fort, which they judged had been built by Christians.

On examining the creek seen from the ship, they found it to have two branches (Hopkin's Creek and Pamet River), and there they saw two canoes, but having orders to stay out only two days, they could explore no further, so they returned to Fresh Water Pond and spent the night there, the rain pouring down in torrents, so that their muskets in the morning were too wet to go off. They lost their way too, when they began the homeward march, and wandered in the woods; and Bradford, examining a noose arranged to catch deer, and wondering at its use, was caught by the leg in it, and tested its working effectually.

Bucks, partridges, wild geese, and ducks they saw

round them in abundance, as they marched by woods and sands, sometimes in the water up to their knees; and at last they came in sight and sound of the ship, shot off their pieces for a signal, and were taken aboard, thankful indeed to have found a store of corn, and to have come safely home.

Meanwhile, the rest of the people had been seeking wood and sawing timber to build a new shallop, but the harbour was inconvenient, and all work was greatly hindered, since only by wading could they land, except at high water. "Oftentimes they waded to the midle of the thigh, and oft to the knees, to goe and come from land. Some did it necessarily and some for their own pleasure, but it brought to the most, if not to all, coughes and colds, the weather prouing sodainely cold and stormie, which afterwards turned to scuruey, whereof many dyed."

As soon as the shallop could be used, even before the repairs were fully completed, a second expedition was sent out, this time consisting of about thirty-four men, ten of them sailors. Master Jones, Captain of the *Mayflower*, was made leader out of gratitude for his kindness and help. Part were to go in the shallop, part were to be taken ashore by the long boat, and to travel by land. They started in a terrible storm; the shallop could not keep the water, and had to harbour almost immediately for the night, and though the land party went on some six or seven miles, the weather was so fierce that many "tooke the originall of their death here. . . . It blowed and did snow all that day and night, and froze withall."

The next day being finer, all went aboard the shallop and sailed to Pamet river, the creek they had formerly discovered. There the men landed, and marched along it for four or five miles, till night came on and they encamped, resolving to follow the river to its head the next morning. But so hilly was the soil, and so unsatisfactory the harbour, that next day they decided to turn to the other branch of the creek (Hopkin's Creek), and to look for the rest of the corn which they had left behind. They found a canoe to carry them across, and came to Cornhill, where they found not only the corn they had left, but a bottle of oil and several other heaps of corn and beans. The ground was now frozen hard and covered with snow, and but for their first discovery they could never have found the corn, and would have had none to plant in the following spring.

Bad weather was coming on, and Jones with some of the weaker people went back in the shallop, leaving eighteen men to spend another night there. Next day, these marched five or six miles into the woods without finding any people, and came back at length to the broad beaten path they had started from. Here they dug up a grave, and found in it the skeletons of a man and child, embalmed in a fine red powder, and buried with them many bowls, trays, dishes, and trinkets. The child was decorated with strings and bracelets of fine white beads, and by its side was a little bow, three quarters of a yard long. They took some of the prettiest things, and covered up the corpses again. Many other graves were around, and at last two of the sailors who had come back with the shallop espied two houses built of young sapling trees bent, with both ends stuck into the ground. They were round, and covered down to the ground with thick mats; the chimney was a wide hole at the top with a mat to cover it; and the door was not more than a yard high, made of a mat to open. Within were finer and newer mats, which formed walls, flooring, and beds, and in the centre four stakes knocked into the ground, with sticks laid over, on which the Indians hung their pots for cooking. In the houses, too, were wooden bowls, trays, and dishes, earthen pots, handbaskets made of crab shells, and an English pail or bucket, besides baskets of every kind. The men took some of them, and of the mats, and went away, meaning to make payment for them when they had the chance, as indeed they did six months later. The shallop had come back for them, and they got aboard the *Mayflower* the same night.

After this second expedition, there was long discussion amongst the whole body of the Pilgrims as to where they should settle. Many thought that the newly discovered Cornhill would be a good place ; it gave harbour for boats, though not for ships ; it was evidently good corn-ground ; it would be near the abundant fisheries of Cape Cod, it seemed healthy and defensible, and further exploration was risky in such severe weather, with people greatly weakened by coughs and colds, and in danger of scarcity of provision.

Others were in favour of Agawam (Ipswich) to the north, having heard good reports of it, and they disliked the idea of fixing on Cornhill as yet, since there might be a much better place for a settlement close at hand. There was some fear about the water too at Cornhill ; it had to be carried up a steep incline, and the summer supply was doubtful.

At last a third expedition was decided on, not to go so far as Agawam, but to look at a place of which Robert Coppin, the pilot, told them, on the side of the bay opposite to Cape Cod, where there was a good river and harbour. On Wednesday, December 16th, a party of twenty men set out, including Bradford, who afterwards wrote the story of this discovery. It was so stormy that they had difficulty in clearing the sandy point, and so cold that the water froze on their clothes and made them like coats of iron. After coasting along for six or seven leagues without coming to either river or creek, they saw a sandy stretch of land jutting out to a point (Billingsgate Point), and sailed across Wellfleet Bay to come to it. On the shore, busy over some black object, were ten or twelve Indians, who ran away as the boat approached, and when the men landed, and encamped for the night behind a barricade of stakes and pineboughs, they saw no more of the savages than the smoke of their fire.

They called the place Grampus Bay, for they found that it was a grampus that the Indians had been cutting up, and they themselves the next morning saw one on the sands, and others lying dead at the bottom of the bay, frozen to the sands when the tide went out. They soon found that the place had no river, and not a very fruitful soil, though there were running brooks and some fresh water. The expedition followed the track of the Indians' bare feet into the woods by the side of a pond, and came upon a great burying place, palisaded round with young saplings, like a churchyard, and open grounds where corn had been planted long ago. Then they found four or five deserted houses, but no people, and no more corn, and at sunset the land party left the woods to join their companions with the shallop, and wearily prepared to camp once more for the night. Once while they slept they were roused by their sentinels' cry, "Arme! Arme!" and awoke to hear hideous sounds in the distance, but when they had fired off a couple of muskets the noise ceased, and they guessed it had been made by wolves or foxes. In the morning, however, they heard it again, and a moment after the Indians were upon them with their arrows. The Englishmen were just returning to their shallop, and had already taken some of their muskets to the shore, but the four who were armed defended the encampment until the rest came up, and in a few minutes the Indians were driven off. No one was injured, though the arrows flew thick and fast, and from this first brush with the Indians the place was named "The First Encounter." The attacking party belonged to the Nauset tribe from which Hunt had kidnapped his slaves, and this was the reason of their hostility.

From here they intended to sail to "Thievish Harbour," the place of which Coppin had spoken, so called because there some Indians had stolen a harping iron from his fellow sailors, and which was indeed Plymouth, their future home. All day they sailed along the coast in that direction, without seeing harbour or creek to put into, and with the afternoon came snow and rain and such a storm of wind as tossed their little boat most dangerously. The rudder broke, and they steered makeshift fashion with two oars; they put on so much sail in their haste to reach the harbour that the mast split in three pieces, and only a favourable tide carried them in. Then the pilot mistook the harbour, and all but cast them away on the rocks, but "a lusty seaman which steered bad those which rowed, if they were men, about with her, or ells they were all cast away; the which they did with speed."[1] Finally in the darkness and rain they came under the lee of a small island (Clark's Island), and on it spent that night and the two succeeding days, utterly exhausted with fatigue and anxiety.

On Monday, 21st December 1620, they sounded the harbour, and the first of the Pilgrim Fathers set foot on Plymouth rock. The good harbour, and the fruitful land with its corn-fields and running brooks, convinced them that they had at last found the right place for a settlement. They realized some of its deficiencies later,[2] but it was so much better than their earlier discoveries that they were glad to accept it, and hastened back to the ship with their good news. The joy of their return was marred, for Bradford's young wife Dorothy had been drowned off the *Mayflower*, whilst he was seeking for a home to bring her to.

The Indian names for the place were Patuxet and Accomack, and Smith wrote of it as wanting only industrious people. He called it Plymouth on his map, and partly for this reason perhaps, partly because Plymouth was the last town they had touched at in Old England, and they remembered gratefully the kindness of the people there, the Pilgrims kept the name.

Three days after this expedition returned, the *Mayflower* weighed anchor, and after a day's delay through contrary winds, came safely into Plymouth Bay. Then they

---

[1] Bradford MS., p. 52.    [2] *Ibid.*, p. 53.

examined the coast to find the most convenient spot for
building the first town. The look of the bay was encouraging, with its abundance of fish, shell fish, and fowl ;
the land seemed good and well wooded, many kinds of
herbs grew there, and there were brooks of fresh running
water. First a spot three miles inland up a creek
(Kingston), and then Clark's Island, were discussed, but
the first was thought to be too far from the fishing and
too near to the woods where the Indians lurked, and the
second was bleak and overgrown with trees, and doubt-
fully supplied with fresh water.

There was little time for discussion, since it was the
29th of December already, and soon the majority decided
to settle on the mainland, on a piece of high ground
where they would have fresh water, ground ready cleared
for corn-growing, and a good harbour for boats and
shallops. Near by was a hill on which they would build
a fort and plant their ordinance, and from which they
could see far out across the bay, and get timely warning
of the approach of any enemies.

At once the building began, and all set to work on the
common house, or storehouse, which was to hold their
provisions and arms, and perhaps to serve for hospital
and church as well. It was slow work, for timber had to
be felled and sawn, and carried a furlong's distance to
the spot ; and almost every day the work was interrupted
by storms of wind and rain, which sometimes made it
impossible to leave the ship. Then, too, provisions were
running short, they had no small hooks with which to
catch fish, and the shooting of an eagle, the catching of a
herring, is recorded with the interest of hungry people.
On Christmas Day [1] all would have had to drink water,
but that the master of the ship took pity on this
melancholy festival, and sent them beer.

On the 7th of January the ground was measured out
for the private houses, which were to be in two rows near

January 4th.

the fort, and paled in for greater security. The houses
were the merest huts, built of hewn planks, with windows
probably of oiled paper.   Single men agreed to join with
some family, that the work of building and impaling
houses might be less, and the company was thus reduced
to nineteen families.   For the same reason the plots were
small; each measured $2\frac{3}{4} \times 16\frac{1}{2}$ yards, and lots were cast
to decide where each family should build.   The men
were allowed to work each on his own house when the
common house was nearly finished, in hopes that the
building would thus be quicker done, but twice the
thatched roof of the storehouse, packed with sick
people, caught fire, and though no lives were lost, the
extra work involved came hard upon men spent with
illness and privation.   And to keep them in constant
suspense and fear was the smoke of the Indian fires to
the southward, more menacing than any hardships.

Exposure and fatigue soon did their work; coughs,
colds and scurvy devastated the company, and out of
the one hundred and two persons who landed at Cape
Cod, fifty-three died during this first winter.   Bradford
was seized with illness, but fortunately for the future of
the colony he recovered.   He speaks gratefully of the
devotion of Standish, Brewster and others to the sick; the
sailors on the other hand treated them brutally, refusing
the few little comforts and attentions that were in their
power to give, but soon the sickness spread to them too,
and they learnt the extent of their cruelty.   The mortality
was not here, as in Holland, mainly among the children,
the wives suffered most, and out of eighteen who voyaged
in the *Mayflower*, only four saw the beginning of a second
winter.   One by one the members of the little company
were carried to Burial Hill, where their graves were
planted with corn and unmarked by any memorial, lest
the Indians should know how great their losses were,
and guess their weakness.

In this plight the Pilgrims were not likely to make

PLYMOUTH IN 1622

W.L.Williams. DEL.

much advance in trade or discovery, or any other work
which was not absolutely necessary. Captain Standish,
with some others, went out to look for any friendly
Indians who might help them, but found no one ; Francis
Billington, one of the boys, exploring with a sailor, came
upon a great water (Billington's Sea) divided into two
lakes three and six miles in circuit, from which flowed
the brook which watered Plymouth ; at another time
two of the company wandered away in an interval of
work and lost themselves, but made no particular
discoveries, and almost perished with cold and hunger.
They found " Neither harbour nor meate, but in frost and
snow were forced to make the earth their bed, and the
Element their covering, and another thing did very much
terrify them, they heard as they thought two Lyons
roaring exceedingly for a long time together." The lions
proved to be wolves, for one of the two men saw them
a few days later, when he was out trying to use his frost-
bitten feet.

Nothing more had been seen of the Indians, but there
had been many alarms, and some tools had been stolen
from the woods where the men were working, so on the
27th February it was determined that military orders
should be properly established, and Miles Standish was
chosen Captain. Whilst the meeting to discuss this was
being held, two savages appeared over the top of a hill a
quarter of a mile away, making signs that messengers
should be sent to them. Standish and Hopkins at once
crossed the brook to meet them, but the Indians fled.

Not knowing whether this was a sign of peace or
enmity, the company determined to be prepared, and a
few days later the Master and his sailors brought ashore
their four cannons of different sizes, and mounted them.
They made a feast of the occasion, the Master bringing
with him a fat goose, and the Pilgrims contributing a fat
crane, a mallard, and a dried neat's tongue, " and so wee
were kindly and friendly together."

About a month later a second meeting was held to conclude about military orders, and again an Indian appeared to interrupt it. This one had no fears at all, but marched boldly into the town as far as the Common house, where he was stopped. He bade the Englishmen welcome in their own language, and they found that his name was Samoset, and that he had learned English among the fishermen at Monhegan. He was a native chief of Pemaquid (Bristol, Maine); he could tell the Pilgrims many things about New England and its inhabitants, and they learnt that Patuxet, the place where they lived, had been swept clear of its native population four years before by an extraordinary plague, which left neither man, woman, nor child. The Indians had taken this plague to be a vengeance on their having murdered and enslaved the crew of a French ship, and so it inspired awe and terror of the white men.

Plymouth's nearest neighbours, Samoset told them, were the Massasoits, a tribe sixty strong; the Nausites were to the north-east, one hundred strong, and it was they who had attacked the exploring party at the First Encounter.

The planters cast a horseman's coat around Samoset's naked body and made much of him, giving him strong water to drink, with biscuit, butter and cheese, some pudding and a piece of a mallard. They did not altogether trust him, however, and would have been pleased if he had gone before nightfall, but he stayed, and they lodged him in Stephen Hopkins' house and watched him. Before he left next morning, they gave him a knife, a bracelet, and a ring, and he in turn promised to come again, and bring others with him to do trade with them. Sure enough, he came the very next day with five others, all leaving their weapons outside the town; and the planters entertained them, but would not truck with them that day, as it was Sunday. The four friends went away, promising to bring more beaver skins, and to return the

tools which had been stolen, but Samoset was so charmed
with his new acquaintances, that he would not go, and
stayed four days feigning illness.

A third meeting was held to settle military affairs, and
a third time it was interrupted by savages, who appeared
with signs of enmity, but fled once more, when two or
three went out to meet them. But next day came
Samoset again, and with him Squanto or Tisquantum, the
only surviving native of Patuxet, who had been carried
away by Hunt and so had escaped the plague. Hunt
had sold his captives in Spain, where the friars tried to
nurture them in the Roman Catholic religion, and took
them out of slavery; Squanto had made his way to
England, and was brought back to America by Mr
Dermer in 1619, when he came to try and make peace
between the Indians and the whites. He was not very
successful, for the natives killed his men, and wounded
him so severely that he died of his injuries later in
Virginia. Hunt's cruel action brought trouble on many
later explorers, for the Indians tried to avenge it on any
of the white race who came near them, and when the
Pilgrims came, they feared that they were come to
punish them in their turn, and met to curse and execrate
the newcomers in a dismal swamp. But Squanto's
knowledge of English, on the other hand, was of the
greatest help to the Plymouth men; he had lived in
Cornhill with Master John Slaney, the treasurer of the
Newfoundland Company, and spoke English well enough
to be their interpreter in these first negotiations.

On his first visit to the settlement with Samoset, he
was accompanied by three other Indians, carrying beaver
skins to truck with, and they brought news that their
Sagamore Massasoit was near by with his brother
Quadequina, and wanted to parley with them.

So the Pilgrims prepared for their first formal meeting
with the natives. King Massasoit appeared in about an
hour with his sixty men at the top of a hill, and Winslow

was sent out to confer with him, and to represent the wish of the newcomers for peace and trade with his tribe. Winslow took to the King a pair of knives, and a copper chain with a jewel in it, and to Quadequina also a knife and a jewel to hang in his ear, besides some provisions. He greeted Massasoit in the name of King James, and desired him to come and speak with the Governor, which, after some hesitation and the leaving of hostages on both sides, the King consented to do. He was taken to a newly built house, and seated upon a "green Rugge" and three or four cushions, and having partaken of a hearty meal, he concluded the following treaty :—

1. That neither he, nor any of his, should do hurt to any of our people.

2. And if any of his did hurt to any of ours; he should send the offender (to us) that we might punish him.

3. That if any of our tools were taken away, when our people were at work, he should cause them to be restored ; and if ours did any harm to any of his, we should do the like to them.

4. If any did unjustly war against him, we would aid him. If any did war against us, he should aid us.

5. He should send his neighbour confederates, to certify them of this, that they might not wrong us ; but might be likewise comprised in the Conditions of Peace.

6. That when their men came to us, they should leave their bows and arrows behind them, as we should do our pieces when we came to them.

7. Lastly, that doing this, King James would esteem of him as his friend and ally.

In this treaty the foundations of all their future Indian relations were laid. The signing of the treaty must have been a strange sight; on the one side the King, seated upon his cushions, attired like his men, but with a chain of white bone beads about his neck, a bag of tobacco hanging down behind, and a knife also hanging from a string in his bosom. His head and face were oiled so "that hee looked greasily"; his followers had their faces painted black, red, yellow or white; some wore skins and some were entirely naked. On the other side the Governor, John Carver, and the chief of the Pilgrims, haggard and emaciated, with every sign of their poverty and weakness upon them, yet firm and resolute, whilst King Massasoit trembled for fear.

When the negotiations were over, the Governor took King Massasoit to the brook, where they embraced and parted, but soon came a message that Quadequina was coming too, and he arrived with a troop of his men. They too were entertained, but by nightfall all had departed, and the hostages were exchanged. Only Samoset and Squanto remained, the rest camping with their wives and families half a mile away. Next day, Standish and Allerton visited the King in his camp, and were entertained in their turn with three or four groundnuts and some tobacco, and then Massasoit and his company went their way.

On the same day, April 2nd, the military orders were at last concluded, and John Carver was confirmed in his previous appointment as Governor.

Spring had come at last, and for two weeks they had been planting corn and garden seeds. Squanto helped them to set their corn, showing them how to manure the ground with fish, for otherwise the land was too exhausted to give good crops. With fishing he helped them too, treading out eels with his hands and feet, and showing them how to take the fish which came in abundance up the Town Brook.

With the end of the winter the settlers hoped that their worst sufferings were over, and when the *Mayflower* set sail about the 5th of April not one of them decided to return. The ship had stayed longer than was intended, for it was the end of December before they had any storehouse, and could unlade their goods, and a fortnight later the store was burnt, and they were still dependent on the ship. It was, indeed, their one stronghold and defence, and not until March 28th, when the carpenter, who had been long ill of the scurvy, fitted out the shallop and brought all from aboard, did they finally leave it. When they first arrived in the country, the shipmaster had been eager to get back, and brutal in his threats of deserting them, but the sickness of his crew, and the stormy season, soon made him as loth for the voyage as the settlers were to have him go.

With the departure of the *Mayflower*, their last link with the Old World was broken, and perhaps nothing in their long sufferings would be so hard to bear as this feeling of isolation. But there is not a trace of discouragement or complaint in their own accounts; they were now heart and soul committed to their enterprise, hiding their weakness, looking only on its hopeful side, and determined that the lives which had been sacrificed for it should not be in vain, but should be so many pledges for its final success.

They had, indeed, done more than they seemed to have done in this first winter, for they had practically established their political freedom. Their landing in the wrong place had freed them temporarily from the authority of either the Virginia or New England Companies, and it never afterwards made itself felt; their failure to obtain a charter from the King made it possible for them to exercise far greater freedom in practice than he would ever have allowed them on paper.

Entirely on their own responsibility, the general body chose their place of settlement, distributed land for the home lots, appointed officers, established military orders, and made terms with the native tribes. The same might have been done by any expedition which laid claim to no political powers whatever, but the Pilgrims had by the compact at Cape Cod practically declared themselves to be the source of power in the colony, and volunteered to abide by the laws which they as a " Civil Body Politic " should make, and this declaration gave a political significance to their ordinary acts. Moreover, it gave weight and authority to all that their officials did ; they had in fact already embarked on that training in self government which had such important results later. With all their references to King James, and the solemn oaths of allegiance to the crown which all their officers were bound to take, these first inhabitants of New England had begun even now to prepare for independence, and to fit themselves for the later Republic.

NOTE.—The rock on which the Pilgrims landed was originally just below Burial Hill, so called because it was the resting place of the many who died in the first winter.

In 1741 Elder Thomas Faunce (born 1646, died 1745) learnt that a wharf was to be built near or over the rock, and fearing that it might be destroyed or covered, and that thus an interesting memorial would be lost, he journeyed to the place, and before several witnesses pointed it out as the actual landing-place of the Pilgrims, many of whom he had known.

At the time of the Revolution an attempt was made to remove the rock to the Town Square, for purposes of political excitement. The granite boulder was loosened, but split in two, the lower part was left behind, the upper part was dragged to the Town Square, where it served as a pulpit for revolutionary orators.

At a later date it was again removed to its present position in front of the Pilgrim Hall, Plymouth, and enclosed by a railing.

the merchants who were eagerly awaiting some interest for their money.

However, as spring drew on, and the corn was all planted, several trading expeditions were undertaken to neighbouring tribes, and when in November the *Fortune* appeared, there was a fair cargo of beaver skins and clapboard ready for her. Bradford writes that it was not so large as they could have wished, but enough to show their good-will and intent to keep their share of the bond.

The *Fortune* brought word from Weston that a patent had been procured from the New England Council for the territory in which they had settled. This patent was taken in the name of "John Pierce and his associates," and Weston wrote that it was better than their former one.

But with this welcome news came serious complaints in a letter from Weston to Carver, about the delay in sending back the *Mayflower*, and her lack of cargo. He spoke roughly of their excuse of weakness, thinking it was rather weakness of judgment than anything else, and urging that more efforts should be made. Bradford's answer was as touching as it was dignified. He wrote of the death of Carver, and of the hardships they had undergone, and then went on to say, " At great charges in this aduenture I confesse you have beene, and many losses may sustaine, but ye loss of his (Carver's), and many other honest and yndustrious men's liues, cannot be vallewed at any price ; of ye one ther may be hope of recouery ; but ye other no recompence can make good, . . . It pleased God to vissite us then, with death dayly, and with so generall a disease ; that the liuing were scarce able to burie the dead, and ye well not in any measure sufficente to tend ye sick. And now to be so greatly blamed for not fraighting ye ship, doth yndeed goe near us, and much discourage us."[1]

[1] Bradford MS., p. 68.

Their condition was not likely to be much better in the following winter, for the *Fortune* had brought over thirty-five more of their company (including Robert Cushman), and misled by the cheerful accounts of some of the first comers, who in the plenty of harvest time forgot their early privations, they had come almost unprovided, and would have to be fed by the settlers till harvest came again. All were put on half allowance, and even with this precaution, their stock of food was finished by May. "I have seen," wrote Winslow, "men stagger by reason of faintness from want of food,"[1] and only some timely supplies from a fishing boat saved them from actual starvation. In gratitude for the patent which had been obtained, and feeling no doubt that some reparation was due to the Adventurers, the Pilgrims at last agreed to sign the conditions which they had refused at Southampton, and a signed copy was returned in the *Fortune*. The ship too was loaded with all speed, and sailed for England early in December, but was captured by the French, detained, and robbed of her cargo. Worse still from our point of view, she was apparently robbed of her papers, including an account by Bradford of the voyage and first winter, so that the account we have in "Mourt's relation" is unofficial, and was published against the will of its writers.

Possibly this second disappointment was too much for the Adventurers. They had invested a large sum of money in the undertaking, and would probably have further demands upon them, and they were not willing to await the slow returns which were all that could be expected from men labouring under so great difficulties. As early as 1622 came rumours of the possibility of breaking up the joint stock company. The hungry planters, who had lived with difficulty through the second winter, and were straining their eyes for a glimpse of the first ship which should bring them

[1] "Good News from New England," Dedicatory Epistle.

supplies, were doomed to disappointment. A ship came, but brought no provisions, only letters of complaint with mysterious hints of disunion and bad faith ; a later ship brought only news of Weston's retirement from the company, and of the robbery of the *Fortune* ; and from this time onward the settlers were left to depend entirely on their own resources for food. It had been understood that the merchants would not stop short at landing them in the colony, but would supply them with clothes and other necessaries until they were fairly established, repaying themselves out of the trading profits of the colony during the seven years of partnership. But fearing, evidently, that they had already sunk their money in a most unprofitable enterprise, the merchants declined to back it up, and were only anxious to break off the contract, and get some compensation for the initial outlay. Weston had left the company to start a more profitable plantation on his own account, hoping to usurp a part of the lucrative fur trade, and the bad character of his men, and their unscrupulous demands on Plymouth colony, were a source of much trouble and friction later on. The Pilgrims never forgot that he had befriended them ; they found him food and shelter, and goods when he was ship-wrecked ; a kindness of which he proved himself quite unworthy ; and even tried to defend and excuse him when he had brought himself within reach of justice.

The first movement of discontent came therefore from England, but it was not only to the merchants that the partnership grew irksome. The Pilgrims soon found that it not only cramped and retarded their material wealth, but that it was likely to prove fatal to their ideals of civil government and religious life.

The chief drawback to prosperity was the communal system. It was found to be impossible to get the maximum of work out of men when they were robbed of the stimulus of self interest and family affection, and this although the people were as conscientious and public spirited as any could be, full of sympathy and mutual helpfulness, as their conduct during their early hardships showed. As Bradford says, the failure of their honest attempt at communism speaks badly for the system. They gave it a fair chance, but in the spring of the third year, when they realized that nothing but a good harvest could save them from starvation and ruin, it was decided that to each man should be given a small plot of corn-growing land for himself. The allotment was only for present use, not for inheritance, but the plan proved successful. Not only did the men work harder to save their own families from want, but women and children who could not have been urged to work in the common fields without seeming hardship, went willingly to work on their own small piece of land. The position of the women and servants had been the most unsatisfactory feature of the communal plan, men disliking that their wives should work for other men, and feeling that the servants they had brought over with them were no advantage, seeing that they could not command their labour.

A year later the communal system was still further abandoned, for an acre of ground was granted to each man in perpetuity, as near to the town as might be.

It was, however, the danger to their civil and religious life which chiefly concerned the Pilgrims in their relation with the Adventurers, for the latter sent over both persons unsuitable in character, and persons who were not to live entirely under the control of the colony, and so were to a certain degree irresponsible.

In 1623 the *Anne* and *Little James* brought over sixty new planters, many of them members of the Leyden Church. The condition of the first colonists, their haggard faces and tattered clothes, shocked these newcomers, and the utmost hospitality that could be offered was a lobster, or a piece of fish, without bread or anything else but a cup of fresh water. With these came some who were to be "on their particular," that is, they were to be subject to the general government of the colony, but yet were to have lands definitely assigned to them, and to enjoy the fruits of their own labour without contributing to the common stock. They were not, however, to be allowed to trade in skins, and were to settle only where the Pilgrims pleased.

The disintegrating influence of such an arrangement is obvious. The position of these "particulars" would be an anomaly; it would be apt to provoke envy among the original settlers, and the government of the colony would be complicated by having to deal with two bodies of people living under totally different conditions, and over whom it exercised a different degree of control. The "particulars," in absolute possession of their own land and its produce, would naturally be far more independent than the "generals," who depended on the governor for the allotment of land, and every necessary from the common store.

However, Bradford was not in a position to refuse the Adventurers' demands, and received these people, contenting himself with defining their position by the following conditions :—

1. Proper places should be allotted to them, and they should receive all kindness from the general company.
2. They should be subject to the laws and order of the colony.
3. They should be free from all common employments, save those connected with defence.
4. Every male above sixteen should pay one bushel of wheat yearly toward the maintenance of the government.
5. They should not trade for furs, etc., until the end of the commonalty (*i.e.* the seven years' joint stock partnership with the Adventurers).

In the following year, as might be expected, some discontented members of the general company desired to join these "particulars," and Bradford permitted it on the same conditions, to which were added two clauses :—

1. That they must remain in the country until the general partnership was ended.
2. That they should pay into the general store one-half of what they raised beyond their food, to pay off the outlay already made for them.

So far, the partnership had resulted in grave drawbacks to the Pilgrim enterprise, but it was soon to prove inconsistent with the welfare of their church, and so with the *raison d'être* of the colony. In 1624 Mr Winslow returned from a visit to England, in the *Charity*, bringing with him the first cattle to the colony. He reported a strong faction against the settlers amongst the Adventurers, which was strongly set against their dearest wish, the bringing over of John Robinson and the rest of the Leyden Church. Probably the reason for this was that Robinson had become by his writings a very well-known Separatist, and to countenance him in any way would have prejudiced the Adventurers in the eyes of the New England Council, which objected to Brownists, and accepted the Pilgrims as tenants very unwillingly. This was why the Adventurers would send over no minister of any power or significance. This faction was willing, and even eager, to break off the joint stock company. Some were more friendly, but the adverse faction sent over a long list of objections which Bradford answered with characteristic shrewdness and humour.

The general complaint was of "Brownism," and they cloaked their discontent under the name of religious scruple. To their complaint of diversity about religion he answered that they knew none ; of the neglect of family duties on Sunday, that it was not allowed, of the want of both Sacraments, that it was inevitable until their pastor was permitted to join them. That children were neither taught nor catechized he denied, though it was true that they had as yet no common school. They complained further that the "particulars" refused to work for the "general"; that the water was unwholesome, and the ground barren, that the fish would not take salt, that the colony was full of thieves, of foxes and wolves, and mosquitoes; that the Dutch were near and would overthrow their trade. But Bradford made short work of such fanciful and unreasonable objections, which served chiefly as an excuse for their dislike to the adventure.

In the same ship were sent over to the colony a carpenter, a saltmaker, and a preacher, and the adventures of this last, John Lyford, caused the final break-up of the partnership, and convinced the Pilgrims of the impossibility of continuing an arrangement which threatened their religious privileges as much as their civil unity.

The church was only too anxious for a preacher, and Lyford conducted himself at first with such extreme humility, that he took everyone in, and was not only well entertained, but received into the church and deferred to on all occasions. Bradford, however, was gifted with clear sight and a good judgment of men, and this cringing humility first disgusted him, and then roused his suspicions. He noticed that Lyford's chief associate was one John Oldham, who had come over on the *Anne* as a "particular," and who had already got into trouble by sending to England false reports damaging to the colony. These two made a faction, countenancing all evildoers against the church; and, suspecting their correspondence with England, Bradford intercepted some of their letters, and found not only copies of private letters from Winslow to Brewster and Robinson, which Lyford had purloined and copied with scurrilous comments to send to their enemies in England, but letters divulging a plot on the part of Lyford and Oldham to reform the Pilgrim Church and administer the Sacraments. Their disloyal conduct became more open about this time; they began to pick quarrels on every occasion, and when, one Sunday, Lyford and his accomplice set up a public meeting apart,

Bradford judged it to be time to reveal all that he had discovered against them. Before the whole company, they were charged with ingratitude and with the stirring up of sedition, civil and ecclesiastical, and no one found anything to say in their defence. The charges made in letters of the intolerance of the church towards any not of the separation, and of injustice and cruelty to the "particulars," were disproved on the evidence of the very men said to have been injured; Lyford's plans for preventing the arrival of the Leyden people, of reinforcing the "particulars" that they might sway all, and of supplanting Standish by a new Captain of his own choosing, were exposed. Oldham was banished from the colony at once, and Lyford, who pretended repentance, was granted six months' grace, to see whether his repentance was sound.

Needless to say, it was not, and he was soon found writing more letters to the Adventurers, justifying what he had done on the ground that it was for the sake of the poor souls shut out from the Church, stating that his one fault was that he had preached to the general, and signing himself "John Lyford, Exille." After this, he went away and established himself with Oldham at Nantasket, where he did damage to the fishing of the colony.

In proof of the injustice of his accusations, many who had not before joined the church, did so now, seeing that it was being unfairly attacked, and being anxious to give it support. But in spite of the obvious ill faith of Lyford, and the proofs of his previous misconduct in Ireland, which were brought before the Adventurers, they chose to make these disturbances the final ground for a break-up of the joint stock company. They accused the Pilgrims of dissembling about the French discipline, which they, however, denied, saying that they had followed it as far as it followed Christ; they demanded that the Adventurers should become partners in the government of the colony, as well as in its trade; that the French discipline should be practised, and that the Leyden people should not be permitted to join the Pilgrims, until they became reconciled to their Church.

To accept a further partnership on these conditions, would have been to abandon everything for which they had suffered, to renounce entirely their independence, both civil and ecclesiastical, and to banish for ever the hope of union with their Leyden brethren; but by the same ship came a letter from four out of the company of Adventurers who were friendly to the colonists, and who proposed that the general stock should be kept up, and that they should help them to pay off their debt to the Adventurers, which then amounted to £1400. Standish went over to confer with them, and to arrange for obtaining trading goods at reasonable prices, and to get help from the Council for New England to prevent the Adventurers from keeping the planters bound to their agreement, if they themselves were to be free. But he was very unsuccessful, for the state of England was unsettled, the plague rife, and the Adventurers poor, and he returned after doing little but get a supply of trading goods. With him came news of the death, not only of Robert Cushman, but of John Robinson.

Meanwhile, the settlers had been sending over cargoes of beaver and other furs at every opportunity to pay their debts; they were thrown entirely on their own resources for trading and planting, and could they have obtained trading goods and clothing at moderate prices from home, would speedily have become prosperous. But the knowledge of their necessities gave everyone an opportunity to swindle them, and they had to pay whatever price was asked. Moreover, there was some competition now. In 1626, feeling that they must come to a definite understanding with the Adventurers, Isaac Allerton was sent over to England to arrange terms with them, and he effected an agreement by which they gave up all claims, past and present, on the planters, in consideration of £1800, that is, they sold their rights in the plantation to Isaac Allerton and his associates for £1,800, to be paid at the rate of £200 yearly to five of their number, Pocock, Beauchamp, Keane, Base and Sherley.

Thus the colony bought out the interest of the English partners, Bradford and seven others (together with the four London merchants who had before offered to support them), becoming bound on behalf of the whole colony for £1,800. The responsibility for the debt was divided amongst a partnership consisting of all heads of families and able young men in the colony, to each of whom shares in the plantation were given, and who in return promised to pay each a sum proportionate to his shares towards clearing off the debt, should the trade of the community not suffice. The land and cattle were now divided, to each was appointed by lot twenty acres of land, besides the one acre which they already had, and to keep the people close together, it was agreed that those who had their lots nearest the town should allow the others the use of part of their land for four years, after which they should have the use of as much land in the outer lots for the same length of time. No meadow land was given, as they had little of it ; it was allotted each year, and no permanent division was made until 1633. Then the Governor and a few others had their houses given to them ; and those belonging to other men were valued, each keeping his own, and those who had the better ones giving something in compensation to those who had the worse.

Bradford, Standish, Allerton, Winslow, Brewster, and three others, who had on behalf of the colony accepted liability for the £1800, as well as other debts amounting to £600, determined to hire the trade of the whole community for a term of years, to enable them to discharge it. They were to have the exclusive use of the pinnace, the bass boat, and the trading stores; they were to have the whole produce of trade in skins, etc., for six years, and each purchaser was to pay to them three bushels of corn or six pounds of tobacco yearly for six years. In return

15

they undertook the debts, and promised to bring over £50 worth of shoes and hose to sell to the planters for corn at six shillings a bushel, and at the end of the six years the whole trade was to return to the use of the colony. This agreement was signed by Bradford, Brewster, Standish, Allerton, Winslow, Howland, Alden, and Prince, who were called the Undertakers, and also by the four London merchants, who had promised to support them, Sherley, Beauchamp, Andrews, and Hatherley, and it was taken to England in 1627 by Allerton, to be ratified by the Company of Adventurers.

With this composition of the Undertakers, the life of the colony entered upon a new phase. It was no longer conducted on entirely communistic principles; it was no longer subject to any interference in church or civil matters, save from King James and his delegates, it was at liberty to decide for itself who should and who should not become settlers within its limits. The load of debt was no less heavy, but it could be cheerfully carried when it did not involve also moral obligations which warred against the dearest principles of the Pilgrim Church.

Their trade had been rapidly improving; from their early dealings with the Indians near at hand and around Massachusetts Bay they had gradually extended operations over a larger area. In 1624 a patent was granted to Cushman, Winslow, and their associates, for Cape Ann, and although the grant was probably invalid for technical reasons connected with the position of the Plymouth Virginia Company, they had a trade depot there for some time. The next year Winslow and some others had gone to the Kennebec river on a trading expedition, and had been so successful that they decided to get a patent for Kennebec, where they built a house and furnished it for trade. They were, too, the first English to possess a settlement on the Connecticut River. Their success enabled them to send over large cargoes of beaver to pay their debts, and had they been better provided with trading commodities from home, they would soon have been in a position to free themselves. But they could obtain none from the Adventurers, and all they could get from stray ships, or other trading stations were at a very dear rate. Corn was therefore their main staple of exchange, and after the granting of land in particular, they had a plentiful supply of it, and did well, until the envy and thoughtlessness of other traders led them to undersell. The *Little James* was sent over by the Adventurers in 1623 to stay in the plantation and trade, but she had such a bad crew and was so ill provided with trading goods, that the scheme was an entire failure, and after being wrecked and recovered, at great expense, she was sent home again.

Fishing, that mine of wealth which had roused Smith's enthusiasm, the planters had no success in whatever from first to last. Either from want of experience, or want of proper implements, every such attempt ended in disaster. But with this exception, the efforts of the colonists at trade and agriculture prospered when they depended on themselves alone, whilst those which were dictated by the Adventurers and governed by them, were frequently a failure.

Freed from the hampering conditions under which they had been working, there was every prospect of speedy prosperity, and a final liquidation of their heavy debts. Sherley was the chief of the four London merchants, sometimes called the "Friends of the Pilgrims"; a man of whom Cushman wrote that he had "by his freeheartedness been the only glue of the Company" before the final disunion of the Adventurers, and he became their agent or factor in England, Beauchamp being associated with him for the purpose.

The first use the Pilgrims made of their freedom was to send for the remainder of their friends from Leyden, and in 1629, at great expense, they managed to get them transported to the colony in the *Talbot* and the *Mayflower*. The Leyden Church was united once more, although its pastor was dead, and only his widow and children were left to join the flock, and one great hope of the settlers seemed to be realised.  They were now able to regulate both the ecclesiastical and civil government of the colony according to their ideals, but its financial position soon became very precarious.  Whether it was that the distance from England robbed men of any feeling of responsibility towards them, or whether their helplessness made them legitimate prey to all unscrupulous persons, they were certainly cheated and deceived on all hands, and often with a show of religious feeling and parade of piety that would make frank knavery seem pleasant.

It soon became obvious that Sherley, who had seemed to be their friend, was playing them false for his own interests, and worse still, that Isaac Allerton, who had been their emissary in the negotiations of the last few years, was not only conniving at Sherley's doings, but trying to profit himself to the hurt of the community.  He first roused their displeasure in 1628, when he brought over a crazy minister, whom they were at great charge to send back ; and also brought goods of his own to trade with, as well as those brought for the colony.  He had no clear account, or distinction between them, so that those which sold readily he declared to be his, and those that were left, he said belonged to the colony.  The following year, in spite of his dissatisfaction, the Governor felt obliged to send him again, as he was in the middle of various complicated negotiations which no one else would understand, he could best help the Leyden people over, and he was trying to get them a new patent, defining the limits of their territory both at Plymouth and Kennebec, and granting them powers of government by royal charter. So Allerton was sent in 1629 with strict injunctions to run them into no expense, and to bring only the trading goods according to his instructions.  Again he played them false, bringing many things which they did not want, and although he apparently procured a new patent granted to William Bradford, his heirs, associates and assigns, from the Council for New England, he did not obtain a royal charter. Bradford thought that he purposely delayed this on some excuse about freedom from customs, in order that he might be sent again the next year to conclude. The delay was fatal, and a royal charter was never obtained.

Although Bradford was angry with Allerton for this breach of trust, he disliked quarrelling with him, since he was son-in-law to Brewster, whom all loved and respected, and also he judged him charitably, thinking he erred from lack of judgment rather than intention.

Meanwhile they had reason to think that Sherley, too, was taking advantage of them. He and the other London partners, sent over in 1629 a young man named Edward Ashley to trade at Penobscot, inviting the planters to become partners with him, or in any case to give him all the help they could. They knew him to be a bad character, and greatly disliked the venture, but seeing that he would in any case be better supplied with trading goods than they were, and would ruin their trade in the district, and fearing to offend their London partners if they refused, they accepted the offer of partnership, and joined with Ashley a man from Leyden on whom they could rely. But this arrangement led to great complication of accounts. Moreover, Ashley managed to get most of the supplies from England, and much from the plantation, and whilst he let these stand on the general account, and refused to pay for them, he sold his beaver in England without sharing with the planters.

In despair at the difficulty of getting trading goods, the Pilgrims, in an unhappy moment, conceived the idea of hiring a ship in the West of England, which should come fishing for them, and could bring their trading goods instead of salt, of which they happened to have a large supply. The Governor was not in favour of the scheme, he knew how fatal fishing had always been to them, and the misfortunes which had come upon any ship attached to the colony, but finally it was decided to refer it to their friends in England. Allerton was sent once more to conclude about the patent, to get a clear statement of their accounts; and if their friends approved of it, to hire a ship on condition that it was laden with trading goods for them and Ashley, but without trading goods, no ship. They thought they had given Allerton strait instructions enough, but the following spring came supplies to Ashley, and none to them, and no news from Sherley or Allerton. Later they heard rumours that one ship had been sent out to them for fishing, and had been driven back by foul weather, and that another ship had been bought by Allerton, in which he was on his way to the colony. Filled with consternation, they sent over Edward Winslow with their store of beaver, to find out the truth of things, for they felt they could no longer trust Allerton either to do their commissions, or to keep exact account of their debts and payments. There ensued lengthy disputes about the *Friendship* and the *White Angell*, the two ships of which they had heard, for the four London men wrote to say that they had hired the former for a fishing ship, and bought the latter for trading, and although all this was clean against the instructions of the planters, and although the *White Angell* did not even bring them the supplies they wanted, an attempt was made to charge the enormous expenses of both ships to their account. Allerton of course was dismissed from their employment, and Winslow sent them over trading supplies, but for years the dispute lasted as to whether the ships belonged to the colony, to Allerton, or to the four London merchants. Hatherley, another of the four, came over to the colony, and thoroughly investigated the plantation and trading houses, and he admitted that Allerton was obviously playing his own game, at the expense of the partners at either end, but he admitted also that if the venture were disastrous, as indeed it was, neither Allerton nor the four partners would own responsibility for it.

Bitterly the planters repented that they had entertained the idea of a ship at all; the suggestion had come from them first, and then had been taken up by Allerton and the partners, as the business of Ashley had been, in the hope of private gains if it did well, and with the intention of charging it on the plantation if their schemes miscarried. Hatherley was not a consenting party to this, and swore that neither ship had been set out for the colony. Allerton finally swore the same, and the planters refused to have any dealings with the ship at all, but Sherley would not consent to have it taken off their account. He hired the *White Angell* out to Allerton, who brought it to the colony and rivalled the trade of the planters everywhere, until the French, seeing that he was damaging their trade too, killed two of his men, and took all his goods. Finally, Allerton bought the ship for £2,000, and during the two years given him to pay for it, he collected all the money due to him as agent for the plantation and claimed it for his own. He was soon in difficulties again, and was being sued on all sides for debt, but though the planters had lost the most by him, they were apparently the only people who got nothing. Indeed, he tried to make out that they were in his debt for goods delivered, charging Brewster, for instance, with £200, and this he did out of meanness, knowing how it would grieve him to seem guilty of extravagance, and that the company would never let one so much respected fall under this burden of debt.

Their accounts were now in the wildest confusion, there was the general account with the company for supplies, the account for supplies sent to them in partnership with Ashley, and the account for the two ships. According to Mr Sherley, they now owed £4770, 19s. 2d., besides the £1,000 purchase money still due to the Adventurers; many things were charged twice over, and the accounts took years to unravel. Winslow's younger brother was sent over as accountant, and they hoped to get things straightened up, but there seemed a fate against them, for the ship in which the copies of accounts, and a list of exceptions to them, were sent to England, was cast away, and not only these papers, but their beaver, was lost.

To compensate for all their misfortunes, trade was excellent in these years, and though the Penobscot house was robbed by the French in 1632, and the colony was devastated by fever in 1633, they were able to send over enormous consignments of beaver, and other skins. It seemed like pouring water into a sieve, their debts grew no smaller, and in 1634 Winslow was sent over to try and finish off the accounts with the partners. He was not successful; Sherley declined to take off the *White Angell* account, and supplied them with goods without either invoice or prices, so that they had no guide as to their position. Moreover, although their accountant had begun well, he had later neglected his accounts, and then had fallen ill, so they felt themselves also to blame. As a climax, in 1636 and 1637 came letters from Andrews and Beauchamp complaining that they had had no money since 1631, when £1100 was owing to each of them, and that Sherley was constantly demanding more money from them. Nothing could be proved, and it was decided to send some beaver direct to them and to discharge Sherley from his agency, Beauchamp suing him without result.

In 1642, feeling that the tangle of accounts could never be unravelled, a composition was decided on. A meeting was called and the remains of the stock valued at £1400 in which valuation the planters really cheated themselves considerably. In payment of all debts and charges they became bound in £2400, for payment in £1200, to be paid £400 in two months, and £800 in yearly payments of £200. This arrangement was accepted by the London partners, and the proportion of payment to each was agreed upon, Andrews frankly admitting that he thought the planters had been wronged. But the Undertakers were growing old, and they were anxious for some composition which should not leave a legacy of debt to their successors; moreover the growth of the colony, and the increase of cattle, had turned men from trading to pastoral pursuits; they were more independent of English help, and anxious to make an end of the wearisome disputes. So, after more than twenty years, the connection with the Adventurers and their successors, the four London Undertakers, was at an end. Few of them visited the colony, but three of them, William Collier, William Thomas, and Timothy Hatherley, made it their home. The last, after several visits, settled at Scituate about 1635, became a freeman of the town, and a prominent member of the colony.

In their poverty and isolation, and ignorant of much business method, the colonists had suffered a great deal at their hands, but it must not be forgotten that, but for them, the enterprise would not have been, and that a few of them did sympathise with the Pilgrims, and had some thought beyond the success of the money venture. The Pilgrims at least were not ungrateful; in 1660 came an order of the Plymouth Court to send £20 to Mr Ling "one of the Marchant venterors att our first beginnings, being fallen to decay and haueing felt great extremity and poverty."[1] The money was to be raised by voluntary subscriptions from the townships, and any deficit was to be made up out of the Country Treasury.

With the grant of the patent to William Bradford, a patent which he resigned in 1641 to the freemen of Plymouth, and with the termination of trade relations with the English partners, Plymouth ceased to be in any sense proprietary, and her trade, her land system, her civil and ecclesiastical rule, were henceforth directed solely by the General Court of the colony itself.

[1] Records, iii. p. 191.

# CHAPTER XII

## NEIGHBOURING COLONIES

LONG before Plymouth had become commercially as well as politically independent, other colonies had settled on the shores of New England, and those relations had been entered upon which ended only in her absorption by Massachusetts.

The Plymouth Virginia Company, founded in 1606, had been much less vigorous and enterprising than the London Company, and had done very little in the way of colonization. Its members were few and poor, the only successful settlement on its territory was that of the Pilgrims, and this as we have seen had been purely accidental. Smith writes that although many ships went to New England for fishing after the publication of his "Relations," nothing was done for a plantation until some Brownists of England, Amsterdam and Leyden settled there. He had been made Admiral of the Company for life as a reward for his services, an office, however, which seemed to mean little or nothing. But at length, roused perhaps by Smith's untiring enthusiasm and glowing descriptions, or more probably by some desire to vie with the London Company, the Plymouth Virginia Company did make some deliberate efforts.

As soon as they began to take any interest in the matter at all, they discovered that their boundaries were very ill-defined, and so were their powers of jurisdiction, and to remedy this they applied in 1620 to King James for a new charter. They asked for the land between the fortieth and forty-eighth degrees, stretching

234

from sea to sea, with an entire monopoly of trade within their boundaries, and of fishing along their coasts. This raised an outcry, for hitherto the two Companies had had the right to fish in each other's waters, but in spite of the protests of the London Company, and long discussions on the legality of such a monopoly, the Charter was finally granted without any concessions being embodied in it. The charter re-established the Company as the "Council for the affairs of New England," and gave to the forty patentees, not only an enormous tract of land, but powers of legislation and jurisdiction throughout it, the right to appoint officials, and to instruct magistrates.

Far from being overwhelmed by the greatness of the favour conferred upon them, the patentees were very little interested. In plain language, they did not see what they were going to get out of it; the contributions of £100 which each member was asked to give towards starting the enterprise, were very badly paid up, and little was done. In June 1621 a patent was granted to the Pilgrims (in the name of John Pierce and his associates) authorising the settlement they had already made, but there was small demand for patents, and the enterprise threatened to languish once more.

To remedy this Sir Ferdinand Gorges, one of the few active members of the Council, issued a book called "A Briefe Relation of the Discovery and Plantation of New England," sketching the plan of the proposed colony, and the forms of government which the Council meant to adopt, and an attempt was made to organise the country on these lines.

There was really very little to organise. Besides the patent to John Pierce and his associates, which was in the nature of a public grant, the Council had issued a few private patents. Thomas Weston had obtained one of these, and in June 1622 sent over fifty or sixty men at his own charge to form an independent plantation. They were a thoroughly worthless set, and after having injured the Plymouth men as far as they could, and abused the natives in every possible way, they narrowly escaped being massacred altogether, and abandoned their settlement at Wessagusset.

But in spite of the emptiness of the country, the Council determined that its government must be put upon a proper footing. To Robert Gorges, son of Sir Ferdinand, was granted for the sum of £160 a tract of land extending ten miles along the coast of Massachusetts Bay, and thirty miles into the interior,[1] and he was at the same time made general Governor of the country. Francis West was sent out with him as Admiral, to regulate the fishing, and Morrell, a clergyman of the Church of England, to superintend the churches, and ensure their orthodoxy. About the same time, the domains of the Council were divided by lot amongst the patentees, and a portion of land definitely assigned to each. But even this failed to arouse the interest of most, and the efforts of the Council seemed doomed to failure.

Gorges started a settlement at Quincy, but his men were too few, and stayed little more than a year in the country.

As Governor-General he was no more successful. He apparently claimed no jurisdiction over Plymouth, though he was well received there, and given much sound advice by Bradford. He did attempt to bring Weston to book for the conduct of his men, but there was little to be gained by that, and the futile quarrel was abandoned.

Apparently West's powers as admiral were no more effectively enforced; and Morrell, who might have interfered uncomfortably with the liberties of the Plymouth church, contented himself with writing a dull poem describing the country.

Gorges soon gave up the government in despair and

---

[1] S. P. Col. vol. ii., no. 14, Dec. 30th, 1622.

abandoned his claim, which passed at his death first to his brother, and then to John Oldham and Sir William Brereton.

Sir Ferdinand Gorges was full of schemes[1] for developing the country; a tract of land on the Sagadahoc was to be reserved for a public plantation, with a great public city in the fork of the two rivers, which they would petition the king to name; a proposal was made to send out poor children of the age of fourteen and upwards, who might under a statute of Elizabeth be bound as apprentices to the colony. Another proposal was made to settle a "strength" in New England, consisting of two hundred men at a charge of £4,000, some gentlemen who could bear arms and attend the Governor, some handicraftsmen, and some husbandmen. But for lack of money and enthusiasm among the patentees, all his schemes came to nothing.

The one thing which the Council could do was to grant lands, and this it did feverishly, without noticing very much whether the new grants overlapped or superseded the old ones. Even in granting lands it was hampered, for so few people cared to have them, and so the few received enormous territories. The two men who chiefly benefited were Sir Ferdinand Gorges and John Mason. In 1622 Mason received a grant of the land between Naumkeag and the Merrimac, and a few months later he and Gorges together were given the great stretch of land between the Merrimac and Kennebec rivers. This included the land between the Merrimac and Piscataqua, which in 1629 was regranted to Mason; and on the following day he and Gorges together received a grant of the district called Laconia, about Lake Champlain. Mason in 1635 received a further grant of the land between Salem and Piscataqua.

As a result of these grants, a plantation was started in 1623 at Piscataqua under David Thomson, and another

[1] S. P. Col., 1622 and 1623.

at Monhegan, which had hitherto been only a fishing
station, but neither of these grew or prospered for many
years.  The settlements at Piscataqua were the origin of
the state of New Hampshire, and would have been under
the absolute ownership of Mason but for his death in
1635.  The property proved so expensive to his family,
that it was before long divided among his servants and
feudatories, and they became practically free both as to
tenure and government.  Round Monhegan gradually
grew up the state of Maine, but grants of land there were
made so rapidly, and their boundaries were so ill-defined,
that small settlements were scattered all along the
coast, and organised colonization was delayed.

The land about Massachusetts Bay, which Smith calls
"the paradise of these parts," was the most favourable
place in New England for a settlement.  Weston's men
had tried it, Captain Robert Gorges had tried it, and in
1625 came one Captain Wollaston, with three or four
more eminent men and many servants, to found a colony
near Wessagusset, at the place now called Braintree.
They called their settlement Mount Wollaston, but it was
soon known to fame as the Merry Mount, for with them
was Thomas Morton, the "Lord of Misrule," whose name
spelt anathema to the Puritans.  Wollaston and his
friends, finding little profit or pleasure in the place,
moved on to Virginia, leaving a man called Fitcher in
charge.  Morton quickly drove him out, made himself
"Myne Hoste of Māre Mount," and led in all its revels.
He determined to celebrate the new name of the
settlement, set up a maypole, brewed beer, provided a case
of bottles, and kept open house for all comers.  A song
was made to be sung with a "corus," performed in a
dance hand in hand round the maypole, whilst one of the
company sang and "filled out the good liquor like
Gammede and Jupiter."  Such revels were heathenish in
the eyes of the Plymouth men, and the maypole seemed
to them hardly less evil than the golden calf.  "They

termed it an Idoll ; yea they called it the calfe of Horeb ;
and stood at defiance with the place, naming it Mount
Dagon ; threatening to make it a woefull mount, and not
a merry mount." [1]

But worse still, they found that Morton and his men
were selling firearms to the natives, and teaching them
their use. This was a real danger, and the Plymouth
men determined to join with those at Piscataqua and the
other scattered settlements, at the expense of sending
Morton back to England.

They gave him fair warning, telling him of the
proclamation of King James forbidding anyone to trade
with the Indians in firearms and ammunition. His reply
was a defiance ; complaints were made of him to the
Council for New England, and Standish was sent to take
him by force. But he escaped and went to England, not
as a culprit but as a hero, at least in his own eyes, and
triumphing over the annoyance of the Plymouth men.
"Captaine Shrimp tore his clothes for anger. . . . The
rest were eager to have torne their haire from theire heads,
but it was so short, that it would give them no hold." [2]
He returned to New England, in spite of their attempts to
keep him away, and published a scurrilous account of his
doings and of their attack on him. But he was not to
triumph long, for other settlers came to Massachusetts
Bay, who would tolerate such men as he as little as the
Pilgrims would ; his maypole was cut down, he was " set
in the bilboes, and sent prisoner to England," and there
lodged in Exeter Gaol.

These three attempts to colonize Massachusetts had
effected nothing, except to raise up a host of difficulties
for future comers. But no failures could disguise the fact
that it was an ideal spot for a settlement, and one was
soon begun on a much larger scale.

On January 1st, 1624, the Plymouth men had gained a
patent for Cape Ann in the names of Cushman and

[1] Morton's " New English Canaan," p. 134.          [2] p. 140.

Winslow, and in the autumn of the same year they sold to a fishing company of Dorchester a piece of land there, on which a community might be established for farming and hunting, so as to make a sort of home for the fishermen of Dorchester and other West of England towns, who were often for months upon the coast without any facilities for religious worship or instruction.

The Rev. Mr White, a Puritan minister of Dorchester, had long been anxious to do something for them, and the year before had sent out men to found a colony, but they had been unsuitable in various ways, and nothing was done.   Meanwhile, the Plymouth men had started a trading house at Nantasket, and to it went Roger Conant, Lyford and Oldham, and some others who were discontented with the religious views of the older colony.

When therefore in 1624, White and the Dorchester Company, having purchased their land, sent out a second relay of colonists, they invited Roger Conant, and one or two other men of ability and experience, to undertake the conduct of the new plantation and to become agents for the adventure.   Once more, however, the scheme was abandoned by the merchants, who saw that it could not be profitable unless organised differently ; they paid all wages and offered passage money to all their employees, and most of the colonists departed in 1626.   Conant decided to remain, and with three companions removed to Naumkeag, afterwards called Salem, on Massachusetts Bay, but so great were their hardships that they were on the point of returning, when letters came from White persuading them to remain a little longer and promising them help and support.

White had now resolved on establishing a place of refuge for persecuted Puritans, and in March 1628, six gentleman of Dorchester, presumably of his way of thinking, bought from the Council for New England a belt of land from the Atlantic to the Pacific, three miles south of the River Charles and Massachusetts Bay, and three miles north of every part of the River Merrimac. This purchase gave them no rights of government, but they were to hold the land direct from the king, and not from the Council, and so were freed from its jurisdiction. Unfortunately, part of the territory sold to them had already been granted to Captain Robert Gorges, and this led to disputes with Oldham, who had succeeded to his claim, and to unceasing enmity with Sir Ferdinand Gorges.

These six patentees were free to associate others with themselves, and White found no difficulty in discovering kindred spirits. About the same time, a number of men in Lincolnshire were anxious to plant the pure Gospel in America, and to live there in peace, and their plan became known to people in London and the West Country.

Amongst these Puritans were Winthrop, Dudley, Johnson, Pyncheon, Eaton, Saltonstall, and Bellingham. These bought up the rights of three of the Dorchester men, and with the remaining three, Humphrey, Endicott, and Whetcomb, became the founders of Massachusetts Colony.

They already possessed a patent for the land, and on February 27th, 1629, this was confirmed,[1] and they were permitted to incorporate themselves under the name of the Governor and company of Massachusetts Bay in America. A few days later, they received a royal charter granting them definite powers of government and legislation.

The Crown was to nominate the governor and assistants for the first year, after which the corporation was empowered to elect them annually ; and in their general assembly, which was to meet four times a year or oftener, they might pass any laws not repugnant to the laws of England.

Their religious position was interesting. The governor was permitted to administer the oaths of supremacy and

[1] S. P. Col., vol. v., 1629, Feb. 27th.

allegiance, but was not compelled to [do so, and he was also permitted to transport to the colony any persons who wished to join it except such as were restrained " by special name." So although no provision was made for religious liberty, and although the members of the corporation were not professedly Separatists, it followed naturally that the emigrants would be chiefly those Puritans who could not live peaceably at home, and that the religion of the colony would soon differ widely from that of England.

An equally great departure was made from the spirit of the Charter in political matters. Powers of government had been conferred, not on the colony as such, but on a trading corporation in England, which could regulate its affairs at will. Some of the earliest emigrants even complained that they were slaves to the corporation. But a proposal was made and finally agreed to, that the Charter should be transferred from the whole Company to those only who should emigrate to the colony. There was nothing in the Charter to decide where the corporation should have its seat of government, it had the right to admit others to its body as freemen, and by this transference the emigrants secured rights of self-government, and Massachusetts became practically independent of outside control.

Long before the question of the Charter was finally settled, the stream of emigration had begun.

In June 1628 Endicott was sent out in charge of the first company, numbering about 100. No doubt Conant and his fellows rejoiced at this accession of strength, but the sufferings of the newcomers were at least as great as theirs had been. Samuel Fuller, the physician of Plymouth Colony, was with them tending the sick throughout the whole winter. Most of them settled with Conant at Naumkeag, but a few strayed through the woods to what is now Charlestown, then inhabited by one solitary Englishman.

By the following year (1629), the enterprise was more widely known, the position of the colony was securely established by its Charter, and two hundred people sailed on the first of May with the Rev. Francis Higginson. He himself has written an interesting account of their voyage and early days. He was an ideal leader, enthusiastic and tolerant. He was a nonconforming minister, and persecuted as such, but was so far from bitterness against England that, as the ships lost sight of land, he bade his followers look lovingly back and say not " Farewell Rome, Farewell Babylon," but " Farewell dear England; Farewell the Church of God in England, and all the Christian friends there." Higginson was a man rather of the type of John Robinson and the Pilgrims, than of the later more rigid Puritans, and the colony had a great loss in his death during the first winter. His followers settled, some at Salem with Endicott, some at Charlestown.

In 1630 about 1500 people sailed from England, including John Winthrop of Groton in Suffolk who was to be Governor, and the whole body of assistants, bearing with them the Charter on which all their liberties depended. The Charter itself became an object of the greatest veneration, and Morton's jeering allusions to it, and its case, were considered almost greater offences than his violation of the proclamation of King James. Winthrop had it carried with him as he made his progresses, and Morton declared that the common people took it for a musical instrument, and " thought. . . this man of Littleworth had bin a fidler."

Winthrop's landing must have been a sad one; the first comers were wasted by disease and on the verge of starvation; instead of helping, they had to be helped. Building began at once, but the company scattered somewhat, driven afield in search of food. Charlestown was favoured first, but the water there proved bad, and some moved to Noddle's Island, some to Dorchester, others, invited by Blaxton, a settler who had remained when Gorges' plantation broke up, came to a place called Shawmut, and bought out any rights which Blaxton had in the locality. They called it Trimountain, from the three hills near by, but it is famous under the name of Boston, given out of compliment to the Lincolnshire men, and especially John Cotton, a clergyman of Boston in England.

The first winter was a terrible one, as it was to all colonies. Building went on slowly, and tents for a long time were the only protection they had against the bitter weather. Hardship and change of climate produced a fatal sickness; Lady Arabella Johnson and her husband, two chief promoters of the colony, died before many months were over, and multitudes found in the new country not a home, but a grave. About one hundred deserted and returned to England, but for the most part the colonists kept a brave heart, and were upheld by a sense of their great mission. A solemn awe hangs over the stories of their sufferings, but there is in them nothing of the sordid ignoble character which had made the adventures of Weston's men so despicable. The sufferers seemed to be uplifted, and something of their influence touches even those who read, and makes it possible to understand Governor Winthrop's words to his wife : " I thank God," he wrote, " I like so well to be here, as I do not repent my coming. I would not have altered my course, though I had foreseen all these afflictions. I never had more content of mind."

With the establishment of Plymouth and Massachusetts colonization in New England had seriously begun, and was to advance with great strides in the years which followed. The two colonies had many points in common ; both had their origin in religious enthusiasm ; in both the settlers had aims of their own, quite distinct from those of the Adventurers who sent them out, aims which encouraged them to overcome the early difficulties of a settlement, and which prevented their enterprise from ever being wholly, or even largely, commercial. Both colonies became very independent in government, Plymouth through the accident of her first arrival, Massachusetts through her Charter and through her own liberal interpretation of the rights it gave.

These two, the first successful colonies in New England, had each been established independently of the efforts of the New England Council, and that Council, and particularly Sir Ferdinand Gorges, had very little good to say about them. They were objected to for their lack of commercial ambition, for their independence in civil government, and for the irregularity of their religious views. Gorges in 1634 complained that the Plymouth people were disaffected to the Government, and would seek to fortify themselves by the aid of the Dutch; he accused them of inviting the Dutch to settle at Hartford in Connecticut, and asked "whether it be not more than time these people should be looked into."[1]

But Plymouth was unaggressive, and had no chartered rights to attack, and the bulk of opposition was directed against Massachusetts. Many attempts were made to check emigration without licence, constant complaints were made about the discontented and factious people who resorted to the colony, and a determined attack on its franchises, begun in 1637, was only obviated by the confusion of affairs in England.

There is little doubt that the founders of Massachusetts deliberately intended to start an independent form of government. In buying their land from the New England Council, they had arranged to hold it directly from the King, instead of through the Council, as Plymouth did, thus getting rid of one source of interference with their actions. And by removing their corporation and the Charter to the colony, they had very largely lessened any

[1] S. P. Col., vol. viii., no. 34.   November (?) 1634.

chance of interference by the Crown, or by their merely commercial associates.

They aimed at an equally complete independence in religious matters. They had come out nominally as Puritans of the Church of England, but no sooner had they arrived than they set up churches which resembled far more closely the churches of the Separatists, and to these churches they demanded strict conformity throughout the colony.

Before Winthrop reached New England at all, the note of religious conflict had been sounded. Higginson's followers subscribed a covenant by which a self-constituted church was set up, asking no consent from king or magistrate, electing its own officers, and rejecting both liturgy and ceremonies. Such a church might have been expected by anyone who understood the conditions under which the colony had been established, but apparently it came as a shock to some of the emigrants. John and Samuel Browne, both influential and able men, refused to join the church, and gathered a company to worship according to the Book of Common Prayer. They were no doubt justified by the letter of the Charter, which assumed the laws of England to hold good in the colony, but to the Puritan colonists the act seemed to violate their place of refuge. It was treated as sedition and mutiny, and the Brownes, who would not be suppressed, were sent like criminals to England. That the episcopal system from which they had suffered so much, should ever gain a footing in the colony, was a horrible thought to its leaders, and having now the power to repel it, they did so. They thought they were driving out the serpent from their paradise; but they were coming perilouly near to the persecution which had dimmed the records of the English Church. They had had glimpses of the principle of liberty of conscience, but saw its bearing only on their own case; and the great aim of religious peace, which had supported them through untold sufferings, was so imperfectly understood, so narrowly interpreted, that the credit of having such an aim at all has been almost blotted out.

Not only did they insist on conformity, and that to a system which would gain no support in England, but they bound the ideas of church and commonwealth so closely together, that an attack on the one meant an attack on the other.

This created great difficulties, and led to very harsh measures, for many of the colonists were of a dissenting nature, and yet the slightest criticism of the Massachusetts system, the slightest divergence from uniformity, was crushed down at once with all the weight which clergy and magistrates could bring to bear upon it. No one could become a freeman of the colony, who was not also a church member, and as only a freeman could share in legislation, the election of officers, or any other work of active citizenship, the government of the colony was confined to a comparatively small oligarchy whose views were orthodox. Legislation and jurisdiction were in the hands of this oligarchy, led by a united body of magistrates and clergy, and so the spheres of Church and State became really identical, and their interests were inseparably linked.

Of the narrow, limited state of society which resulted, and of the repressive measures taken to prevent the introduction of any new ideas, no more can be said here than will explain the upgrowth of other colonies which had their origin in religious dissent.

The first serious trouble which the Massachusetts system brought upon its authors, was in the matter of Roger Williams. He came to the colony a few months after Winthrop's arrival, "a young minister, godly and zealous." He was a Puritan; educated at Charter House and Cambridge, and was probably at one time admitted to orders, for he appears to have been chaplain in 1629 to Sir William Masham of Otes in Essex. Sir Edward

Coke had been his friend, but Williams became discontented with the ceremonies and principles of the English Church, and was forced to fly from its consequent persecution. Coke had no words bad enough for him after his apostasy; it is said that his daughter kept some letters of Williams' that their evidence might hang him if ever he set foot in England again. With this deadly enmity behind him, he sailed for America, but found no more congenial views surrounding him there.

He stayed for a short time in Massachusetts on his first arrival, and there gave offence by refusing fellowship with the Boston church, because its members had formerly been in communion with English churches, and would not declare their repentance. As Massachusetts still kept up a nominal friendship with the Church of England, such advanced Separatism seemed to them dangerous and compromising.

Further, he denied the right of magistrates to punish offences against the first four commandments, and this seemed like an attack on the Calvinistic system, which demanded state support in enforcing every kind of church discipline.

The Presbyterian instincts of Massachusetts took fright, and when Salem, always the most separatist church of the colony, invited Williams to be its teacher, it was discouraged, and Williams retired to Plymouth.

Whilst there he committed a further offence. Throughout his life he showed extraordinary affection and sympathy for the Indians, carrying it so far as to learn their difficult language, to which in later years he wrote a "Key." This sympathy led him to champion their rights, and he declared that a patent from King or Company was no just claim to the country, which in truth belonged to the natives, and on this subject he wrote a treatise. His act seemed to Massachusetts to be a direct attack on their precious Charter, and, when after two years in Plymouth, Williams returned to Salem, he was severely censured by the Court at Boston. At first he seemed to retract, but a year later, he attacked the Charter once more, denounced the Church of England, and in 1634 refused to take the resident's oath, on the grounds that an oath was an act of worship, not to be imposed indiscriminately upon pious and impious men.

At this rather inauspicious moment, the church at Salem invited him to be their teacher. Williams was admonished by the Court at Boston, and " dealt with " by the church; Salem was accused of insubordination, temporarily disfranchised, and denied a grant of land for which it petitioned.

After a lengthy and complicated dispute, Salem renounced Williams, and Williams renounced all the churches of the colony, and, as he continued to maintain his opinions, he was finally ordered to leave the jurisdiction within six weeks. Then he was said to be ill, and the Court granted him leave to remain until the spring, but his utterances were so unguarded that it repented of its mercy, and decided to send him to England.

But when Williams received the summons to come to Boston and embark, for the first time he failed to appear. He had left Salem and fled into the woods in the bitter winter weather, to find amongst the Indians more kindness than amongst his own people. They repaid his friendship now with shelter and protection ; Massasoit of the Pokanokets, and Canonicus of the Narragansetts were his friends for life, and he could make peace between them and the English, when all other means had failed.

He thought first of settling at Seekunck, close to Narragansett Bay, but a letter from Winslow advised him that it was within the bounds of Plymouth, and so he crossed the water, and, with five companions, settled at the place which they called " Providence," and so the foundations of the state of Rhode Island were laid. There was some idea that this place, too, was within the Plymouth bounds, but Bradford declared that, even if it were so,

Williams should not be "molested and tossed up and down again, while they had breath in their bodies." Winthrop himself, who had always befriended him, suggested this place of settlement, urging its freedom from English claims or patents. Williams gained a title-deed to the land from Canonicus and Miantonomoh, the Narragansett chiefs, but wished to reserve nothing to himself, but to give away lands to all who came. Nor was he more greedy of political power; a community gathered round him and was governed on purely democratic lines, a compact being made by the settlers to submit themselves to the laws and magistrates that they themselves had set up, but in civil matters only. Thus entire religious and intellectual freedom was secured, and Williams was at last at liberty to work out his principles to their logical conclusion.

It is a disputed point whether the banishment of Williams could be considered an act of religious persecution. It appears from his own testimony, as well as from that of some contemporaries, that his assertion of "soul liberty," his determination to separate civil and ecclesiastical matters, were not the chief charges against him. It was his attack on the Charter, and his tendency to involve the colony with the English Government, which were his unpardonable sins. But the pressure which was brought to bear upon him by the churches, and their interference with the independent action of the church at Salem, gave the whole affair an ecclesiastical significance, and illustrated the extent to which clergy and magistrates stood together in any attack on either. And the later development of Williams' views on the sanctity of conscience, and on the powerlessness of the magistrate to control opinion, or to compel forms of worship, placed him in a light of opposition to the Massachusetts Puritans, and insensibly leads people to believe that his religious ideas were the real, though unacknowledged, reasons of his banishment.

One more colony owed its origin to the severity of the Massachusetts system, but in this case the dangers which led to persecution were probably more real than in the case of Williams.

Nothing had steeled the hearts of Elizabeth and James against the Puritans more than the fear that, by permitting freedom of religious opinion, they would undermine their civil authority, and no accusation had been more fervently denied. And yet as soon as the Puritans were in the position of rulers, they took the same view. To them, religious dissent and political sedition seemed necessarily to go together; they had built up their little state with difficulty, and dreaded to see its solidarity endangered by too much freedom of opinion. But some of the later settlers felt this responsibility less, were even more interested in nice theological divergences than in the consolidation of the colony, and they soon found themselves in opposition to the conservatives. Amongst the several extreme parties which gained a hearing was that of the Antinomians, who asserted the doctrine of justification by faith alone, and the entire uselessness of good works.

Their leaders, Mrs Anne Hutchinson, and her brother-in-law John Wheelwright, declared that all the ministers of the colony except Mr Cotton, who hovered on the brink of Antinomianism, were under "a covenant of works," and thus the ministry was discredited in the eyes of many. The whole town of Boston was very much affected by the heresy, which gained a political significance through the favour which Governor Vane showed to it, whilst Winthrop, the ex-Governor, was its sternest opponent. Obviously too, the doctrines were dangerous and awkward, not only to the ministry, but to any office holders, since it was asserted that a right to direct belonged only to those who, by their inward conviction, felt themselves to be worthy, and to none other was obedience due.

The magistrates came to the aid of the traduced ministers; the general court of election was removed from Boston, to escape Antinomian influence, and Winthrop was chosen Governor. The men of Boston, who had acted as sergeants to Vane, refused to follow the new Governor; and not a church member of Boston would serve on the levy for the Pequod war, because the army chaplain was one of Mrs Hutchinson's greatest enemies. But the rebellious church was crushed down with an iron hand. All the other churches of the colony united in a Synod to condemn the followers of Mrs Hutchinson; the newly elected magistrates formed a strong conservative majority, and the Antinomian leaders were banished from the country. Wheelwright added to his offence by threatening appeal to England, and so turning a religious dispute into a political attack on the independence of Massachusetts. With some friends, he founded the town of Exeter on the Piscataqua, but Anne Hutchinson and the greater number of their followers went southwards. Invited by Roger Williams, they settled for a time on the island of Rhode Island, and prospered in spite of some dissensions amongst them. Their government was a democracy, and " it was further ordered that none be accounted a delinquent for doctrine."

But Mrs Hutchinson later removed into the territory of the Dutch, for one of her sons and a son-in-law, venturing to plead her case before the Court at Boston, were sentenced to long imprisonment, and she feared that her retirement to Rhode Island would no longer serve to protect her. An insurrection among the Indians was provoked by Kieft, her house was set on fire, and of the whole family, only one child remained alive.

Not all the colonies which sprang from Massachusetts had such an unhappy origin. So great was the stream of emigration to the older colony before the Civil War, that some outlet had to be found for it. As early as 1635 a little band of pioneers made their way inland to Concord, now by its associations one of the most interesting towns of New England, and almost at the same time came the migration to Connecticut.

This beautiful valley was owned under a grant from the Council for New England by the Earl of Warwick, and was afterwards assigned to Lord Say and Seal, Lord Brooke, John Hampden, and others. But before they could take steps to colonise it, it was made known to the Plymouth men by the Dutch, and later by some Mohegan Indians, who had been driven out by the Pequods, and wanted the white men's help against them. They invited them to trade there, and the Plymouth men asked Massachusetts for help and co-operation, but failing to get it, established a trading-house alone at Windsor in 1633. The right sachem was reinstated, and a tract of land was bought from the Indians, but everything seemed to conspire against their peaceful possession of it. The Dutch regretted their information, and threatened to set up a rival trading-house at Hartford ; by reinstating the Mohegan sachem, they had made enemies of the powerful Pequods ; and in 1635 the Massachusetts people, who had at first looked coldly on the adventure, began to hanker after the Connecticut River territory.

In the autumn of 1635 some sixty men, women, and children, of Roxbury and Watertown, having gained a tardy permission from their government, migrated westward, but the season was too late. Winter overtook them before their houses were built, their cattle were destroyed, and many of them were driven to face the perils of the return journey, rather than live on under such privations.

But in the following year came a much greater migration, chiefly from Newtown and Dorchester, led by Thomas Hooker. Driving their cattle with them, camping by the wayside, about one hundred settlers made their way slowly through the forests. Some of the best spirits of

Massachusetts were amongst them; Vane, Peters, and the younger Winthrop were all active promoters of the new colony. Winthrop had been appointed Governor by the Warwick patentees, and was able to pacify all previous claims to the land, save that of the Dutch, who were constantly hostile.

For a year the colony was governed by rulers named in a commission issued by the General Court at Boston, but Connecticut was a true child of Massachusetts, and showed herself as independent of the older colony as that colony had been of England. At the end of a year, she took the reins into her own hands, and set up a form of government slightly more liberal, slightly more democratic, than that of the parent colony, but resembling it in many important particulars. Towns rapidly sprang up, and its rich meadows, its convenience for trading purposes, made the Connecticut valley seem, in spite of surrounding dangers, a veritable land of promise. Not until 1662 did it receive a charter from England, but this charter gave liberal powers of government, and extended the bounds of Connecticut to include the colony of New Haven, which had been founded in 1639 by John Davenport.

Davenport too had emigrated from Massachusetts after a very brief sojourn there, and had established a colony on strictly Puritan lines. His government was equally independent of Massachusetts and of England, and was based solely on the "worde of God." Its history, however, up to 1662 was uneventful, and the colony was only of importance to Plymouth as being a member of the later confederacy.

Such, roughly speaking, was the origin of the states which grouped themselves around Plymouth colony, and which drew her from the isolation of her early years. Her own expansion brought her into touch with them, and to them she naturally turned for help and association when perplexed by questions of general policy, and threatened by dangers from without. Naturally too the association, particularly with Massachusetts, grew closer as years went on, and as the Pilgrim leaders, with their strong individuality, gave place to weaker men, whose training had lacked the influences which gave to Plymouth her distinctive policy.

## CHAPTER XIII

### INDIAN RELATIONS

WHENEVER a colony of white men is planted successfully amongst savages, there may be found on the reverse side of its history, a tale of undeserved suffering, of ignorance driven to despair, of a weaker, more backward, race trodden down by the newcomers.

In the case of New England, the result is made almost more melancholy by the good intentions of the settlers. One of the chief reasons given by Bradford for coming to America was the hope that they might lighten the heathen darkness, and Cushman bases on their missionary endeavours his justification of their sojourn there. But they showed their good will in other ways than this, and followed the advice of Lord Bacon: "If you plant where savages are, do not only entertain them with trifles and gingles, but use them justly and graciously, with sufficient guard nevertheless." Each tract of land which they occupied, they honestly bought; everything they took in the way of corn, and utensils on their first landing, they paid for as soon as the owners were known, and outrages against the Indians were punished so severely that some of the community complained.

The laws and court regulations of Plymouth concerning the Indians are of various kinds.[1] Some are merely restrictive, in self-defence, and these vary, as the feeling between the races was friendly or the reverse. Chief of these were the laws forbidding truck with the Indians in

[1] Records, vol. xi.

guns, powder, ammunition or horses, boats or rigging; the laws against making payments to them in gold or silver (on account of the scarcity of coin), against admitting strange Indians into the jurisdiction, and against allowing them to come to Plymouth during court meetings, or to trade with foreign vessels in the harbour. Another class of laws is evidently meant to protect the Indian, both from himself and from unscrupulous white men. Such are the laws against buying, hiring, or receiving as a gift, any lands without the consent of the government, the frequent orders against selling wine, strong waters, beer or cider to the natives, the order for fixing boundaries between the lands of the English and the Indians, and for fencing in their cornlands.

A third class is both interesting and unique, for it aims at establishing a jurisdiction over the natives which would draw them into line with the English, and bring them, in certain respects, up to the same level of conduct. Laws were passed forbidding them to work on the Sabbath, to shoot either at night or on the Lord's Day, to become drunk, or to live idly. They were to receive justice for the trespassing of animals on their lands, their affairs were to be heard on a special day in the October and July courts, and minor disputes were to come before the select men of the townships. Their testimony was admitted without oath, their claims to land were to receive a fair hearing, and they were to be given due notice of any trial to be held. In later days, a magistrate was specially appointed to hold courts in their reservations, from which appeal could be had to the Court of New Plymouth.

In 1627 De Rasières wrote, "The tribes in their neighbourhood . . . are better conducted than ours, because the English give them the example of better ordinances and a better life, and who also, to a certain degree, give them laws, by means of the respect they from the very first have established amongst them."[1]

[1] Rasières' letter in Palfrey, i. 220.

17

Williams, too, observed that the savages watched the lives of the English very narrowly, and that they were specially impressed with the idea of keeping a day of rest.

The Pilgrims went far beyond mere justice towards the natives in their times of sickness, helping and tending them, burying their dead in the terrible epidemics of smallpox, and they earned a gratitude that safeguarded them more than fortifications and arms.

Friendship with the Indians was of the utmost importance to them in their early days; all the success of their trade, as well as the safety of the tiny colony, depended on it. Chance had tossed them to a lonely and somewhat barren part of the coast; to the north the nearest settlements were those of the English at Newfoundland, and Monhegan, and of the French at Nova Scotia, gradually extending towards Penobscot. To the south were the Dutch settlements at Manhattan, and the English in Virginia, 500 miles away. Until they had ships of a very different type from their little shallop, it was useless to rely on any of these for regular trade, much less for help in an emergency.

Owing to the great sickness which had swept over the district only a few years before they landed, there was no one to dispute their settlement at Plymouth, and so there was no immediate friction. One writer of 1643 gives a list of the ways in which God had blessed New England, and heads it with the sweeping away of the natives by smallpox.[1] As soon as a means of communication was found through Samoset and Squanto, the planters set to work to establish their position by obtaining the consent and goodwill of the neighbouring tribes. The chief groups with whom they came in contact at first were the Nausites, who owned the land around Cornhill, and with whom they had fought at the "First Encounter"; the Massasoits or

[1] New England's First Fruits.

Pokanokets to the south-west of Plymouth; the Narragansetts further south still, and the Massachusetts around Boston Bay.

After three years' life among these tribes, Winslow has left an interesting description of them and of their customs,[1] and his account may be enlarged from that of Roger Williams, who knew them perhaps more intimately than any white man of the day. Their instinctive devotion to the idea of a God, their interest in religious questions, their curious doubting attitude towards their own deities, are noted by every writer. They were always a little half-hearted about their own particular creed, a little doubtful as to the omnipotence of their gods, and very willing to learn something of a God who might be greater. "They have," writes Williams, "no clothes, Bookes, nor Letters, and conceive their Fathers never had; and therefore they are easily persuaded that the God that made the Englishmen is a greater God, because Hee hath so richly endowed the English above themselves : But when they heare that about sixteen hundred yeeres agoe England and the inhabitants thereof were like unto themselves, and since have received from God, Clothes, Bookes, etc., they are greatly affected with a secret hope concerning themselves."[2] According to Winslow, they acknowledged many divine powers, working under one supreme deity which had existed from all eternity. This was Kiehtan, "the very aged one," the chief and maker of all. Kiehtan had peopled the earth, and dwelt in the heavens, and to him, when they died, went all men, good and bad, to knock at his door. The good were admitted at once, but to the bad he said "Walk abroad," and so for ever "they wander in restless want and penury." Kiehtan no man had ever seen, but Hobbamock, the spirit of evil, appeared in many shapes, mostly in that of a

[1] Good News from New England. Arber, pp. 581-592.
[2] Williams' " Key." To the Reader.

snake, to holders of high office and renown, and "all of them strive to attain to that hellish height of honour." Others worshipped the far south-west, where the great god Cantantowwit held his court, and where dwelt the souls of their forefathers. From the south-west, they believed, came all their plenty, sprung from a grain of corn, a French and an English bean carried by a crow from the fields of the Great God. "And indeed," adds Williams, "the further north and west from us their corn will not grow, but to the south, better and better." The crow for this reason was sacred, and no man would ever kill one, however mischievous.

However they might divide the Godhead, all Indians believed that God made all, and that He would reward or punish, and that the soul was immortal. "Though the natives hold the soule to live ever, yet not holding a Resurrection, they die and mourn without Hope." They would disturb no man, themselves, the English or Dutch, in their conscience and worship.

The ruler over each tribe was a sachem or governor, whose office was hereditary; the greater sachems, such as Massasoit of Pokanoket, and Canonicus of Narragansett, were kings; the lesser were under their protection, and did homage to them. Each sachem knew the bounds of his own territory, and out of it he granted land to his people for corn-growing, receiving in return a yearly tribute of corn, and of venison also from the hunters.

The sachem could conclude nothing which concerned all without the consent of the people, but the administration of justice was one of his chief cares. He not only passed sentence upon wrongdoers, but executed it with his own hands, unless a mutiny was feared. Then he would send one of his warriors to "fetch off a head" unexpectedly. To his care were left the aged and destitute, the widows and fatherless, and Williams says that no beggars were found among them, nor fatherless children unprovided for. The sachem, too, dispensed the hospitality of the tribe, and in his house all travellers and strangers were lodged. The hospitality was sometimes rude, as Winslow himself experienced, but it was ungrudging. Anything they had to eat they would share with a stranger; Williams found more free entertainment among them than among Christians: "In wildernesse, in great distresse, these Ravens have fed me."

Chief among the men of every tribe were the Powahs or medicine men, who were supposed to have intimate dealings with the devil, and who exercised strange rites over the sick and wounded; and the Pineses, who were men of great courage and wisdom, chief in the field and in council. They stood as much upon their reputation as any men, and scorned deceit, discourtesy, or cowardice. They were men of great stature and strength, trained to hardness in their youth by extreme severities, and their fortitude under pain and torture was extraordinary. Toothache was, said Williams, "the onely paine that will force their stout hearts to cry"; to cry out under punishment was counted far greater shame than any fault, and under the most prolonged tortures the victim at the stake would heroically sing his death song, and hurl scorn upon his enemies and tormentors.

The men of the tribes spent their days in hunting and fishing, the women tending the [corn and doing all household duties. The only labour in the fields which men would do was setting tobacco, which was their sovereign remedy for colds, toothache and exhaustion. In any special work, such as the breaking up of fields, or the cutting up of a whale, the whole tribe worked together, the women doing most, but the men sometimes helping a little.

There was little reverence from man to woman, but much from youth to age, for the younger folk would do all mean offices for the elder, even if they were strangers. On the other hand, Williams says that their strong love towards children made those children sometimes "saucie, bold and undutiful."

They showed great kindness to one another in sickness; they had no remedies, so the only consolation was in the visits of friends. If a person were ill, the women and maids blacked their faces; if he died, the men would do it too, and would remain so for weeks and months in token of mourning. They disliked to mention the name of a dead person, and if any one else had the same name he would change it. Often too they would desert the place where one had died, and move their huts elsewhere. The chief possessions of a man were buried with him.

They were naked generally, save for a skin or mantle hanging over the shoulders, and a little apron. Indoors they would take the mantle off, for their houses were hot, and they kept fires burning all night, instead of bed-clothes. Sometimes they had a coat or mantle, curiously made from the feathers of turkeys, woven by the old men of the tribe who could no longer hunt or fish. They had leather leggings and stockings in one, with moccasins made of deerskin, and the women and girls decorated themselves with strings of beads about their legs.

English clothes, and mantles of Dutch and English cloth they prized greatly, so much so, that they would taken them off when it rained, and go naked so as to keep them dry.

For food, they lived mostly on parched meal, with a little water either hot or cold, save that three or four hundred miles inland was a tribe that lived on the bark of trees, mixed with the fat of beasts, or of men. These were the "Tree-eaters," the terror of the neighbouring tribes.

Their language was very copious and difficult, and varied somewhat in different districts. They counted with grains of corn, and measured their days by the stars, for they slept chiefly in the open air, and were very observant of the heavenly bodies. They had many towns, but moved often, and very quickly. Williams tells how once on a journey, he lodged in one of their houses, and hoped to do so again on his return, the next night, but the house had vanished, and he was glad to find shelter under a tree. "This question they oft put to me : Why come the Englishmen hither ? and measuring others by themselves they say, It is because you want firing; for they, having burnt up the wood in one place (wanting draughts to bring wood to them) they are faine to follow the wood ; and so to remove to a fresh new place for the wood's sake." [1]

Instead of written history, they had a volume of tradition. Where any notable act had been performed, a round hole was dug in the ground near by, that all who saw it might ask its meaning, and hearing it, might tell others. It was a primitive means of record, but by it a journey became a lesson in history and patriotism, and things of great antiquity were kept in remembrance.

The first object of the Pilgrims was to ensure their safety from attack, and to establish trade relations. With their honest intentions and straightforward dealing, they were not long in gaining the confidence of the savages. The treaty with Massasoit was the first bond between them, and it held good for fifty years. The king was persuaded by Squanto that if the English should be his friends, he need not fear any enemies in the world, "so did he become a wall to the English at Plymouth against other Indians." Moreover, their success at the first encounter had impressed the natives, and so did their habit of prayer and fasting. When, after a long drought, rain came in answer to their prayers, falling gently and gratefully upon their parched crops, the Indians were filled with respect both for the English and their God.

The first treaty was followed up by an embassy to the king. Governor Bradford, Stephen Hopkins, and Edward Winslow, guided by Squanto, and bearing a horseman's

[1] Key, p. 60.

coat of red cotton as a present, and a copper chain to be the badge of the king's messenger, went to continue with the king the league of peace, to ask him to restrain the disorderly visits of his followers, whose appetites were quite out of keeping with the poverty of Plymouth, and to make payment for the corn which they had taken on first landing at Cape Cod. Travelling from morning till night, resting in the open fields, and being well entertained and kindly treated by the Indians everywhere, they came after two days to Pokanoket. Massasoit received the coat with pride, put it on at once to the great admiration of his followers, and granted their requests. Then, gathering his men around him, he asked them was he not the king, and were they not all his people, and should they not bring their skins to these traders, and one by one the men from thirty towns agreed, so that thankful as they were to get their trade started, the Englishmen soon grew weary enough. They then had a taste of savage hospitality. Massasoit had but just returned home, and to his great chagrin had no food to offer them ; a bed the emissaries shared with the king and his wife and two of his chief men. They stayed another day and night, completing their negotiations, and then, weary and half starving, but happily finding food on the journey, they made their way home, well satisfied with their work.

It was soon the Englishmen's turn to carry out their part in the treaty of mutual defence, for Corbitant, a petty sachem of the district, in league with the Narragansetts, began to stir up revolt against Massasoit, and the planters heard that he had been put from his country, and that their interpreter Tisquantum had been killed. This news proved false, but Standish with ten men marched to Namaschet, where Corbitant had been, and struck awe into the hearts of his followers, making them answerable for Massasoit's return, and threatening them with vengeance if any violence were offered to him or to his subjects.

More serious alarms came later, from the Narragansetts

and the Massachusetts, who were to be a menace to the English for many years to come. The Narragansetts hated Massasoit and his friends, and when in 1621 fresh colonists came in the *Fortune*, all unprovided and ill-fitted for the place, and the colony was put to its direst straits, their chief, Canonicus, sent by a messenger a bundle of new arrows wrapped in a rattlesnake's skin, in token of his defiance. But the handful of colonists had staunch hearts, and Governor Bradford came of a good Yorkshire stock, which was not likely to be cowed by a threat. So they put a bold face on their weakness, and sent back the snake's skin filled to the brim with powder and shot, with a message from the Governor to say that only lack of ships prevented him from sending his men to Narragansett, and saving Canonicus any long journey to attack him. The bold stroke told; the awful implements of war and the undaunted message terrified the king, the rattlesnake's skin he dared not touch, and by one messenger and another it was passed on, until it came back unopened to Plymouth. The planters did not content themselves with bold words; they knew their weakness, and lost no time in taking what precautions they could. A palisade was put around the town, and regular guards appointed for defence, and in the following spring a fort was built on Burial Hill, from which could be obtained a wide view of the surrounding country, and timely warning given of any threatened invasion.

So far they had had few dealings with the Massachusetts. A voyage had been made to establish trade there and to make a compact of peace, but though the emissaries admired the country and did good trade, the voyage was fruitless in some respects, for they could not see the queen, and could make no treaty. A second expedition was about to start, when they were warned that the Massachusetts were allying with the Narragansetts against them, that the former intended to cut off Standish and the members of the trading expedition whilst they were with them, and that the latter would attack Plymouth in their absence. In spite of the warning, they decided not to show fear, nor to mew themselves up in their enclosed town, since not only would it be impolitic to show their weakness, but to live much longer without fresh supplies of food would be impossible.

Further alarms delayed the expedition, but either these were exaggerated by Squanto, who liked to make himself of importance, and to think that he could lead men to peace or war as he wished, or else their boldness had the desired effect, for no trouble ensued.

For the first two years, therefore, in spite of some rumours of war, and much uncertainty and fear as to the temper and good faith of the savages, the good judgment, courage, and honesty of the Plymouth men maintained peace, and had they been left to themselves, they might have extended their treaties to all the neighbouring tribes, and lived in safety for many years. But, just as they were beginning to live down the hatred of the English which Hunt the slave dealer had inspired, it was justified and revived by the ill-doing of some of the later plantations.

In June 1622 came two ships of Mr Weston's, the *Charity* and the *Swan*, bringing fifty or sixty men sent over at his own special charge, to plant for him. Weston cared only for speedy profits, and the men had no higher motive; moreover, they seem to have been improvident, lazy and worthless, without a particle of the industry or judgment necessary to found any colony. They landed at Plymouth, and were entertained there until they could make a settlement, and badly they abused this hospitality, which, indeed, the Plymouth men could very ill afford. They stole the corn before it was ripe; they spread abroad slanderous tales and complaints of the rulers of the colony, and mocked at its poverty and weakness, boasting of the great things that they would do, being all strong men, unhampered by women and children. From what they saw of them, the

Plymouth men from the first dreaded their treatment of the natives, and when Wessagusset (Weymouth) was chosen for their plantation, and they removed there in the autumn of 1622, it was but a short time before the Governor's ears were filled with complaints from the Indians there, that Weston's men stole their corn and abused them in other ways. The two plantations joined in partnership to trade for corn at Manamoycke, Massachusetts, Mattachiest, and Nauset, and everywhere Weston's men spoiled the trade, giving more for a quart of corn than had formerly been given for a beaver skin, and everywhere the Indians renewed their complaints of their conduct. Tisquantum died on the first of these voyages, the Plymouth men lost both a guide and an interpreter in him, and the expeditions were fraught with a danger that only the vigilance of Standish contrived to elude.

From the time Weston's men arrived, there seemed to be a disposition to treachery all around, and finally Standish, on one of these expeditions, and Winslow, on an errand of mercy, simultaneously discovered a plot to kill the men at Wessagusset, and knowing that vengeance from Plymouth would surely follow, to destroy that colony too.

Hearing that King Massasoit was ill, and knowing that the Indians in times of sickness liked to receive visits from their friends, Winslow and Hamden, guided by Hobbamock, had gone on an expedition to Pokanoket, taking with them such simple remedies as they thought might be of use. On their journey, they heard many reports from Corbitant (the next heir) that the king was already dead, but though they knew that, if so, their lives were in danger from his enemies, they determined to go on.

Arrived at Pokanoket, they found him still alive, though far gone in weakness, surrounded by medicine men "making such a hellish noise as it distempered us that were well, and therefore was unlike to ease him that was sick." They gave him some remedies which speedily took effect, he ate and slept, and made a marvellous recovery. "Now," said the king, "I see that the English are my friends and love me, and while I live I will never forget the kindness they have shown me." He kept his promise, and as an immediate sign of gratitude, revealed to Hobbamock the conspiracy against the two plantations. The people of Nauset, Pamet, Succonet, Mattachiest, Agowaywam, and the Isle of Capawack were all joined with the Massachusetts. Massasoit alone, in deference to the treaty of peace, had refused to help in the plot.

Winslow returned to Plymouth to find that Standish had heard the same news at Manomet, and with the Governor they debated what should be done. They disliked greatly to shed blood unprovoked, yet feared to let the Indians strike the first blow, and being assured of the truth of the plot, it was made known in public court, that the permission of the whole court might be obtained for war. The business was difficult and grievous to all, but finally Bradford, Allerton, Standish, and any others they chose, were appointed to decide the matter, and they agreed to take a strong body of men to give warning to the English at Wessagusset, and then to go on, under pretence of trade, amongst the Boston Bay Indians, to take notice of their behaviour. If there were any need to fight, Standish was to bring back the head of Wituwamat, "a notable and bloody villain," who had been foremost in insulting him on their former expedition.

Dire reports came as to the state of things at Wessagusset, how Weston's men made themselves servants to the Indians for bread, and had been so dishonest that they could no longer either buy or borrow corn. They thought of taking it by force, and had fortified their town, but Bradford wrote and strongly dissuaded them from such an outrage.

The departure of Standish and his eight men was hastened by the coming of one of Weston's men, Phinehas

Pratt, who reached Plymouth half dead with exhaustion, with pitiful accounts of the colony, and of its subjection to the Indians. To satisfy them, a man had been hanged for stealing corn. As the thief was strong and well, they thought of putting his clothes on a sick man and hanging him instead, "but that one with a ravenus voyce begunne to croake and bellow for revenge."[1] Still they feared to hang the strong man, so took him and bound him, as it were in jest, and then hanged him in earnest. The Indians were not propitiated, the colonists were naked and starving, scattered and defenceless, and the Indians took their food and ate it before their very eyes.

On hearing Pratt's story, Plymouth was put in a state of defence, an Indian who came to spy upon them was chained up in the new guard-room, and Standish set out. He landed near Wessagusset, told the heads of the plantation of the plot, and of Bradford's offer to receive them at Plymouth for a time, collected all the people in the town, and put them on an allowance of food, having brought some corn spared out of their seed.

An Indian came presently, to spy under pretence of trading, thinking something was amiss; Standish gave no sign, but the man saw anger in his eyes, and knew that the plot was discovered. Signs of insult and defiance occurred daily, but still the Captain made no move, until one day he came upon Wituwamat and Pecksuot, two of the chief aggressors, and two of their men, together in a room. Then having four also on his side, Standish gave the word; Wituwamat, Pecksuot, and another were killed, the fourth was taken and hanged. Two or three more were killed by another company, but one Indian escaped, warned the tribes, and so disappointed their hope of avenging the whole conspiracy. A few went in pursuit, but with Obtakiest their sachem,

---

[1] Morton's "New English Canaan," p. 110.

the Indians entrenched themselves in a swamp, and the Captain was forced to return, sparing the native women and children, and not allowing the least discourtesy towards them.

Master Weston's people had had enough of Wessagusset, and determined to go to Monhegan, to get passage to England in one of the fishing ships. The scorn of Captain Standish at this desertion can be imagined; he told them he durst live there with fewer men, but according to his orders, he gave them all the corn he could spare for their provision, and any that wished he took with him in the shallop to Plymouth.

This was Standish's triumph, his notable adventure, and he returned from it, bearing the head of Wituwamat with him. He had ample proof that the bloodshed was not unnecessary; one of the Boston Bay Indians, always a friend to the English, told the Captain that the conspirators were only waiting till Weston's men had made them two more canoes, and that they then meant to take the ship and kill all. When the expedition got back to Plymouth, the spy confessed the same, and he was sent back to Obtakiest with a strong warning and justification of what had been done. Obtakiest was also requested to give up three Englishmen of Wessagusset who had sought his protection, but after a long time, word came by a woman that they had been already killed, and that the sachem feared to come before the English to make his peace.

Justifiable and necessary as this punishment had been, it was an episode regretted by all, and when Robinson heard of it in Leyden, he wrote to the Governor, sadly lamenting that the blood of any Indian should have been shed before one had been converted.

But the severity of Standish had done its work. The tribes who had joined with the Massachusetts, seeing their punishment, were filled with fear. They ceased to plant their corn, and hid in swamps and places so unhealthy that many of the chief of them died; the rest of them dared nothing against the English, and for many years peace reigned around the colony of Plymouth.

But the Pilgrims could not fail to be involved in the troubles which came upon the neighbouring colonies, whose settlement interfered more directly with the lands and liberties of the Indian tribes.

As the white population grew and spread in all directions over New England, the natives began to feel the pressure, firm and relentless, of an unwelcome civilization. By an ironic fate, it had been through the enthusiastic descriptions of three Indians who had been brought to London, that the zeal of Sir Ferdinand Gorges had been aroused for colonizing New England, and the coming of the white men does not seem to have been much resented at first. The Pilgrims were, on the whole, well received: Miantonomoh of the Narragansetts became the friend and guest of Winthrop, and when Massachusetts colony was founded, one tribe after another offered alliance and craved protection, until finally even the fierce Pequods brought gifts and attempted to make a treaty with the English.

All the New England states made great efforts to deal fairly and equitably with the Indians ; all had a body of laws like those enacted at Plymouth, regulating inter- course between the two races. Each state in turn was founded with the consent and sometimes at the request of the neighbouring tribes; the land required was fairly purchased, though doubtless for a very inadequate price, and in 1676 Josiah Winslow could write, " I think I can clearly say that, before these present troubles broke out, the English did not possess one foot of land in this colony but what was fairly obtained by honest purchase of the Indian proprietors. Nay, because some of our people are of a covetous disposition, and the Indians in their straits are easily prevailed with to part with their lands, we first made a law that none should purchase or receive of gift any land of the Indians without the knowledge and allowance of our Court. . . . And if at any time they have brought complaints before us, they have had justice impartial and speedy, so that our own people have frequently complained that we erred on the other hand in showing them overmuch favour."

The Indians were like children, living altogether in the present ; they were willing enough to sell their lands, thinly populated as they were, in return for comforts and necessaries which, for the moment, meant much to them ; they were willing enough to offer friendship to men whom they knew to be powerful, whom they felt to be trustworthy and kindly towards them, in return for protection, for food when they were in want, for help in the awful epidemics of smallpox and fever from which they suffered. But presently they began to feel that the price was too great, that the English demanded in their allies conformance to an impossible standard. They were asked to forego their primitive joys of revenge, and the exercise of power, to submit to arbitration which could take small account of their tribal differences, of their traditions of love and hatred. They felt cramped and restrained, and finally the vision of their future, ever driven back into narrower, more limited territories, ever more and more bound down by laws which they had not made, until finally their land, their creed, even their nationality, would be wrested from them, rose before them, and goaded them to a passion of hostility that nothing could allay.

The first serious conflict, the Pequod war, followed closely on the settlement of Connecticut, but it was probably caused less by hatred of the English than jealousy of their action in supporting the Mohegans against the Pequods. It is hard to know what else could have been done : the Mohegans offered honest friendship, the Pequods were obviously treacherous, and moreover the Mohegans were in the right in their dispute. But to interfere in tribal warfare is dangerous, and the Pequods never forgot their grudge.

In 1633 two traders named Stone and Norton, sailed up the Connecticut River to trade with the Dutch there. They took some Pequod Indians on board, and were murdered by them in the night. Representatives of the tribe, however, on being summoned to Boston, urged that they had acted in self-defence, and the plea was accepted. Stone was not a very desirable character ; not long before he had seized a barque belonging to Plymouth traders, and it had only been rescued by the help of some friendly Dutch seamen, so it was felt that he might have given the Indians some extreme provocation to violence.

The Pequod chief promised to surrender the only two assassins who were still living, to pay a tribute to the Court in Boston, and to cede some ground for a settlement. At the time, he was on bad terms with both the Narragansetts and the Dutch, and feared to make enemies of the English also, but when he had made his peace with them, they in turn negotiated peace for him with the Narragansetts, and his position became more secure.

In 1636, feeling able to defy the English once more, some Pequod Indians murdered John Oldham, a man of eventful history, who had been expelled from Plymouth with Lyford, but had apparently later redeemed his character, had been with Conant at Cape Ann, had succeeded to part of Gorges' claim in Massachusetts, and was one of the earliest explorers of Connecticut. A small boat belonging to him was seen off Block Island, evidently in the hands of inexperienced sailors, and when it was approached, the deck was seen to be covered with Indians. Some of them jumped into the water, some were taken prisoners, and the dead body of Oldham was found on board. In command of about ninety men, Endicott and Underhill, a soldier who had served in many countries, undertook to punish this assault, but though they did much damage

18

and lost no men, they seem to have exasperated rather than intimidated the Pequods.

Thirsting for revenge, their chief sought to ally with his old enemies, the Mohegans and Narragansetts, that together they might wipe out the whole of the New England settlements. Such a combination would have been dangerous in the extreme, and Roger Williams, who had been one of the first to hear of it, and to warn the Governor of Massachusetts, spared no effort to prevent its taking place. Relying on his friendship with the Indians and his influence with them, he made his way to the house of the sachem of the Narragansetts. The Pequod ambassadors were already there, and Williams describes the horror with which for three days and nights he endured their presence, feeling that they reeked of the blood of his countrymen, and looking for their bloody knives at his own throat also. But his mission was successful ; the wavering Narragansetts gave him their promise that they would not move against the English, and even advised how the campaign should be conducted ; the Mohegans also refused to join the conspiracy, and the Pequods were left to stand alone.

Their murderous attacks soon roused Connecticut to action, and sixty men under John Mason, joined by twenty from Massachusetts under Underhill, commenced the attack. One hundred and sixty men from Massachusetts, and forty from Plymouth were promised as reinforcements, a slender army against the one thousand Pequods already in the field, and the large numbers held in reserve. But before the Plymouth men had started, they got word to stay, as the victory was won. Mason had chosen the least expected point of attack ; leaving the mouth of the river, he had sailed easterly into Narragansett Bay in full view of the Pequods, who thought he was retreating. Landing there, and advancing towards the rear of the Pequod camp, he fell upon them two hours before dawn, when the Indians, worn out with their war songs and rejoicings over a terrified foe, were sleeping in fancied security.

Mason on one side, Underhill on the other, leapt within the palisade that guarded the fort, and held their own alone, until their men cut a way through and joined them. The struggle was desperate, and Mason, fearing to be overpowered by numbers, gave the word to burn the Indians out. The matted roofs of the wigwams flamed easily; the English stationed themselves outside the palisades, shooting all who sought to escape. They lost but two men, the Indians more than six hundred. Mason, on landing, had been joined by large numbers of Narragansetts and Mohegans, but though faithful, they took little part in the struggle, soon falling to the rear and leaving all the fighting to the English. To the natives, according to Bradford, was due the horrible suggestion of burning the camp, which even the plea of necessity finds it hard to excuse, for it held women and children as well as warriors. But the complete extermination of the race had been determined on, and Mason vigorously followed up this first victory. Those of the Pequod tribe who remained, were remorselessly pursued and killed, their wigwams were burned, their land devastated: Sassacus, their chieftain, fled in despair to the Mohawks, who slew him, and then the feeble remnant of the tribe surrendered to the English. Some were sent as slaves to the Bermudas, some were incorporated with the Narragansetts, some with the Mohegans, some with the Niantics; their country fell under the jurisdiction of Connecticut, and the Pequods as a nation existed no more.

This horrible war secured peace for a time, though the questions arising out of it required careful adjustment and arbitration, and were an immediate cause of the Confederation of the New England Colonies, whose Commissioners first met in 1643.

Seeds of jealousy had been sown between the Narragansetts and Mohegans, when the English divided the remnant of the Pequods between the tribes, for the Narragansetts thought they should have had sway over all, whereas the English favoured Uncas of the Mohegans, who had put himself under their protection, and whom they made responsible for collecting the tribute due for the Pequod captives. Moreover, both chiefs were a little jealous that the English should have gained so complete a victory over any of their race. They thought their success was ominous, as indeed it was, and they resented the complete control which the English assumed over the fruits of their victory. The tribute fell into arrears, and the Pequods were constantly trying to free themselves from the control of Uncas, and to be taken directly under the government of the English.

In 1640 Miantonomoh of the Narragansetts had been accused by Uncas of treachery against the English, and had been summoned to Boston to explain himself. This he managed to do satisfactorily, but in 1643 further fears were aroused, for it was said that he had attempted to murder Uncas, because of his accusation, and his friendship with the white men. Again he was summoned to Boston, and again he answered the charge, but so strong were the suspicions against him that all was held in readiness for war with the Narragansetts.

Miantonomoh gained further disfavour from his connection with Samuel Gorton, an enthusiast with awkward opinions and not very nice ideas of conduct. Gorton had fallen foul of the Massachusetts people on account of his Antinomian views; had been expelled from Plymouth for questioning their judicial procedure, and championing a woman who had transgressed their rule of conduct, and had been whipped out of Rhode Island. He then settled at Shawomet, getting a deed for the land from Miantonomoh, which was witnessed also by Pumham, the petty sachem of the district. But he got into difficulties with some English settlers near by, who had bought their land from another petty sachem,

Sacononoco, without the consent of Miantonomoh, their chief. Under the influence of these settlers, the two petty sachems asserted their independence of Miantonomoh, and asked to be taken under the jurisdiction of Massachusetts, Pumham declaring that he had been forced into selling his lands to Gorton. Massachusetts consented to protect them (overlooking the fact that their land was within the Plymouth patent); Gorton was summoned to answer for his conduct at Boston, and finally brought there by force, tried, and sentenced first to imprisonment, then to banishment.

This complication blackened Miantonomoh in the eyes of the Massachusetts government; his right to sell the land at all was questioned, and in any case, it was taken ill that he should have sold it to one of their enemies.

He was summoned to Boston once more to support his claim, and failed to do it satisfactorily. Full of anger and chagrin, feeling that life had no zest where such interference and humiliations were possible, the Narragansett chief, with his warriors, fell upon the Mohegans, in defiance of the treaty of peace made in 1638, by which it had been agreed to submit all disputes to English arbitration, instead of going immediately to war. His army was defeated, and he himself brought prisoner to Uncas, who, with the permission of the English Commissioners, given after anxious deliberation, and under their strict supervision, took his rival beyond the limits of the white men's jurisdiction, and put him to death.

Miantonomoh was proved to have plotted against the life of Uncas in time of peace, and to have tried to arouse a conspiracy against the English, but the reasons for his execution read unconvincingly, when one thinks of him as the faithful friend of Roger Williams the champion of the Rhode Island settlers.

The Narragansetts burned to avenge his death; outrages occurred, and they demanded of the Commissioners leave to take the life of Uncas, on the ground that he had received a ransom for Miantonomoh, and then executed him. But the English still stood by Uncas, and after careful examination of the evidence, it was decided that no ransom had been taken. In 1645, Williams contrived a meeting at Hartford; the Narragansetts promised to restore all they had taken from Uncas, and to pay a fine to the English for breaking their former treaty; both sides promised that they would give thirty days' warning to the Commissioners before commencing hostilities, and so they were forced to a reluctant peace.

The troubles with the Pequods had been rather the affair of Massachusetts and of Connecticut, than of Plymouth, though deeply affecting all the colonies. But the next great struggle, after many years of peace, came nearer home, and almost wrecked the slowly growing prosperity of the little colony.

The early treaty of Plymouth with Massasoit had been the basis of a long-lived peace, but with the death of the actual parties to the treaty, it became less of a reality. Brewster died in 1644, Winslow in 1655, Standish in 1656 and Bradford in 1657; Massasoit their faithful friend died in 1660, and thus the personnel of both sides of the treaty was changed.

Although nominally the alliance continued, it was perceptibly weakened when the old bond of personal friendship was no more. The Pokanoket Indians, too, repented the alienation of their best lands; they resented the English rights of jurisdiction they had themselves consented to; even in their old pursuits of hunting and fishing they saw themselves outdone by the English with their superior methods and weapons. For greater security, they had been driven gradually back into narrow strips of sea-girt land; and, hemmed in, oppressed, and restricted, with the sense of their nationality, the remembrance of their old freedom burning within them, the Pokanokets at last turned upon the English, in a war more fatal than any that had gone before.

In 1675, when the war actually broke out, it found Plymouth somewhat unprepared, somewhat enfeebled in fighting capacity, since the days of Standish's notable adventure—those early days, when they were conscious of carrying their lives in their hands, and every man was trained for military defence and strategy.

But there had been signs, since Massasoit's death, that might have given them warning. He had been succeeded by his sons Wamsutta and Pometacon, who, asking from the General Court of Plymouth the gift of English names, were called Alexander and Philip.

Alexander, the elder, had given some cause for suspicion, and it was said that he died as a result of the anger and shame of being called to account for it at Plymouth. His brother succeeded him, and was summoned to Plymouth to give solemn assurances of his fidelity. But this practice of calling Indian chiefs to answer charges against them, was one of the most galling results of English domination; it made them feel that they were dependents, and not allies, and Philip bore it no better than Miantonomoh had done. Being suspected of alliance with the French and Dutch in 1667 and 1671, he was forced to surrender the English arms possessed by his tribe, to find part of the expenses of the expedition sent to summon him, and to pay a heavy tribute; and when he was once more informed against, this time by a converted Indian of Natick called Sausamon, the informer was murdered, and Philip showed himself openly hostile to the English. For the murder of Sausamon was punished by the execution of three Indians, and their comrades, thirsting for revenge, killed several English people, and Philip was thus forced into a war that he only half desired.

He must have known that his cause was desperate,

that even with the alliance of other tribes he could not hope for ultimate success against the English, with their supplies of arms and of food, their superior houses and fortifications, but to live longer in subjection was impossible. " For them as a nation there was no to-morrow," and they fought to the last breath, meaning, if ruined they must be, to carry many with them in their downfall. Not unattended would each warrior go to knock at Kiehtan's door; before him he would drive the souls of the white men whom he had slain for their attempt to rob him of all that he cherished most, even the faith of his fathers, and from within the gates of Paradise he would glory in their dismissal.

The war was at first confined to the places around Mount Hope, Philip's stronghold, which was in Plymouth territory. The English were quickly alive to their danger; Plymouth sent to Boston for help, and the little town of Swansey, which was first attacked, was speedily reinforced by troops from the two colonies. Philip and his companions, driven out of their own country, took their canoes across to the eastern shore of Narragansett Bay and entrenched themselves in a swamp. There the Plymouth men mounted guard over them, but could neither get at them nor prevent them from raiding the towns of Dartmouth, Taunton and Middleborough, burning and massacring wherever they met.

The Massachusetts forces meanwhile had marched into the Narragansett country, hoping by an armed demonstration to persuade this tribe to keep peace. The move was dangerous, more likely to provoke than to intimidate, for the sachem, Canonchet, was son of Miantonomoh; they remembered their own wrongs only too clearly, and their promises of peace were worth less than nothing.

Before the troops were reunited, Philip had escaped from his swamp and made his way into Massachusetts, where, in spite of all attempts at dissuasion, he was joined by the Nipmucks. The seat of war had now removed to central Massachusetts and the Connecticut valley. Mendon was attacked, Brookfield was besieged and partly burnt, the inmates being rescued only by the timely arrival of Major Willard, an old man of seventy, in command of forty-seven horsemen. So stubborn had been the defence, and so vigorous his onslaught, that the Indians lost eighty men killed and wounded. Tales of heroism were many, though the English had been so awed at the opening of the war that they read portents in the sky, and augured ills for themselves from the howling of wolves and the moaning of the winds.

Connecticut was now drawn into the struggle, and began to take vigorous measures for defence; the Commissioners took affairs in hand, and voted a further levy from each of the colonies, but to find men enough to defend and to attack was difficult, for the Indian raids were as unexpected as they were fatal. Deerfield and Northfield were attacked during the temporary absence of the troops; Hadley was surprised when the inhabitants were at church, and was only saved from panic and utter annihilation by an unknown man, white-haired and wearing garments of antique cut, who appeared in their midst and directed the defence with the skill of a practised soldier. The Indians were driven out, and the people turned to thank their leader, only to find that he had vanished. It was the regicide Goffe, in hiding from the vengeance of the Stuarts, and this heroic incident is the last record of his life.

The worst disaster of all occurred near Deerfield, at a place which was ever afterwards known as the Bloody Brook. A convoy under Lathrop attempted to bring the harvest loads from Deerfield down to the lower towns, and apparently no scouts were sent ahead of the teams. Thick woods hung on either side of the brook, and as they reached it, the soldiers, laying their arms in the waggons, scattered right and left to gather grapes from the vines along the banks. They paid dearly for their rashness; a host of Indians surprised them, Lathrop was shot dead, and only seven or eight escaped to tell the tale of their disaster. The ambush was punished by Moseley, who secured the return of the waggons, but Deerfield was abandoned, and the Indians remained supreme in the district.

The towns in immediate danger naturally wished to concentrate on defence; those at a safer distance advised a vigorous attack, and the work of the Commissioners and the commanders was not easy.

But the tide began to turn, as it was bound to do. By this time winter was setting in, and the Indians suffered even more heavily than the English. They gained less advantage from the woods, ever their securest point of vantage, for in open field the English always gained the day, and they decided to take refuge with the Narragansetts, and postpone their devastations till the spring. The Narragansetts refused to give them up, as in their treaty they had promised to do, and so the suspicions of their bad faith were confirmed.

The Commissioners issued general orders for an expedition, and in December 1675, the troops of the United Colonies, and one hundred and fifty Mohegan warriors made a determined attack on the principal forces of the Narragansetts.

Josiah Winslow, son of Edward, and Governor of New Plymouth, was in command, and hearing from a prisoner where their chief camp was situated, he set out, with the united forces of New England at his back. The camp was near the present town of North Kingston, and after sleeping in the open and marching from early morning over the snow-clad ground, they reached the spot, and opened their attack. The fighting was desperate, for the Narragansetts were prepared, and after some three hours, when leader after leader had lost his life in trying to gain ground within the palisades, Winslow, like Mason before him, decided to burn the wigwams.

It was done, and the victory was complete. Not only
did hundreds of men, women and children perish by sword
or fire, but the wigwams, their only shelter against the
storms of winter, all their stores of food, their treasures of
mats and wampum, were destroyed. Church, one of the
attacking officers, protested against this needless waste,
urging the comfort that the warm wigwams would be to
the wounded English, many of whom died with cold
before they could be got under shelter; the value to
themselves of the stores of corn and provisions. But
Winslow was inexorable. As Mason had been bent on
reducing the Pequods at any cost, so he had determined
on the downfall of the Narragansetts, and he spared nothing
to achieve it.

Living in swamps, protected only by the boughs of
trees, digging under the snow for acorns and nuts to save
them from starvation, the tribe was reduced to the depths
of misery. The greatness of their spirit is revealed by the
bearing of Canonchet under these appalling disasters. To
the last man he declared they would fight rather than be
slaves to the English; he preferred death to a treaty with
his enemies, and welcomed its coming before he should
have said anything unworthy of himself.

The downfall of the Narragansetts did not end the war,
though it made the issue certain. The remnants of the
tribe allied with the Nipmucks, and devastated the border
towns of Massachusetts, of Plymouth and Rhode Island. In
the early spring town after town was harried in one or
another of the colonies, Lancaster, Medfield, Weymouth,
Groton, Marlborough, Scituate, Rehoboth, Providence,
Northampton, Hadley and Hatfield, and many others.
Mary Rowlandson of Lancaster has left a pitiful account
of her captivity among the Indians, when with her
house burnt, and her children killed, she was driven
with one poor wounded child in her arms through the
snowy forests, having for days no food, no resting-place
but the frozen ground, and forced, when death ended the

piteous plaints of her child, to leave it behind on the snow, and follow her captors with every circumstance of privation and insult, the unwilling witness of their barbarities and pillage.

But the sufferings and reverses of the savages led to divisions and complaints among themselves. Philip became the scapegoat; on him, as the first insurgent, all their disasters were blamed, and there grew up a party amongst the Indians willing and even anxious for peace. Some surrendered, encouraged by a government proclamation promising mercy; others wandered off to join the tribes of the north; the English were successful in the field, and active in detaching from him Philip's less devoted allies, so that finally he was left with but a handful of warriors.

Peace he would not hear of, but in the summer of 1676, he determined to go back once more to his own country and meet openly the fate which should await him. His followers attacked several places in Plymouth colony, but with small success. Church determined to hunt them down, and to capture Philip, and on August 12th Philip was surprised by an ambush, and shot dead by a man of his own race. His only son was transported as a slave.

The war had been one of excessive cruelty on both sides, and in the whole story of the relations between the races, it is impossible not to give one's sympathy to those whose only crime was a backward civilization.

The New England Colonies were, indeed, disastrous to the natives, who rejected much of what was highest and best in the civilization which came to them, and drank to the dregs what was degrading and bad. All their primitive virtues were tarnished; they had shown manly trust at first, but only servile subjection now; their industry was undermined when they realised that, by selling lands and goods for the moment useless to them, they could live with comfort in idleness. They had learnt an immorality, not natural to them, from the vicious offscourings of the

English community ; drunkenness, with all its attendant
vices, had become more and more common ; oppression
had fostered in them a cruelty greater than the ordinary.
By destroying their independence, the English had destroyed their self-respect, and had brought to the fore
the weak and worthless who would bear the yoke, whilst
the noble and high spirited had no refuge but in revolt
and death.

Surely great wrongs are done in the name of civilization. If one studies the history of these Indians, even
the success of the New England Colonies, even the greatness of their future, seems to have been too dearly
paid for. And yet the colonists could hardly be
blamed ; they had striven for peace and justice, they
were only the instruments of a great principle. The
Indians were doomed by the fact that the white men
came at all, though neither the one nor the other realised
it, till the inevitable results had come.

# CHAPTER XIV

## THE GOVERNMENT OF THE COLONY

IN nothing was the work of the Pilgrims more lasting and more important than in the form of civil government which they established, and nowhere was their actual position more different from their nominal one.

With their relations to the Merchant Adventurers and to the New England Council, and their allegiance and submission to the English king, it would have been natural if their government had borne signs of proprietary, feudal, or monarchical influence. To all appearance they were a community possessing no intrinsic rights whatever, ruling only through a patent from the New England Council, which granted them, together with land and trading privileges, permission to issue necessary ordinances, and to elect officers to enforce them. Some further rights of government were promised in the future, but such favours were entirely invalid without a charter from the king, for the New England Council had no power to grant them. Even this precarious claim to government was not in their own hands at first, but in those of the Adventurers to whom they were bound, the patents of 1621 and 1622 being taken out in the name of John Pierce and his associates. In 1629, when they were freed from the joint-stock company, another patent was taken out in the name of William Bradford, and the colony came more nearly into possession of its own liberties. This it finally did in 1641, when Bradford resigned his patent into the hands of the freemen of the colony, who formed the General Court.

In holding these patents, the colonists were liable to many dangerous attacks on their privileges, from the Adventurers, the New England Council and the king. Pierce in 1622 attempted to become proprietor instead of trustee of the colony, obtaining instead of his patent a "deed Pole," by which he could make the colonists "to hold of him as tenants, and sue to his courts as chiefe Lord." [1] His design was fortunately frustrated, though not without great expense to the planters. The interference of the New England Council, its efforts to establish government through Gorges, West and Morrell, and its constant attempts to embroil the colonies in some difficulty with the king, have already been noticed. In 1635 the Council yielded up its Charter, and King Charles assumed direct government over the colonies, proclaiming in 1637 that he did so, "knowing it to be a duty not to suffer such numbers of his people to run to ruin." [2]  As a result of this cession, and of Laud's enmity to the Puritan colonies, the Commission for regulating Plantations was established in England.  Massachusetts armed herself to the teeth on hearing of it, but the Scotch War and the opening of the Long Parliament checked the proposed policy of interference, and not until after the Restoration did it have any active influence.

It was not however on grants or patents, vague and liable to change and revocation, that the government of Plymouth colony was really based.  Its form was neither proprietary, feudal, nor monarchical, but democratic, and it stood firm as a rock through storm and tempest, supported by the voluntary compact made in the cabin of the *Mayflower*, deriving its power from the men who by this act had become the first freemen of the colony.

As almost all the male passengers signed the compact, practically the whole company would be freemen at first and the government of the colony was in the hands of this

[1] Bradford MS.
[2] S. P. Col., 23rd July 1637, vol. ix. no. 60.

General Court, or primary assembly. Bradford gives many examples of the kind of business that was put before it. It chose the Governor, first Carver, and then, on his death, William Bradford, with Isaac Allerton as his assistant. It elected too a military commander, and that meeting at which Standish was chosen, and military orders settled, and which was so often interrupted by the coming of the Indians, has been already noticed. Besides exercising elective functions, the members of the General Court decided on the place of settlement and the laying out of the town; they were consulted about the danger from the Massachusetts, and sent Standish off on his notable adventure. They were consulted later as to the conditions on which the "particulars" should be admitted to the colony, and they agreed upon the division of lands and cattle at the break-up of the joint-stock sytem. Finally, the whole company was summoned to do justice in the case of Lyford and Oldham.

Later on, when ship after ship had brought colonists to Plymouth, and other freemen had been admitted on the approval of those who signed the compact, the General Court still remained the source of power, but it became impossible for it to remain a primary assembly. Other towns had grown up, and the number of freemen had greatly increased; it would have been difficult for all to attend, and business would have been impossible in such an unwieldy gathering. So it came about that the general body met as a rule only once a year, at the great meeting in which officers were elected, and laws were framed or repealed, and which was held originally on the first Tuesday in March, but later, on account of the severity of spring weather, and the difficulties of travel, on the first Tuesday in June. Other courts were held, in March and October, and these were also called General Courts, but to them the freemen might send elected deputies instead of coming themselves. The tendency was for the primary assembly to let its powers lapse; in 1658 voting by proxy was allowed even at the June Court, and the freemen were not obliged to appear in person unless some special reason, as for instance the repeal of various laws in 1659, made it necessary. As early as 1652, aged freemen had been permitted to send their votes sealed up, a presage of the ballot system which came probably from Holland, where it was used largely in the elections of the Reformed Church. Finally the primary Court did little beyond electing officers,[1] and all the other business of the colony was done by the Governor and assistants, who had increased in number from one to seven, as the work became heavier. It was done either in their own monthly courts, or in the three annual General Courts, in which they were joined by deputies or committees from each of the towns.

But although with the growth of representation each freeman no longer had a personal share in the decisions of the colony, it did not cease to be democratic. The machinery of government, the legislative and judicial systems, landowning, finance, and military matters, all showed the same principle of equality, and all were ultimately controlled by the will of the people.

It is true that the conditions of the franchise were strict, for although freemen were not, as in Massachusetts, compelled by law to be church members, it is certain that these would be most readily approved. But the limitation was one of character and not of wealth, and not until 1671 did active citizenship involve the possession of property.

All offices were elective, they could not be refused, and few if any had regular salaries attached to them. The chief civil officers of the colony in early days were the Governor and assistants, who acted as magistrates; the treasurer, who managed the finances; the constable, who saw to the keeping of the peace, and was responsible for the payment and collection of rates; and the marshal, or

---

[1] Records xi. p. 79, 1658.

19

messenger, who had to enforce the decisions of the Court. He collected fines, and was apparently the executioner too, for one Jonathan Pratt in 1675 undertook to do all the duties of a marshal, "excepting puting to death," which the Court promised to arrange for otherwise. In 1646 a receiver of excise was appointed in each town, and a town clerk to keep the registers of marriage, birth, and burial; and in 1658 a coroner was appointed, whose office was to be as like that in England as possible.

All these officials, great and small, were elected annually at the June Court, and as has been shown, election was the function of all others which was most actively exercised by every holder of the franchise.

Legislation, which was perhaps the next most important work of the General Court, was of a very varied character, local and temporary regulations finding a place amongst general laws and moral restrictions. For sixteen years the colony was governed by the laws of England, but in 1636 a special committee of men from each township, together with the Governor and assistants, drew up a code more suited to their needs. This was revised and added to several times during the century, the special co-operation of all freemen, either personally or through committees, being invited in the work. The interests of all classes of persons, English and Indians alike, were safeguarded, and legislation was generally impartial. But the codes show a growing tendency towards the severity of the Jewish law, and laws dealing with religious matters became more frequent in later years.

In jurisdiction the General Court was supreme, and formed a court of appeal; it assumed the right to inflict capital punishment for wilful murder, compact with the devil in witchcraft, treason against king or commonwealth, of England or the colonies, and the wilful burning of ships and houses. In some other offences against morality it might be decreed at the discretion of the magistrates.

The first recorded law of the colony (in 1623) established trial by jury, the code of 1636 applied it to all cases, and provided also for a grand jury of presentment. The Governor and two assistants were allowed to judge cases of less than forty shillings, and minor powers of jurisdiction were granted to the towns as they grew up, though Plymouth parted with her powers reluctantly, and always reserved a right of appeal to herself.

Justice was dispensed as impartially as laws were framed, and though penalties were severe, and in some cases brutal to modern minds, they were for that age comparatively mild. Here again, however, the growing religious intolerance after the death of the first settlers marred the records of the colony, and the treatment in Plymouth of witches, Quakers and other persons anathematised by the church became only a degree more just than that which they met with in the stricter colonies.

The granting of land was another important function of the General Court, which was practically in the position of a proprietor. To have the ownership of the colony vested in all its freemen led inevitably to a democratic state of society, and this was perpetuated by the way in which these freemen made their grants. They were almost all made to towns, thus putting other freemen in a similar proprietary position; other grants made to individuals were as a reward for some signal service, usually in connection with the founding of the colony or town. For instance the Purchasers or Old Comers, who had borne the burden of the debts of the colony, were in 1652 permitted to choose some lands for themselves. But even this was exceptional in Plymouth, and as mining, trading and manufacture were less lucrative pursuits than agriculture, the lack of extensive land proprietors made any great inequality of wealth impossible.

Land in Plymouth was invariably granted in the town meeting; it was not sold by the colony to its settlers and very rarely leased, and even after a tract of land had been granted for a town, the General Court exercised a good deal of control over its distribution and the government which might be established. In spite of the democratic element in the land-system this distribution was by no means rigidly equal, for regard was had both to the expense and trouble which any particular inhabitant might have had in the founding of the town, and to his ability to be of value and service when it was founded. At first too an inhabitant was liable to own several pieces of land scattered about the settlement, as the tract granted to a town was usually divided into home lots, meadow land, marsh, etc., according to the quality of the ground, and a share of each was given to every man, but by exchanges, sales, inheritance and marriage, a greater consolidation of estates gradually came about. And although the distribution was not equal, it was usually fair; great efforts were made to suit the grant to the individual, and to remedy natural inequalities in estates, and an appeal was almost certain to bring justice to any injured owner.

The General Court controlled the finance of the colony and had at once assumed the right to levy taxes, and to allocate the sums necessary to support its government. Taxation, like military service, was a burden which fell on the freeman and the mere inhabitant alike, and a very early law prevented the freeman from taking advantage of his position as a legislator to secure exemption from or reduction of his taxes.

The financial work of the Court was made peculiarly difficult, if interesting, by the extreme scarcity of coin in the colony. Taxes, like wages, had to be paid in kind, and to fix the current price of corn or cattle, to assess and levy with any degree of fairness, must have added greatly to the ordinary difficulties of making up a budget. The perplexities of the treasurer were not at an end even when this was done; these cumbersome and perishable commodities had to be collected, and in 1666 the

constable was authorized to press boats and carts into
his service for bringing in the rates. When collected
they had to be stored until they could be made use of;
stockyards must be impaled for the cattle, granaries
built for the corn, and the government was liable to heavy
losses through the spoiling of its goods.

Taxes were levied strictly in proportion to what a
man was able to pay, "according to goods, lands, improved
faculties and personall abillities." It is to be feared that
a tendency to disguise this ability existed even in those
days, for in 1676 the rules for rating various towns end
with this significant sentence, "if any haue not given
a true list of his estate it may happily be discouered
and made manifest by some naighbours."[1] The lump
sum needed by the government was divided between
the towns, each of which was responsible for assessing,
and collecting from its own inhabitants. Each town
chose men to make a list of its rateable property; this
was read and corrected in the town meeting and handed
on to the General Court, and then the treasurer
empowered the constable to make his collection. It
was an onerous task; in 1643 it was ordered that
the constable should pay the rate himself if he neglected
to bring it in; fines for non-payment were frequent,
and in 1658 the constable was made responsible for
these also, so that he had a strong personal interest in
doing his duty by the government.

Plymouth never levied either a poll tax or an income
tax, but like all the other New England colonies she
added to her revenue in later years by indirect taxation, the proceeds of which seem usually to have been
devoted to some special work. Timber, boards, planks
and tar, oysters and iron were all subject to an export
duty, and an excise on the sale of wine and strong
drink, tobacco and oil, imposed in 1646, went to defray
the charges of the magistrates' table. A receiver was

[1] Records xi. p. 242.

nominated in every town, who received the excise on four days in the year, and paid it to the treasurer annually. Besides the licences for keeping inns and ordinaries, without which no man might sell wine save in case of sickness, there was a licence fee for fishing at Cape Cod, collected by a special "water bayley," and appropriated to the support of schools. The Court also demanded some share in the profit of drift whales cast up upon the coast, and the money thus raised helped towards the maintenance of the ministry.

Most of the money raised was used for defence; some of it went in pensions or as rewards for public services. Few of the officers of the colony appear to have had a regular salary at first; in some cases, as for instance that of the magistrates, their expenses were defrayed whilst they were on duty; in others they received gratuities varying in amount, and at more or less irregular intervals. For example in 1633-4 Standish and William Holmes were appointed to teach the use of arms in Plymouth and Duxbury, " to be paid £20 for this present year."[1] In 1639 it was ordered that £20 should be paid to the Governor, as well as a contribution from each town. The deputies from the townships were paid daily wages, and so were the Commissioners of the United Colonies, and by degrees the gratuities of other officials became so regular as to amount to a salary.

Finally the General Court controlled the military as well as the civil government of the colony, issuing military laws, appointing commanders, and ensuring, through the clerk of the military company, regular attendance at trainings and an efficient supply of arms and ammunition.

As the colony grew and towns multiplied, powers of local government were granted. The court of each township, the town meeting, had in a lesser degree the same duties as the General Court of the colony. It too was composed only of freemen as active members,

---

[1] Records i. 38.

though non-freemen apparently voted sometimes for deputies, for there was a complaint in 1658 that as the inhabitants outnumbered the freemen, unsuitable persons were often chosen.[1] In 1667 too came an order that no one might vote in military matters unless he were an inhabitant over twenty, and had taken the oath of fidelity,[2] so apparently all voting was not strictly confined to freemen.

Each township had its own officials, a constable, select men, receivers of excise, a clerk to keep the registers, all elected by its own freemen. Towns might distribute and dispose of their lands, subject to the approval and occasional interference of Plymouth ; they might make orders for themselves which were not repugnant to the general law, but each must possess a book of the laws of the colony, to " bee read oppenly once euery yeare." [3] They had their magistrates, one of whom was specially authorised to perform marriages in the district; their select men were empowered to judge minor disputes, to enforce fines, to levy rates and to distrain for non-payment. Each town had to provide itself with a place of defence, and to see that its inhabitants had the regulation supply of arms, and attended the military trainings. Each was responsible for its own poor ; for the keeping of its boundaries, the repair of its highways, bridges, and fences ; and in later years each was compelled by law to build a meeting-house at public cost, to enforce church attendance, to collect the maintenance of ministers, and to support a school.

Thus the towns of Plymouth colony possessed all the elements of self-government, and were practically in the position of small republics, just as the Dutch cities were. The town meeting was the scene of the citizen's greatest power, the school of his training, but

---

[1] Records xi. 91-92.   [2] Ibid. xi. 219.

[3] Ibid. xi. 121.

local and central government were linked by the annual meeting of all freemen, by the sending of deputies from each town to the other meetings of the General Court, and by the right of townships to nominate candidates for the assistantship, who were voted on by the whole country. After the Confederation was formed in 1643 the General Court of the colony was linked in its turn with the government of New England through the meetings of the Board of Commissioners. Thus local and central government alike were in the hands of all who possessed the franchise.

For more than thirty years Plymouth was fortunate enough to enjoy all the benefits of popular rule with very few of its drawbacks. The ordinary evils of democratic government, its tendency to encourage place-seeking, to be unstable and to lack unity in its component parts, were all held in check by counteracting influences. And the chief of these influences was the personality of Bradford.

He it was who put self-seeking to shame, and stimulated public spirit by holding office without salary, and by introducing social and philanthropic reforms; he it was who promoted unity in the colonial government by insisting on the pre-eminence of Plymouth, and by supervising and controlling the growing townships; he it was who gave stability to the popular government and prevented it from going to extremes, religious or otherwise. So conservative were the people in their choice of officers, so consistently was Bradford elected to the post of Governor, that government, whatever its forms might be, seems to have been summed up in his person, and one is apt to think of the colony as one huge family, guided in every department of life by this wise and kindly leader.

With the exception of about five years, when at his earnest request Winslow or Prince held the office, Bradford was Governor from 1621 till his death in 1657,

COPYRT. A.S. BURBANK, 88

W.L.WILLIAMS. DEL.

GOVERNOR BRADFORD'S HOUSE, 1621

and though nominally the Governor had merely a general power of direction and a double vote on the Board of assistants, a man like Bradford, occupying the position he did in the church and in the commercial system of the colony, with his force of character, could not fail to have an immense influence in guiding its policy.

The change that came over the colony, in the character of its legislation and the spirit of its judicial decrees after his death, is sufficient proof of this.   Public spirit waned, and neglect of civic duties became more common ; very frequent fines had to be imposed for the non-payment of rates, non-attendance at the General Courts, and neglect of military duties.   Religious observance and belief became more and more the subject of legislation, and with this confusion of the duties of Church and State came a sense of greater danger from dissent, and consequently harsher judicial decrees.   The franchise was narrowed, and something like the sectarian oligarchy of Massachusetts grew up in Plymouth also.

And so much of the spirit of the Pilgrims was lost. But their early work is interesting through its adaption of English and Dutch ideas in representation, local government, elective unpaid officials, state registration of births, deaths, marriage and land transfers, state schools and pensions; it is important because so many of its principles and details passed into the later constitution. It had its permanent value as an example and a training, and much that was best in it has survived to the present day.

# CHAPTER XV

## THE CONFEDERATION AND FINAL UNION WITH MASSACHUSETTS

IT was impossible that the colonies of New England could long be blind to the advantages of some sort of union.

Situated as they were, they could have no umpire in England; Massachusetts indeed would have been too proud to appeal to any; Plymouth did appeal on one or two points, but got no answer, and the English government was altogether too disturbed and too unsympathetic at the time to be of any value as an arbitrator.

And yet some arbitration was essential. The old colony at Plymouth, small and weak as it was, naturally had in early years the prestige of experience, and it held out a generous helping hand to all new-comers. Weston's men for some time owed their subsistence, and ultimately their lives, to Plymouth colony; Bradford helped Captain Gorges so far as he was able, and Samuel Fuller, the physician of the colony, was tending the sick people of Salem through the whole of the first winter.

In spite of goodwill, however, collisions were inevitable. The colonists had vague and ill-defined patents, and as they developed their resources, disputes were certain to arise about the boundaries. Plymouth grew slowly, but the energy and determination of the colonists made them put out feelers in every direction. At Kennebec their trade was threatened by the men of Piscataqua, at Cape Ann by the Dorchester fishing company, on the Connecticut by emigrants from Massachusetts, although they had been the pioneers in each of these places. And finally

Massachusetts claimed that the land on which stood Scituate and even part of the town of Plymouth was really included in her grant.

Thus it was absolutely necessary to have some body which could settle the boundaries and just limits of trade for each colony.

Apart from any disputes, the colonies had many common interests about which they would want to consult. Most of them, Plymouth and Massachusetts in particular, had definite religious aims, both as to their own people, and the Indian tribes about them, and they very quickly came to an understanding about church affairs. The first comers to Massachusetts had been prejudiced against the Pilgrims, dreading the obnoxious name of Brownists, but they had not long been at Salem, under the ministrations of Fuller, who was a church deacon as well as a doctor, before Endicott wrote to Bradford that they had been much misrepresented, and that he found their church " far from ye common reporte that hath been spread of you." [1]   When the church at Salem was set up, Plymouth was asked for counsel and help, and Governor Bradford would have been present at the ceremony, but that he was delayed by cross winds, and only arrived later in the day to offer them the right hand of fellowship. When Winthrop landed in the colony he too asked Plymouth for help in church organization, and Fuller wrote to Bradford that the Governor wanted Plymouth to set apart the day on which his church was formed, and to offer up prayers for their help and guidance. In 1632 Winthrop and Mr Wilson visited Plymouth and took part in the church service there ; and as early as 1637 a Synod was held, consisting of all the teaching elders in the country, and messengers from the churches, to debate on the errors of Antinomianism.

So there was likely to be much intercourse in religious matters.

[1] Bradford MS., p. 173.

In external affairs their interests could hardly be separated. Each colony was in danger from the Indians, from the Dutch and French, and from a hostile religious party in England, and an injudicious act on the part of one would be liable to have fatal consequences to all. This was proved by the harm done to Indian relations by Weston's men and Thomas Morton. Possibly it was this sense of mutual responsibility which led Massachusetts to claim a right to interfere in an unfortunate affair which happened in 1634 on the Kennebec. A man called Hocking of Piscataqua attempted to trade within the limits of the Plymouth patent, and as he refused to desist, the chief man there, Howland, ordered his canoe to be cut loose. As this was being done, Hocking in a violent passion shot one of the men who did it, and a friend of his in revenge shot Hocking. The incident was very unfortunate for Plymouth, as Lord Saye and Lord Brooke, who had some rights in Piscataqua, did all they could to enrage the English government against her. Massachusetts, fearing no doubt to be involved in the disgrace, went so far as to imprison John Alden as hostage when he visited the Bay colony, thus making quite unjustifiable claims to jurisdiction. Finally, however, an assembly of ministers decided that Hocking alone was to blame for his death, and the two colonies were reconciled.

In military as well as judicial matters there was the greatest need for combination. The Dutch, in spite of their early overtures to the Pilgrims, did their best to injure the English in Connecticut, where they had undoubtedly prior rights of settlement. The French were also hostile, though their settlements were further north, and collisions less frequent. Twice, however, the trading houses near Penobscot, belonging to Plymouth, were robbed by them. The Indians were a further difficulty, and the first united action of the colonies, except for the subscription to send Morton to England, was in the levy for the Pequod war in 1637. This, together with the Synod held in the same year, led naturally to the idea of some definite confederation.

Massachusetts proposed it first, but Connecticut and Plymouth were unwilling, being afraid probably that they might pay dearly in liberty for the help they gained. In 1643 however, when the air was full of Indian disturbances, they consented to the scheme, Connecticut indeed being the prime mover now, and in May of that year commissioners from Massachusetts, Plymouth, Connecticut and Newhaven met at Boston to consider the terms of their union. Maine was excluded on account of the difference in her civil and religious administration, and possibly the same objection was felt to Rhode Island, which twice applied in vain to join the Confederation.

Possibly the form of union was suggested by the Plymouth men, who had had some experience of the confederation of Dutch states. It provided for a Board of eight Commissioners, two to be chosen annually by the General Courts of each of the plantations, the first delegates from Plymouth being Edward Winslow and William Collyer. The Commissioners were to meet once a year, or on any occasion of emergency, to discuss military and civil questions relating to the whole of the United Colonies, but each of the four was to retain separate jurisdiction within its own limits. No new member was to be received into the League, nor were any two members to be united, without the consent of the rest.

In the preamble to the Articles of Confederation [1] the colonies urged in favour of their union their common aims, their scattered settlements, the dangers around, and the "sad distraccõns" in England. These causes had led to the formation of a "consociation" for mutual help and strength, to be known as the "United colonies of New England." The consociation lasted until the reign of James II., although by that time New Haven

---

[1] For the Acts of the Commissioners, see Records, vols. ix. and x.

had been joined to Connecticut, and Plymouth made some difficulties about continuing a league of three. Its practical importance, however, save for a short time during King Philip's war, ended with the Restoration.

As the chief cause of the Confederation had been danger from without, it followed that its chief functions should be military. It was empowered to decide upon offensive and defensive war, peace, leagues, aids, charges, levies of men, money, and supplies, and to divide the spoils of war. If the danger were slight the nearest colony might help, but on urgent appeal the entire force of the Confederation was called out, the number of men from each colony being fixed by the original Articles, one hundred from Massachusetts and forty-five from each of the three others, proportionately to the number of male adults in the population. No colony could be called upon to pay on behalf of another colony unless the Commissioners declared the war to be a just one, and the booty was divided according to the charges borne.

The Confederation also provided for extradition laws between the colonies, and exercised a general supervision over justice and Indian affairs.

Four Commissioners might act on an emergency, the unanimous vote of the eight became law, a measure could be passed by a vote of six, but was then only advisory.

The weak point of the Board was that it had no executive, and no power to raise money; its real source of power lay in the General Courts. If any colony refused to obey its decisions or changed its religion, it would be held to have broken the Confederation, but there was no way of punishing it. Two members could prevent any recommendation from becoming law, and even if the Board were unanimous it had no means of enforcing its regulations. Its main power, that of deciding peace or war, was called seriously into question, and in 1670 it was finally decided that it could bind the colonies to war only with the express consent of the General Courts.

Thus it was really able only to advise, the efficacy of the advice depending entirely on the co-operation of the colonial executives.

In 1643, when the Board first met, there were many matters for the Commissioners to deal with. The boundaries between Plymouth and Massachusetts had been settled by a special commission in 1640, but similar questions arose in the succeeding years. We find the Commissioners deciding that Seakunck belonged to New Plymouth, Martha's Vineyard and Woroanoke to Massachusetts, and Southampton to Connecticut; there was an interminable dispute between Massachusetts and Connecticut about jurisdiction over the town of Springfield, and later about the sharing of the Pequod country; and another between Plymouth and Massachusetts about the lands of Pumham and Sacononoco, two native chiefs who yielded up to Massachusetts jurisdiction over a tract belonging to the territory of Plymouth. In some cases the Commissioners seem to have supervised not only boundaries but the making of roads between the colonies, for in 1644 they ordered that a way should be made between Massachusetts and Connecticut, the charge of which was to be borne by the whole of the United Colonies.[1]

But their chief sphere of action was undoubtedly foreign policy. From 1643 to 1650 there were constant disputes with the Dutch about their trading house at Hartford in Connecticut and about the encroachments of the people of Newhaven. Kieft the Governor complained in 1646 of "an unsatiable desire of possessing that wch is ours,"[2] and a determination "to fasten your foote neare Mauritius River [the Hudson] in this Province," and threatened immediate war. Complaints were sent backwards and forwards, the English complaining of disorderly trading with the Indians, and of interference with a ship belonging to a Dutch planter

[1] Records ix. 25.　　　　[2] Ibid. ix. 62.

of Newhaven whilst in English waters, the Dutch being
equally urgent about the usurpations and encroachments
of the English, the restrictions imposed upon their
trade, and the detainment of Dutch fugitives in Newhaven.
Finally in 1650 Stuyvesant, the new Dutch governor,
arrived at Hartford to treat with the Commissioners, and
after much negotiation some terms of "neighbourly
union" were ageed upon, and the question of the Dutch
in Connecticut was settled. But only a year later
disputes began about Delaware, and the agreement as
to boundaries was of little avail. In 1663 Stuyvesant
asked once more for some mutual agreement about
trade, and for some kind of neighbourly union of
Christian people living amongst savages, and his proposal
was referred to the General Courts. But he was coldly
answered and there was no cordiality between the two
nations.

There were French complications too at the moment
when the Commissioners first met. Disputes were going
on between Charles de la Tour of St John's River,
and D'Aunay Charnissay of Port Royal, who had
succeeded to the claims of the French governor in
Acadia, and Massachusetts had rashly involved herself
in them. Each asserted his authority in the district,
D'Aunay deriving it from the French crown, La Tour
through the Company of New France.

The merchants of Massachusetts had traded with
La Tour, and when matters came to a crisis he was
permitted to raise a force in the colony to fight for
him. Four ships and seventy men were hired, and
although the leaders became convinced that D'Aunay
was right and refused to attack him, some of their
men engaged in a skirmish, killed three men and
plundered a pinnace-load of furs belonging to D'Aunay.
About the same time another expedition was planned
to make good the injuries done to Plymouth by the
robbing of her trading houses. So that by 1644 D'Aunay

had great cause of complaint. He reinforced himself by having his claim to authority confirmed in France and then threatened to seize the vessels of Massachusetts and to make immediate war upon her for the help given to his rival and the injuries done to him.

By this time Massachusetts began to fear that she had acted foolishly. A large party within the colony condemned her action in persisting in trade with La Tour, partly on the score of his Roman Catholicism, and in allowing a levy of men to be used against the genuine representative of France, and before the matter was brought before the Commissioners she had already decided to try and make peace with D'Aunay. This the Commissioners approved, though they contemplated the possibility of fighting him in defence of La Tour should he continue hostile.

Plymouth, the really injured party, who had been robbed by the French at Penobscot in 1632 and 1635, and who had sent out one fruitless expedition, and vainly asked for help from Massachusetts, now petitioned through the Commissioners for some satisfaction for the second robbery, which had been done by D'Aunay, but was told to wait until an answer had been received to the peace terms, and it does not appear that she ever got any compensation.

D'Aunay however defeated La Tour, and made peace with Massachusetts, and there was little more trouble with the French until expansion towards the north had much advanced.

The Governor of New France in 1651 proposed a league offensive and defensive with Plymouth and Massachusetts, but this was refused for fear of involving the colonies in unnecessary war with the Mohawk Indians.

But more critical even than French and Dutch relations were those with the native tribes. Indian policy played a large part in the work of the Commissioners, for

20

every colony alike had a very strong interest in it. It was important too that this policy should be uniform, and the Commissioners did good work in settling the relations of the various colonies to the natives round them, and in preventing selfishness on the part of less exposed settlements in times of danger.

It was to Indian difficulties that the Confederacy largely owed its origin, and for many years after its formation it was busy settling the disputes which arose out of the Pequod war. The Pequod tribe had been almost wiped out in this struggle, the remnants were forbidden to keep their tribal name, and were divided between the Mohegans, the Narragansetts and the Niantics. But this led to jealousy between Uncas of the Mohegans and Miantonomoh of the Narragansetts; and the death of Miantonomoh at the hand of Uncas, far from settling matters, caused perpetual outrages between the two tribes. By a treaty with the Narragansetts in 1645 the English made themselves arbitrators in their disputes, and exacted a tribute, and much of the Commissioners' time was taken up in holding the natives to their agreement, and in apportioning the lands of the conquered Pequods.

In later years they had to deal with the Indian reservations, appoint their governors, and superintend the administration of justice, and at the time of King Philip's War the Commissioners issued general orders for some of the expeditions, managed the finances, levied men from each colony, and in some cases appointed commanders.

All that they did with regard to the Indians was, however, but a tithe of what was done by New England as a whole, for so vital was the question that every colony had its own distinct legislation concerning it, a body of laws which was constantly being added to or in some way modified.

Not only did the Commissioners set boundaries to the

colonies, and issue advice and orders on foreign policy, but they took an immense interest in the moral and educational welfare of New England.   They seem to have felt responsible for the moral tone of the colonies, the orthodoxy of the churches, and the support of the ministry, and seem to have felt too that Plymouth was the particular member of the Confederation who was most apt to lag behind and fail.

In 1644 they issued orders for the maintenance of ministers, payment from unwilling members to be exacted by the civil power.   A year later it was suggested that the elders should publish a confession of doctrine, which might confirm the weak, and stop the mouths of adversaries abroad, and a year later again religious and moral considerations were set strongly before the league; it was reminded that mutual aid in asserting the liberties of the gospel was a part of its original programme, and that Anabaptism, Familism, and Antinomianism, must be crushed.   The several colonies were exhorted to keep a watch at the door of God's house that none might enter but such as had an effectual calling, and were at union with Christ through their covenant, and that only such members and their immediate seed should receive the privilege of baptism.   Plymouth demurred a little at the last clause, and asked to consider the matter further, but it sounds like a protest against the growing laxity of church membership.   At the same time the Commissioners urged that steps should be taken against oppression either in commodities or wages, against excess and disorder in apparel, and indulgence in drink.

In 1656 Plymouth again failed to come up to the views of the Commissioners, and Massachusetts complained that the people of that colony were wanting to themselves in due encouragement of the ministers of the gospel.   The flood of error was again lamented, this time in reference to the Quakers, and two years later the colonies were advised to pass special laws against them.   In the same year it was proposed that the colonies should make a collection of instances in which God's Providence had been showed towards them in any special way.

In 1667 the Commissioners once more found it necessary to remind people of their duty in maintaining the ministry, and it was ordered that Synods should be held when wanted, at or near Boston. The Commissioners were exclusively appointed from church members, and so were throughout on excellent terms with the churches, and took the advice of the elders on many important points, such as a war with the Narragansetts in 1644, negotiations with the Dutch in 1653, a war with the Dutch in the same year, and in 1654 they requested them to justify to their congregations an Indian expedition which had just taken place.

Their efforts on behalf of schools and colleges were more interesting and valuable. Education was a subject of common interest to all the colonies, and so had its place in the work of the Commissioners, more particularly in regard to its centre, Harvard College. The project of a college had been started in 1636, when the General Court of Massachusetts agreed to give £400 to be paid the next year in two instalments towards a school or college. The first needs of the colony had been attended to, and " one of the next things we longed for and looked after was to advance Learning and perpetuate it to Posterity; dreading to leave an illiterate Ministry to the Churches, when our present Ministers should lie in the Dust." [1] In 1638 John Harvard died, leaving to the College the half of his estate, a sum equal to about £700, and all his library, and in gratitude the new foundation was called by his name. They had other gifts, the state added what was wanting, and the College was built. "The edifice is very fair and comely within and without, having in it a spacious Hall ; (where they daily meet at Commons, Lectures, Exercises) and a large Library with some Bookes to it, the gifts

[1] New England's First Fruits, 1643, p. 23.

of diverse of our friends, their Chambers and Studies also fitted for and possessed by the Student and all other rooms of the Office necessary and convenient, with all needfull Offices thereto belonging.  And by the side of the Colledge a faire Grammar Schoole, for the training up of the young Schollars and fitting of them for Academicall Learning, that still as they are judged ripe, they may be received into the Colledge of this Schoole." [1]  Over the College were twelve overseers chosen by the General Court, six magistrates, and six ministers.

So far the College belonged to Massachusetts, though of course it received pupils from elsewhere, but very shortly came a proposal to found a species of scholarship fund, by gifts from all New England towns, a proposal which stimulated the interest of the other colonies, and resulted in giving the Commissioners some voice in the administration of its affairs.

At the second meeting of the Board a letter from the Rev. Thomas Shepard, pastor to the church at Cambridge, was read and recommended to the General Courts of the colonies.  He urged that from the schools and College would come the future ministry, that parents could not always afford to pay for the education of their children in full, and he proposed therefore that families who could afford it should give one-quarter of a bushel of corn in a year, or its equivalent, for the maintenance of "poor schollers" at Harvard "that Schoole of the prophets that now is." [2]  Scholars from the towns which contributed were later declared to have the first claim on the fund so raised.  He asked for a limited amount of help only, so as not to "suck and draw away all that nourishment wch the like Schooles may neede in after tymes in other Colonies."  The contributions given were more or less appropriated by the Commissioners, for three years later the President, Henry Dunster, wrote to

---

[1] New England's First Fruits, 1643, p. 24.
[2] Records ix. 20, 1644.

in England and with the missionaries about the provision of books and other necessaries, and about the educating of Indians to be teachers of their own race.

In 1653 an additional building at Harvard was proposed to accommodate "six hopfull Indian youthes," and Mayhew and Eliot asked for an allowance from the Society towards the expense. In 1652 the native town of Natick on the Charles River was begun and to it were moved the Indians from the scattered reservations. An order was given for the formation of other similar towns; magistrates were appointed to hold courts amongst them, and they were governed like the Hebrews in their wanderings, by a ruler of one hundred, two rulers of fifties, and ten rulers of tens. An attempt was made to govern by Indian officials, but it failed, and all was under English supervision, one of the most important superintendents being Daniel Gookin, who wrote a valuable account of the work.

After the control had been given into the hands of the Commissioners, missionary enterprise became more general in other colonies. Connecticut had already adopted the reservation system as a means of civil protection, and by that time had two important missionaries at least, but only one small community of praying Indians. In Rhode Island there were none; Roger Williams was an ardent missionary, and believed that no red man existed who had not the impulse of religion, but in spite of his understanding of the Indian language and character, in spite of the warm affection between him and many of the Pokanoket and Narragansett Indians, he effected very few conversions. Any efforts he made, however, were quite outside the influence of the Commissioners, and find no place in their consideration of the work.

The Plymouth men were apparently never very active in proselytising. They had imagined a great missionary enterprise before them when they embarked for America, but probably, taught by their experience in Leyden, they realised the almost impossibility of shaking a faith which had generations of tradition behind it. Winslow, returning from the sick-bed of Massasoit in the early days of the settlement, spent a night in the house of Canonicus, and whiled away the time with theological discussion. Canonicus, with the keen interest in such subjects which all Indians showed, asked many questions as to the faith of the white men. Much of their creed he approved, but objected to the seventh commandment, thinking there were great inconveniences in a man being tied to one woman. There were other cases in which Indians actually sought instruction in the Christian faith, prompted more by the spirit of inquiry than by any thought of adopting it, but though the Pilgrims were always ready to explain their creed and testify to the power of their God, they seem to have relied a good deal on the testimony of their lives, and to have been contented with imposing a superior moral code on the Indians, not interfering very actively in their beliefs. They could indeed have been able to spare little intellect for the missionary field, being forced to work so hard for bare existence that their own educational needs were in danger of being neglected, and moreover the Pokanoket Indians, their nearest neighbours, were of all tribes the most adverse to Christianity. They were far more high spirited and sturdy in their beliefs than the Massachusetts Indians ; Massasoit, friendly as he was to the white men, would have liked to insert in all his treaties a clause, to which they never consented, promising that no attempt should be made to convert any of his followers.

Whatever the reason was, Plymouth seems to have done little missionary work until the Commissioners took it in hand. Then reservations or colonies of praying Indians began to grow up, the most extensive one being at Sandwich. Richard Bourne was recom-

variety of questions, would always work in harmony. As a matter of fact it did not, and the cause of difficulty was always the superior power and pretensions of Massachusetts.

When a union was first thought of by the colonies, Massachusetts, who had least to gain by it, proposed so many clauses which would give her a leading position that the scheme fell through for a time. But a leading position she was determined to have, and when the Confederation actually came into existence, she quickly claimed that her name should have first place on all acts or orders of the Board, and this was permitted, though not as a right. Moreover it was provided by the Articles that meetings should be held twice at Boston for once in each of the other colonies.

These were comparative trifles, but more serious pretensions came later. In 1647 the Commissioners had to consider whether Springfield, which had been declared to be within the jurisdiction of Massachusetts, was bound to pay a custom towards maintaining the fort at Saybrook. Connecticut declared that Springfield benefited by it as much as her own River Towns and had exacted the tax for the past two years, and Plymouth and Newhaven supported her. Massachusetts, angry no doubt at finding herself outvoted, attempted to alter the Articles of Confederation, complaining that her share of the burdens was unfair, that it would be enough for the Commissioners to meet only once in three years, and that it should not always be necessary for the colonies to be guided by their advice. Naturally the rest of the board did not agree, and in 1649 Massachusetts avenged herself for the tax on Springfield by taxing Plymouth, Newhaven, and Connecticut for all goods passing through Boston Harbour, in order to repay the cost of fortification. So Plymouth and Newhaven were punished for giving advice which displeased the powerful member of the Confederation. Finally in 1650 Massachusetts repealed the duty, on

condition that Connecticut did the same with the duty
on Springfield, and apparently this was agreed to. In
the same year it was agreed that the Governor and
Commissioners for Massachusetts should undertake the
affairs of the Board during the intervals of their sessions,
for by this time the work of Indian conversion had been
placed in its hands, and correspondence on the subject
was continual.

In 1651 it was Plymouth who had to complain of the
overbearing ways of the larger colony. Massachusetts
had taken into her jurisdiction the lands of two
sachems, Pumham and Sacononoco, on which Samuel
Gorton had settled. But she failed to keep Gorton in
order, and the matter was referred to the Board of Commissioners. There Plymouth claimed that the lands were
within her jurisdiction and could not fairly be yielded
up to Massachusetts by the sachems; Massachusetts
declared that the Plymouth commissioners had agreed to
it, Plymouth declared that they had not, and that if they
had, they had not the power to bind their colony to any such
cession. The case was decided in favour of Plymouth, after
a great deal of ill-feeling, but the lands finally became
part of Providence plantation. In 1653 Massachusetts
was at loggerheads with all the other colonies. Newhaven and Connecticut, alarmed by a threatened attack
from Dutch and Indians, were anxious to open an
offensive war against them. Massachusetts, being less
concerned, and perhaps realising that the alarm was
false, flatly declined to make war, although the vote of
the Board was in favour of it, and denied that by the
Articles the Commissioners had power to bind their
governments to attack, but only to defend. She
was accused of attempting to destroy the Confederacy,
but held out until the next year, when, all danger of war
being over, she revised her reading of the Articles, and
agreed with the other colonies in their interpretation.
In this case she had done good service, though it was

done illegally, and when the Articles of Confederation were revised in 1667 and 1670, it was agreed that the Commissioners should not be allowed to involve the colonies in any war without the consent of their General Courts.

The Board was undoubtedly of value. It could only advise the General Courts, not compel them, but it did suggest and in many cases impose, a more uniform policy throughout the four colonies than could have been ensured in any other way. In external affairs this was an advantage. It provided a corporate whole with which savage or alien European powers might treat, and although the Confederation was not recognised at all in England except by the Society for Propagating the Gospel, and very slightly by other nations, there was at all events unity on one side in the negotiations, and the danger of colonies taking different sides in a foreign quarrel was avoided.

But on the whole the working of the Confederation was ominous to the weaker colonies. They might benefit by the additional support, but there was little chance that they would get much say in New England policy, in spite of their being equally represented on the Board. As this body had no executive and could only recommend measures to the General Courts, a victory on the Board meant nothing if the stronger colonies chose to defy the rules of Confederation. This both Massachusetts and Connecticut did on occasion, and there was no way of punishing them. Plymouth complained in 1667, when protesting against a confederacy of only three colonies, that the Commissioners' decision was not always attended to even when it was backed by six or eight votes, and that there was no use in belonging to a Confederation if after all the expense and trouble of meeting, the matters agreed upon were not carried through.

As far as Plymouth was concerned its benefits ended, with its support in foreign policy, and were even a little dubious there. Plymouth's relations with the Dutch were more friendly than those of any other colony, chiefly because their claims did not overlap very seriously; in her difficulties with the French she got no help at all from the league; and until King Philip's War she was on completely satisfactory terms with the Indians. In that war however her existence was threatened, and could hardly have been saved but for the support of the Confederation.

In other ways Plymouth suffered greatly by the connection. Her church government was originally conducted on a much more popular and broad-minded basis than that of Massachusetts. When the Synod met at Cambridge in 1646 to decide on a uniform platform, the version sent in by Samuel Partridge, her representative, gave less authority to the elders, less control to Synods, and was far more inclined to limit the power of the magistrate over the church than that finally adopted. In actual life too her churches were more tolerant: a freeman's rights were not limited by law to church members; Williams and other dissenters were less vehemently accused; the Quakers were leniently treated for many years. But after the death of the original settlers, pressed on one hand by the decisions of the Commissioners, on the other by the decisions of the Synods which they encouraged, Plymouth lost much of her independent, individual policy. She became less democratic, more intolerant; laws such as that of 1658 against Quakers follow hard upon the recommendations of the Board, and becoming identified with the harsh, overbearing policy of Massachusetts, she gained a name for aggression which her own inclinations did not warrant. It would be idle to blame the Confederation entirely for this loss of individuality, for the very remarkable character of the first comers was much weakened in the second and third generations, but there is no doubt that Plymouth had lost her true independence of thought and policy before she was finally called upon to renounce independence of government.

Her rulers were conscious of their position—Prince wrote sadly to the Commissioners in 1667, " The truth is wee are the meanest and weakest, least able to stand of ourselves, and little able to contribute any healpfulness to others ; and wee know it tho. none should tell us of it." [1] Their sense of weakness and the constant pressure of the stronger state of Massachusetts probably led to the protest before mentioned in 1667. Newhaven had just been absorbed by Connecticut, and Plymouth, feeling her own independence trembling beneath her, made one last bid for liberty. But neither was the Confederation responsible for her loss of independent government, for though it certainly paved the way for it and made union with Massachusetts seem a natural conclusion to their relations, the act of union was dictated by the English Crown, which had never even recognised the Confederation.

After the Restoration, when England had leisure to appreciate the wealth and honour which her colonies brought with them, their regulation and supervision became a matter of importance, and English policy, ignoring the various circumstances of their origin, aimed at establishing a uniform government throughout New England. Massachusetts, the least tractable of the colonies, bore the brunt of the attack ; in Plymouth the forms of government were very little interfered with— Charles II. had been proclaimed there, though tardily, his Commissioners were so well received that submission disarmed interference, and in 1666 the king issued a circular letter to the New England colonies, commending the attitude of all but Massachusetts.

But in 1684 the charter of Massachusetts was finally cancelled, and with the work of establishing a new government there came a chance to further the aim of consolidation—Plymouth had no charter, and her annexa-

[1] Records x. 325.

tion was an immediate certainty; one by one the other colonies shared the same fate, till Sir Edmund Andros ruled as governor over all New England. Local and individual tendencies, however, proved too strong for this levelling process; simultaneously with the overthrow of James II. came a revolution in New England, Andros was driven out, old forms were everywhere revived, and Plymouth returned once more to the old constitution established on the *Mayflower*.

Under William and Mary more attention was paid to the individuality of the colonies; charters were in many cases renewed, local government usually went on undisturbed, though in central government checks were imposed by a royally appointed governor. But their accession saw little change in the policy of consolidating the smaller colonies; in the charter granted to Massachusetts in 1691 Plymouth was included within its boundaries, and the colony of the Pilgrim Fathers ceased to have a separate history.

# CHAPTER XVI

## LIFE IN PLYMOUTH

TO picture to ourselves the society in which the Pilgrims summed up all their great ideals and all their past experiences, we are left chiefly to the evidence of laws and Court records, and to chance references and criticisms from outside sources. Plymouth had few literary men, and Bradford, absorbed in the history of its government and · commerce, flashes only now and then a gleam of light on the everyday life and social habits of the people.

Above all things, life in Plymouth was a life of defence, on the one hand against external foes, on the other against the powers of darkness. The Pilgrims felt that they were living in a state of siege, and this defensive attitude is the keynote to their society.

Their weakness and constant fear of attack influenced the growth of the colony, its compact, defensible townships differing widely from the large scattered plantations of Virginia; it influenced the very aspect of the towns, with their forts and garrison houses, their stockades and barri-cadoes, with gates upon the highways.

Nothing is left of the ancient town of Plymouth but a fragment of the rock on which the Pilgrims landed, their buildings were too humble to last, and all pictures are more or less imaginary. But we have a description by De Rasières, in a letter to the Hague written after a visit to the town in 1627. "New Plymouth lies on the slope of a hill stretching east towards the sea-coast, with a broad street about a cannon-shot of 800 feet long leading down the hill, and with a street crossing in the middle northwards to the rivulet, and southwards to the land. The houses are constructed of hewn planks, with gardens, also enclosed behind and at the sides with hewn planks, so that their houses and courtyards are arranged in very good order, with a stockade against a sudden attack; at the ends of the streets are three wooden gates. In the centre is a square enclosure upon which four patereros are mounted, so as to flank along the streets. Upon the hill they have a large square house with a flat roof made of thick sawn planks, stayed with oak beams, upon the top of which they have six cannons which shoot iron balls of four or five pounds and command the surrounding country. The lower part they use for their church, where they preach on Sundays and the usual holidays." [1]

The colony, handicapped and poor, grew very slowly, but in 1641 Bradford mentions nine townships, Duxbury, Scituate, Taunton, Marshfield, Sandwich, Yarmouth, Barnstaple, Seekonk, and Nauset. A few more, Rehoboth, Bridgwater, etc., were added later, and probably all were built upon the same lines. The Plymouth people were too poor for the more ambitious architecture found in other colonies, of which Coddington's house at Newport is an example, but the chief feature of every township would be the church and some fortification against attack.

Then there would be the pound, in which animals found trespassing were kept; the stocks and the whipping post, which play too large a part in all New England annals. Plymouth had a prison in 1638, and a house of correction was later proposed for Quakers, idlers, and vagrants. The houses were mere huts and hovels built of logs daubed with earth or clay, and thatched with long grasses, until the danger from fire led to a law that all houses should be roofed and not thatched. The windows at first were not of glass but of oiled paper, for Winslow,

[1] Quoted in Palfrey i. 226.

in 1621, in a letter to coming settlers, warns them to bring a supply of it for the purpose.[1] Possibly the brick pavements, which were a feature of later New England towns and which were copied no doubt from the Dutch, would be found in Plymouth, for bricks were made in Salem as early as 1629.

If the fear of attack had much to do with the arrangement of the towns, it influenced still more the lives and occupations of the colonists. They were farmers for the most part, for corn was their staple commodity. In corn they paid their debt to the Undertakers, in corn they traded with the Indians for furs, in corn they paid the taxes of the colony. For money was scarce, and the little they had speedily found its way to England to pay for the commodities which they were forced to import. They grew other grains too, besides hemp and flax and many fruits and vegetables, both native and English, although De Rasières writes that their land was stony and unsuitable for the plough, and less good than that around New Amsterdam.

Hunting and fishing were other occupations of the colony, but lesser ones. They could get birds and fish for food, but Bradford, as we have seen, spoke very slightingly of fishing as an industry. Even trade with the Indians, at first the great source of wealth, through which the Undertakers were able to pay off their heavy debts in England, in time gave place to agriculture. In June 1639 Bradford and the partners gave notice that they would hold the trade only until the November following ; in the next year it was offered on lease for a year or a term of years, and bought by some of the Company for one-sixth of their profits. With the first-fruits of this lease the prison was built, but it does not seem to have yielded largely, probably on account of the greater competition of the surrounding colonies.

Of manufactures there were few. In 1624 a saltmaker

[1] Arber, p. 493.

had been sent over from England by the Adventurers to start works, and make salt for the fishing. But all he could do was to boil salt in pans, a process in which the colonists needed no instruction, and he ended by burning the house and spoiling their pans. Salt works were, however, established later.

The smelting of iron was also attempted, rather unsuccessfully. Hatherley set up an "iron mill" at Scituate in 1650, and in 1655 three men of Taunton asked to be exempted from military training on account of their duties at the iron works. In 1663 leave was given to the inhabitants of Taunton engaged in the iron industry to cut wood on certain lands for the use of their works, but two years later the Court had received complaints of the bad quality of the iron made there, and issued a mandate concerning it.

Most of the trades which one would expect in a community forced by its isolation to be self-sufficing were to be found in Plymouth. Blacksmiths were requisitioned to mend arms and household utensils; probably all were carpenters as far as their own households went, for the furniture of the houses was simple in the extreme, home made save for the few articles brought out of England. The traders too needed ships, and in 1623 a ship's carpenter came out in the *Charity*, and built them two shallops and a lighter. But they were too poor to do much shipbuilding, and not until 1642 was a vessel of any size constructed in the colony. Then a ship of forty or fifty tons, costing £200, was built at the expense of thirteen men, four of them taking charge of the work.

In a corn growing community there were naturally millers, to whom the people took their own corn to be ground. There were windmills in Plymouth as early as 1634, and in the Court records are found not infrequent charges of dishonesty against the millers for keeping more than their proper due of the flour they ground.

Cloth was at first imported from home, though with the growth of hemp and flax, linen was soon made in New England, and it is hard to believe that the Pilgrims with their Dutch experience did not very early set up handlooms in their own houses. Tailors they certainly had, for in 1641 John Jordaine was presented before the Court "for takeing stuff to line a dublet throughout and yet lyned not the skirts, and restored not the rest."[1] There could have been but a poor living for tailors, for dress was no doubt of the plainest and usually sombre, though Brewster possessed a blue cloth coat, a violet colour cloth coat, and a green waistcoat, and the clothes mentioned in the inventory of Bradford's estate were by no means all " sad-coloured." A pair of red silk stockings however once attracted so much notice in the streets of Plymouth that the matter was investigated, and it was found that they had been stolen from Boston.

There were no shoemakers in the early years, and shoes were the commodity which Bradford specially undertook to import from England when taking over the trade in 1627. £50 worth of shoes and hose were to be brought over yearly to be sold to the planters for corn at six shillings a bushel. But when cattle became plentiful and were killed for food, leather could be obtained in the country, so that the author of " New England's First Fruits" rejoices in 1643 that " God is leading us by the hand into the way of cloathing."

No matter what his occupation might be, however, every colonist had imperative military duties. The colony was carefully organized on the militia system, and the whole male community formed an army, bound to possess adequate arms and ammunition, and to attend the regular trainings which were held six times a year in every township. Again and again towns were presented and fined for neglecting to enforce this stringent

[1] Records ii. p. 5.

rule, they were not even permitted to be "defective for want of a drum."

Cromwell himself was not more careful than the Pilgrims to have in his army men "as made some conscience of what they did"; some townships limited membership of their company to freemen of good repute (though all male adults were liable to be called upon for defence), and great care was taken to ensure a high moral tone by discipline of the strictest nature. The exercises at each training began and ended with prayer, and once a year a sermon was preached before the company, at the election of its officers.

There was no cavalry in Plymouth until 1658, and the companies were not organized in regiments, though towns might train together if they wished, and sometimes did, for in 1668 Plymouth, Taunton, and Yarmouth agreed to hold their trainings at each town in succession. In very early days the body of freemen not only formed the army, but gave its opinion and vote on military projects, but in 1643 a council of war was established consisting of the Governor, three assistants, and Miles Standish, and into its charge this power of direction was delegated. A similar body existed for the same purpose during the whole life of the colony. The chief officer was a Major, but like the President of the Dutch Republic, the Governor of each New England state was commander-in-chief.

From the first, careful arrangements were made for sounding an alarm, and so constantly were the Pilgrims on the alert against attack that De Rasières describes them assembling for their church service "by beat of drum, each with his musket or firelock, in front of the captain's door; they have their cloaks on, and place themselves in order, three abreast, and are led by a sergeant without beat of drum. Behind comes the Governor, in a long robe; beside him, on the right hand, comes the preacher with his cloak on, and on the left hand the captain with his side arms and cloak on, and with a small cane in his hand; and so they march in good order, and each sets his arms down near him. Thus they are constantly on their guard night and day." This was in 1627, and in 1641 it was enacted by law that all should go to meeting on the Lord's Day armed.

But the armour which they wore as they prayed and listened was not only against external foes, it was a visible sign of their attitude to the world and its vanities. All their social as well as their political life was moulded by their religious views, and they regarded anything that trenched upon them as more deadly than the tomahawk of the Indian. And so they armed themselves spiritually and lived in a mental state of defence.

They set a moral stockade around their towns, and would admit none as inhabitants who were not approved by the church or the Court; no one might even take a lodger without special leave. The franchise grew stricter as time went on, the goodwill of those in authority was always necessary, and in 1657 the privilege was definitely denied to Quakers and to all opposers of law and worship. Control was kept over the population too by the prohibition of any sale of lands without the consent of the Court, and land was not granted to any township until its founders showed that they could support a church and a ministry.

The Pilgrims too tried to encase their people in the armour of righteousness, to strengthen them by frequent religious observances, and to arm them with a knowledge of God's Word. They had few educational advantages, fewer amusements, all their lives centred in that Sabbath-keeping, that compulsory attendance at public worship, which seem so wearisome unless one can regain the fervour of the early enthusiasts.

In newer townships the church was the central feature of the settlement; at Plymouth, first the common store-

THE OLD FORT AND FIRST MEETING-HOUSE

house, and then a room under the fort, served for a meeting-house. There they had usually two services on each Sabbath, with extemporary prayers, psalms sung in the metrical version without any instrumental music, and finally a sermon lasting for an hour by the hour-glass. Henry Ainsworth's version of the Psalms was used there for seventy years. Occasionally there might be prophecy, but reading of the Bible without exposition was rare.

Governor Winthrop and Mr Wilson visited Plymouth in 1632, and we have from the Governor's Journal an account of the service there at that date. "On the Lord's Day there was a sacrament which they did partake in, and, in the afternoon, Mr Roger Williams (according to their custom) propounded a question, to which the pastor, Mr Smith, spoke briefly; then Mr Williams prophesied, and after the Governour of Plymouth spake to the question; after him the Elder; then some two or three more of the congregation. Then the Elder desired the Governour of Massachusetts and Mr Wilson to speak to it, which they did. When this was ended, the Deacon, Mr Fuller, put the congregation in mind of their duty of contribution. Whereupon the Governour and all the rest went down to the deacon's seat and put into the box, and then returned."[1]

Baptism took place usually on the next Sunday after birth; marriages and funerals were civil affairs, and had no place in the church service. Bradford writes in 1621, "May 12th was ye first marriage in this place; which according to ye laudable custom of ye Low Countries in which they had liued, was thought most requisite to be performed, by the magistrate, as being a ciuill thing."[2]

There can be no quarrel against the Pilgrims for trying to protect the moral character of their settlers, nor for trying to arm them with the best weapons of which they knew. So long as the first settlers lived and the tone of the colony was largely of their making, it was only the

[1] Winthrop's Journal.      [2] Bradford MS., p. 67.

negative side of their work which could be found fault with, the neglect of many gifts and faculties which might have made life a better and happier thing.

They had set themselves to found a community of saints upon earth, and it was perhaps inevitable that with a programme of such high seriousness some things which we now think valuable should have been left out, those fruits of culture and sociability that only a spontaneous joy in living can produce.

They were not always to blame, for the hard conditions of their lives left little room for recreation, whether learned or otherwise. Brewster's library is the only one of which we know in the colony; the earliest press in New England was not at Plymouth but at Cambridge, Massachusetts, where it was founded in 1639, Joseph Glover giving a font of printing letters, and some gentlemen of Amsterdam contributing £49 to the furnishing of a press.

Neglect of education was one of the charges of the Adventurers against the colony in 1624, and Bradford was forced to confess that the children depended for it on their parents, as they had no common school. They must have had schools of some sort ten years later, for in 1635 the widow of Dr Fuller was allowed to have an apprentice on condition of keeping him at school two years, but common schools were not established in Plymouth until 1677. In that year it was ordered that in every town of fifty families and more there should be a "gramar scoole," for which the town was to pay a rate of £12, the balance being paid by those whose children attended it. The idea of having a school in every town had been mooted in 1662 and a year later it became a proviso in settling new plantations, that they should have a schoolmaster. In 1673 it was proposed that the charges of a free school, calculated at £33 a year, should be paid out of the profits of the Cape Cod fisheries, and after the act of 1677 these profits were divided amongst the towns with schools, not more than £5 being granted to any one. A town with no school of its own had to pay £5 a year to the next town that had one.

Delay in providing education, however, resulted not from any depreciation of its importance or prejudice against secular learning, but from the poverty and toil which were the order of life in Plymouth. The Pilgrims had no time to be cultured, no time to read anything but their Bibles, but recreation in the sense of amusement was taboo for very different reasons.

Without insisting upon the austerity and gloom which obtained in later years, there is no doubt that the Pilgrims from John Robinson onwards would have regarded unrestrained mirth as unseemly, and would have condemned any organised form of amusement as sinful waste of time and opportunity. One cannot think that Bradford, with his kind heart and his keen sense of humour would prohibit innocent pleasures and merriment, but they would have to be strictly kept in their place, and that place would be a very small one. On Christmas Day in 1621 some of the young men had been excused from work because they said it was against their consciences to work on such a day, but as Governor Bradford returned from the fields he found them playing games in the street. He "took away their impliments and told them that was against his conscience that they should play and others worke." On that day he would have no "gameing or revelling in the streets."

Seriousness was indeed the leading characteristic of the Pilgrims, and the one which their rulers took most pains to foster. They had need to be serious, for they felt that they must be always on their guard lest evil should creep in and destroy the fruit of all their labours. But a defensive attitude is not a wholesome one for most people, and they walled in their garden so closely that the fruit grew sour instead of ripening.

In later years, when one portion of the community had

grown lax, and the other unduly severe, the broad-minded tolerant spirit which had been the characteristic of John Robinson's pupils was lost sight of, in social and religious life even more than in civil government. Everywhere restrictive legislation took the place of the old mutual conscientiousness; and the multiplying of sins, the utter loss of all sense of proportion in conduct, led to the growth of that Puritan conscience which had been responsible for so much misery and such a violence of reaction.

There grew up a tendency to regulate man's whole life by law; not only could no one build, keep house, have a lodger or entertain strangers and Quakers without consent of the Governor, but single persons were forbidden to live of themselves, or in any family but such as the select man of the town should approve, and no one might live in an inn or ale house in his own town. Intercourse between certain people was also restricted as the government thought fit, a servant could not be married without his master's consent, no one could be married without the consent of parents or the Governor. Sometimes these restrictions were valuable, as for instance when Francis Crooker, who wished to marry Mary Gaunt, was ordered by the Court to get first a certificate "that the disease from which he is sometimes troubled is not the falling sickness." And indeed the philanthropic regulations in Plymouth as to pensions, the care of pauper children, and of poor and distracted persons were far in advance of the age, and can only be ascribed to Dutch influence.

No one was permitted to live idly; extortion either in wages or prices was severely punished. Presentments were made on several occasions of people who had taken pay for their work and of people who sold wine and beer at too high prices. John Barnes was presented for selling black and brown thread at 5s. 4d. per lb., Peter Hopkins for selling a looking-glass for 16d. which could be bought in the Bay for 9d., and Thomas Clark for extortion in buying boots for 10s. and selling them again for 15s. Thus anything resembling usury was sternly repressed.

The regulations limiting the sale of drink, the keeping of inns and "ordinaries," and the use of tobacco were frequently reinforced and defined. In 1637 the taking of tobacco on the streets was forbidden by law ; this was crossed out, but reinforced later; it might not be taken on juries nor near the meeting-house, and in 1645 persons were again forbidden to take tobacco "in very unciuil manor" on the streets.

Inns were carefully licensed, and no "profane singing, dancing or revelling" was permitted in them. Amusements were more strictly forbidden, though very often there was some aggravating circumstance when "revelling" was attacked and the penalties were not as a rule heavy. A culprit presented for "mixed daunsing" was released with an admonition, and in 1652 a lady with the graceful name of Mercy Tubbs, presented on the same charge, shared no worse fate. The introduction of cards and dice was forbidden by law in 1656, and in 1663 several people were fined twenty shillings each "for play att cards on the Lord's day." This was a double crime, but in the same year five people, two of whom were women, who were fined forty shillings each for playing cards, presumably on a week day, had their fines remitted. In 1637 a man was fined for allowing people to drink and play "shouell board" at his house, but the words "contrary to the orders of the court" are expressly added, the probability being that he had no licence.

Although some of the penalties on the statute book are very severe, particularly for offences against morality, some traditions of mildness lingered in the colony and they were seldom executed in their full brutality.

After the first thirty years of the colony, when a less zealous generation had grown up, there was a good deal of severe legislation on the subject of Sabbath keeping. In 1649 John Shaw was condemned to sit in the stocks for attending to his tar pits on a Sunday, in the following year Elizabeth Edy was presented for wringing and hanging out clothes on the Lord's Day in time of public exercise, and several people were summoned for holding meetings on that day from house to house. Transgressions of this kind led to many acts against vilifying the ministry, profaning the Sabbath, and attempting to set up different churches or meetings. Unnecessary travelling on Sunday was also restricted, and on that day no wine or liquor might be drawn except in cases of sickness, and none might smoke tobacco within two miles of the meeting-house.

Not only was Sabbath keeping strictly upheld, but the maintenance of ministers, formerly the voluntary privilege of the faithful, became one of the cares of a magistrate, who was even authorised for a time to distrain upon those who neglected to take their share of the burden.

Thought and opinion as well as the outward life of a man had to conform to the required standard, still with this rooted idea of sheltering the community from any evil influence. Just as the rulers dreaded any unguarded outpost among their settlements, so they dreaded any alien act or thought which could not be harmonized with their rigid rules of conduct.

Several circumstances, however, mitigated the severity with which new opinions were received in Plymouth. There was less close connection between Church and State than in Massachusetts and relations with the English government were less strained. So that repression of religious views was not confused with political issues ; a difference of religious opinion could neither shake the foundations of government, nor play into the hands of enemies in England, and there was no need to unite ministers and magistrates into one gigantic sledgehammer to crush it.

Moreover they had few ministers, and those not of the greatest. In Massachusetts the orthodox ministry was the learned class, dictating opinion and gaining undue political importance. But Plymouth, first through the lack of sympathy of the Adventurers, then because her poverty and small population offered no attraction, had few shining lights in her churches, and what she lost in learning she gained in secular independence and freedom of thought.

It was only when, through Synods and the Confederation, New England practice became equalized, that difference of opinion was harshly treated in the Old Colony. By degrees there too anything unfamiliar came to be suspected, and if a man lived amongst them who liked to wander outside the barriers, who thought for himself and valued spontaneous instincts above rigid rules, who thought it right to enjoy rather than to question the beauty and wonder of life, it had been better for that man if he had never been born.

Perhaps the picture of life in Plymouth is disappointing when one thinks of the high ideals that had gone to the conception of it, perhaps the spiritual liberty, the freedom from worldly considerations which had been the great cause of Separatism, seem very much obscured.

But to bring practice into line with theory is difficult, and it must be admitted that whilst the Pilgrims lived they had overcome this difficulty as far as human beings could. That they could not bequeath their spirit as well as their system to their children takes nothing from their personal greatness, nor does the overshadowing and final absorption of their colony by Massachusetts take anything from the value of their work. They had been the pioneers, on them had fallen the burden and hardships of any such undertaking, and they have been blamed for faults and failings which were not theirs at all.

With reaction, and a truer view of the elements which went to the making of New England, the great importance of the Pilgrims in the political and religious world becomes more and more clear, and no better epitaph could be found for them than the words written to Bradford by a friend out of England. " Let it not be grievous to you, that you have been instruments to break the ice for others. The honour shall be yours to the world's end."

# INDEX

TURNBULL AND SPEARS, PRINTERS, EDINBURGH